Grammar for Grown-Ups

**A COMPREHENSIVE GUIDE & WORKBOOK
TO BOOST YOUR WRITING SKILLS**

Mark Peters, PhD

Publisher Mike Sanders
Art & Design Director William Thomas
Editorial Director Ann Barton
Cover Designer Laura Merriman
Book Designer William Thomas
Layout Ayanna Lacey
Proofreader Jean Bissell
Indexer Johnna VanHoose Dinse

First American Edition, 2025
Published in the United States by DK Publishing
1745 Broadway, 20th Floor, New York, NY 10019

The authorized representative in the EEA is Dorling Kindersley Verlag GmbH.
Arnulfstr. 124, 80636 Munich, Germany

Copyright © 2025 by Dorling Kindersley Limited
25 26 27 28 10 9 8 7 6 5 4 3 2 1
001-348430-AUG2025

All rights reserved.
Without limiting the rights under the copyright reserved above, no part of this publication may be reproduced, stored in or introduced into a retrieval system, or transmitted, in any form, or by any means (electronic, mechanical, photocopying, recording, or otherwise), without the prior written permission of the copyright owner.

No part of this publication may be used or reproduced in any manner for the purpose of training artificial intelligence technologies or systems. In accordance with Article 4(3) of the DSM Directive 2019/790, DK expressly reserves this work from the text and data mining exception.

A catalog record for this book
is available from the Library of Congress.
ISBN: 978-0-593-96520-7

DK books are available at special discounts when purchased in bulk for sales promotions, premiums, fundraising, or educational use. For details, contact:
SpecialSales@dk.com.

Printed and bound in China

www.dk.com

Updated and reprinted from *Idiot's Guides®: Grammar and Style*

This book was made with Forest Stewardship Council™ certified paper—one small step in DK's commitment to a sustainable future.
Learn more at
www.dk.com/uk/information/sustainability

To Ed and Janet Peters.

Contents

Introduction 7

Part 1: Introduction to Grammar and Style 9

1   Rules and Conventions 11
Brushing Up on Three Key Concepts 11
Understanding Grammar 12
Choosing a Usage Level 14
Adhering to Conventions 15
Appreciating the Purpose of Rules and Conventions 16

2   Beyond the Rules: Writing with Style 25
Defining Style 25
Some Different Styles 26
Style Guidelines 29
Sharpening Your Style 30
Enhancing Your Prose with Literary Devices 31

Part 2: Grammar Basics 37

3   Brushing Up on Parts of Speech 39
Meeting the Actors: Nouns and Pronouns 39
Taking Action with Verbs 45
Getting Descriptive with Adjectives and Adverbs 50
Making the Right Connections with Conjunctions 54
Building Relationships with Prepositions 58
Dealing with Interjections: Yay! 60
Blurring the Lines That Define Parts of Speech 61

4   Recognizing the Parts of a Sentence 65
What Exactly Is a Sentence? 65
Completing Actions with Complements 69
Accentuating Sentences with Phrases 71
Grasping the Basics of Clauses 76
Common Sentence Structures 79

Part 3: Using the Parts of Speech to Build Sentences 85

5   Using Nouns and Pronouns as Subjects 87
Starting a Sentence with a Noun 87
Starting with a Pronoun Instead of a Noun 90
Pronouns and Gender 93
Person-Centric Language 94
Using Expletive Expressions Sparingly 94
Sorting Out *Who*, *Which*, and *That* 96
Knowing When to Use *Who* or *Whom* 97

6   Taking Action with Verbs 101
Recognizing Verb Forms 101
Telling Time with Tenses 107

Making Your Nouns and Verbs Agree 118
Setting the Right Mood 122
Choosing a Voice 123

7 Describing Words: Adjectives and Adverbs 129
Adjectives: Describing Words 129
Types of Adjectives 131
Articles: Little Words with Big Jobs 139
Adverbs: Describing Verbs, Adjectives, and Other Adverbs 140

8 Wrapping Up Action with Complements 147
Linking to a Subject Complement 147
Complementing a Direct Object: The Object Complement 148
Taking Action on Nouns with Verb Complements 150

9 Using Phrases 155
What a Phrase Is (and Isn't) 155
Forming Prepositional Phrases 157
Using Verbs as Adjectives, Adverbs, and Nouns 159
Elaborating on Nouns with Appositives 162
Rearranging Phrases to Clarify and Emphasize 164

10 Adding Clauses 169
Recognizing the Two Main Clause Types 169
Rearranging Clauses to Clarify and Emphasize 176

Part 4: Writing with Style 181

11 The Seven Cs of Good Writing 183
Clear 183
Compelling 185
Consistent 186
Concise 189
Convincing 189
Complete 191
Correct 191
Consulting Style Guides for More Direction 192
Steering Clear of Plagiarism 193

12 Choosing the Right Words: Diction 201
Word Books: Dictionaries and Thesauruses 201
Avoiding the Double Negative 205
Avoiding Vague or Stale Language 206

13 Maintaining Parallel Structure 217
Understanding Parallel Structure 217

14 Varying Sentence Structure 225
Rearranging Words and Phrases: Syntax 225
Combining Short Sentences 226
Giving Long Sentences a Break 229

  Trimming the Fat...230
  Varying Sentence Types..231
  Varying Sentence Beginnings 232
  The Virtues of Variety 233

15 Avoiding and Fixing Common Errors..237
  Repairing Broken Sentences 237
  Clarifying the Relationship Between Ideas 241
  Clarifying Pronoun References...242
  Fixing Misplaced and Dangling Modifiers 243
  Avoiding Shifts in Subject and Verb Forms..243

16 Avoiding Sexism and Other Biases 247
  Maintaining Sex and Gender Equality..247
  Calling People What They Want to Be Called 252
  Maintaining an Objective Viewpoint 257

Part 5: Fine-Tuning the Mechanics 261

17 Basic Punctuation 263
  Putting an End to Your Sentences...263
  Knowing When to Use Commas 266
  Using a Semicolon to Join Items 271
  Brushing Up on Colon Usage...274

18 Quotation Marks and Apostrophes 279
  Enclosing Text in Quotation Marks 279
  Using Apostrophes..284

19 Hyphens, Dashes, Parentheses, and Brackets 291
  Putting Hyphens to Good Use..291
  Making Good Use of the Dash 295
  Enclosing Incidental (Nonessential) Text...296
  Using Brackets [Rarely, If Ever]..299

20 Spelling Rules, Tips, and Tricks 303
  Spelling Phonetically: A Challenge in English..303
  Brushing Up on Spelling Rules 303
  Making Plurals 306
  Attaching Prefixes and Suffixes 310

21 Capitalization, Abbreviations, and Numbers 315
  Understanding Capitalization..315
  Using Abbreviations 322
  Working with Numbers, Dates, and Times 324

A Glossary 327

B Resources 333

  Index 337

Introduction

Welcome to *Grammar for Grown-Ups*! What brings you here? If I had to guess, I'd assume one of the following descriptions applies to you:

- You're a student of some sort. You might be in middle school, high school, college, or even graduate school, but you've realized you need some extra help with grammar and style.
- English is not your first language, and you're struggling to get a handle on English grammar.
- You've received an unexpected opportunity to write something important—like a business report or an article—and you want to brush up on your grammar and improve your style.
- Your supervisor at work (or maybe a kind colleague) suggested you work on the basics of writing so you can present yourself better in emails and other written communication.
- You're a curious person who likes language and wants to spend a little more time learning how it works.

Do you fit in one of those categories? If so, welcome aboard. If not, welcome aboard anyway. As long as you have a desire to learn about the nuts and bolts of grammar and the rules of thumb for style—or just a desire to improve your writing—this book should be educational.

What You Will Learn in This Book

This book is divided into five parts:

Part 1, Introduction to Grammar and Style, provides a look at some of the reasons why grammar and style are important. I'll discuss different usage levels and the importance of writing at the appropriate level, whether you're writing a text message, short story, newspaper article, or dissertation. I'll also discuss literary devices, which aren't just for fiction writers and poets.

Part 2, Grammar Basics, looks at the parts of speech: nouns, verbs, adjectives, adverbs, prepositions, conjunctions, and interjections. I'll introduce you to concepts and terminology that will be important throughout the book, including the different sentence types.

Part 3, Using the Parts of Speech to Build Sentences, helps you utilize some of the building blocks and components of grammar that have already been introduced. In particular, you'll learn about nouns and verbs, which become subjects and predicates in sentences.

Part 4, Writing with Style, looks at various ways you can make your writing not only grammatically correct, but enjoyable to read. Sentence variety is one important aspect of writing with style, and I'll discuss many other ways to make your writing lively and readable. I'll also suggest ways to keep your writing inoffensive and bias-free.

Part 5, Fine-Tuning the Mechanics, will help you with some of the smaller details of writing, especially spelling, capitalization, and punctuation. You'll learn the various uses of commas, which can be very confusing. I'll also discuss parentheses, colons, question marks, exclamation marks, and semicolons. Hint: There are only two uses for semicolons.

Throughout each chapter you'll find practice exercises to help you review what you've learned. At the end of the book, you'll find a glossary of key terms and a list of resources for further reading.

Acknowledgments

I'd like to thank my parents, Edward and Janet.

Thanks to all my writing students over the years. Whether you knew it or not, you helped me learn, too.

I'd also like to thank my dog, Monkey. He has excellent grammar for a dog.

Special Thanks to the Technical Reviewer

Grammar for Grown-Ups was reviewed by an expert who double-checked the accuracy of what you'll learn here, to help us ensure this book gives you everything you need to know about grammar and style. Special thanks are extended to Joy Dean Lee.

About the Author

Mark Peters, PhD, has been writing professionally and teaching freshman grammar for two decades. He has been a writing instructor for Adler University, Capella University, and Empire State College. He has written for *Writer's Digest*, *The Writer*, *The Chronicle of Higher Education*, *Esquire*, and many other publications. He is also the author of *Bullshit: A Lexicon*.

Part 1
Introduction to Grammar and Style

Professional racecar drivers can't go from 0 to 200 miles per hour instantly. They have to gradually work their way up to the high speeds. In grammar you have to start slowly, too. This part will help you begin to learn the parts of speech and elements of grammar that will be crucial throughout the book—and in your future as a writer.

Motivation is also helpful when learning anything new. Maybe you already have strong reasons for learning about grammar and style, but in these chapters, you'll learn many reasons why grammar and style are important.

I'll introduce a lot of rules and conventions throughout this book, but this section will discuss the purpose of the rules and conventions. You'll learn some linguistic concepts such as syntax and morphology, as well as usage levels. Every type of writing is at a certain usage level, and it's important to know what level is appropriate. You wouldn't want to write at the texting level for a résumé.

I'll also discuss some aspects of style, including the use of literary techniques such as allusion, alliteration, and metaphor. Even if you don't want to write fiction or poetry, knowing about the creative potential of English can enrich your writing and make it much more enjoyable to read. Even the driest forms of writing have some art to them.

1

Rules and Conventions

As you set out on your journey to master English grammar and related topics, the first and most pressing question you might ask is: Why do I have to know this stuff? I'm not going to major in English or become a novelist. How is grammar going to help me?

That's understandable. After all, if you can read this book, engage in coherent discourse, and keep in touch via texting, email, Zoom, and other digital media, you might wonder why you need to follow a bunch of apparently arbitrary rules.

This chapter answers those questions and more, as it brings you up to speed on what grammar, usage, and mechanics are all about and why they matter. I think you'll find there's a lot more to grammar and style than you think, and that they can help you not only in school and at work, but in how you present yourself throughout your life.

Brushing Up on Three Key Concepts

One of the keys to good writing is to define your terms, so the reader knows what you're talking about. The following three key terms are discussed in this chapter:

- *Grammar* is the structure of a language that governs how words are formed and arranged to build phrases, clauses, and sentences. A grammarian studies sentence structure.
- *Usage* is the customary way people express themselves in words; for example, formally or informally. Usage isn't right or wrong. It just is.
- *Mechanics* are the minutiae of writing, including spelling, capitalization, and punctuation. Editors focus on mechanics when checking a piece of writing for errors.

All writing and speech are examples of usage, and that usage can contain good grammar, bad grammar, good mechanics, or bad mechanics.

Understanding Grammar

Grammar has two branches: *morphology*, which applies to the formation of words, and *syntax*, which applies to the arrangement of words to form phrases, clauses, and sentences.

Grammar is both descriptive and prescriptive. Linguists approach grammar as descriptive; they analyze and describe the way native speakers actually use a language. English teachers, on the other hand, tend to treat grammar as prescriptive—a set of rules to follow. We like to think of grammar, usage, and mechanics as both prescriptive and descriptive because we all need to agree on some rules to communicate effectively with one another while recognizing the fact that language evolves over time. In other words, we need to follow rules, but those rules are subject to change.

The following sections dig deeper into these two branches of grammar to give you a general understanding of what they're all about.

Morphology: Words

Morphology is the study of *morphemes*—the smallest recognizable units in a language. For example, the word *cats* is comprised of two morphemes—the root word *cat* and the *–s* that makes it plural. The word *inconceivable* contains three morphemes: the root word *conceive*, the prefix *in–* and the suffix *–able*. The word *earring* is a *compound word* (a word made up of two or more words) consisting of two morphemes—*ear* and *ring*.

Morphemes are language's secret code. Knowing something about morphology can help you spell words correctly and determine their meaning without having to crack open a dictionary.

Morphology also applies to the roles that words play in sentences—whether a word functions as a noun, verb, adjective, adverb, or one of the other eight parts of speech described in Chapter 3.

Of course, you can know much more about morphology, including the distinctions between roots, stems, and affixes (such as prefixes and suffixes); free and bound morphemes; and inflectional and derivational morphemes. But such information is of interest only to those working toward a degree in English or linguistics. For the rest of us, knowing about root words, compound words, prefixes, suffixes, and parts of speech is good enough.

Practice

Now let's try a few practice exercises to see what you've learned. In the blank, identify the morphemes in each of the following words.

1. class _____
2. unknown _____
3. infrequently _____

4. boots _____
5. failsafe _____
6. indefatigable _____
7. unsmiling _____
8. spider _____
9. fortunate _____
10. precooked _____

Answers

1. One morpheme (class)
2. Two morphemes (un + known)
3. Three morphemes (in + frequent + ly)
4. Two morphemes (boot + s)
5. Two morphemes (fail + safe)
6. Four morphemes (in + de + fatigue + able)
7. Three morphemes (un + smil + ing)
8. One morpheme (spider)
9. Two morphemes (fortune + ate)
10. Three morphemes (pre + cook + ed)

Be sure you don't identify morphemes that aren't there. For example, *spider* may look like it contains the suffix *–er*, but it does not; *spider* is a morpheme with a complete meaning of its own.

Syntax: Word Order

Syntax applies to the way words are arranged to form phrases, clauses, and sentences. For example, most sentences in English start with a subject (noun or pronoun) followed by a verb with something at the end to complete the thought:

Molly	ran	down the hill.
Subject	**Verb**	**Prepositional phrase as adverb describing *ran***

Syntax also relates to the placement of adjectives (usually before the noun they modify) and adverbs (usually after the verb they modify); the arrangement of words in a prepositional phrase (preposition followed by the object of the preposition); the structure of relative clauses, such as those that start with *who*, *which*, or *where*; and so on. You'll find out more about syntax throughout Parts 1 through 3 of this book.

Practice

1. Which of the following sentences has syntax problems?
    A. Gunther gave the dog a treat.
    B. The dog received a treat from Gunther.
    C. Dog get treat Gunther.
    D. Gunther gave the dog another treat—the third today.
2. Which of the following means the same as *syntax*?
    A. Word meaning
    B. Word order
    C. Word origin
    D. Word pronunciation
3. In English syntax, what usually comes first?
    A. A subject
    B. A predicate
    C. A prepositional phrase
    D. A euphemism

Answers

1. C
2. B
3. A

Choosing a Usage Level

Usage is the conventional use of a language in any given context. You probably change usage levels without ever realizing it; for example, you may talk one way to your parents and another way to your friends. You probably write in an entirely different way when writing an article or essay. Writing a scholarly article and an article for a magazine are also two very different animals. Usage is constantly changing according to the circumstances, especially the audience.

All types of writing vary in usage level. A text message to a friend will be extremely informal (and possibly sloppy). A peer-reviewed research article will be impeccably researched and written in an objective, scientific style (or at least it should be). A newspaper editorial and a personal essay will both be subjective and opinionated but might vary wildly in terms of tone and purpose. An email to a friend will be much more informal than an email applying for a job. Depending on the audience and purpose, you'll have to write at many different usage levels, adjusting your tone, style, and diction.

The term *usage* also refers to the acceptable way of using certain words and phrases. For example, many people use the word *literally* figuratively, as in, "The fans were literally going crazy!" That kind of statement is just fine in a message to a friend, but in any kind of formal writing, you'll want to use *literally*, well, literally.

Computers and smart phones have introduced an entirely new level of usage for informal emails, texts, tweets, and other casual online communication in which abbreviations are common and correct spelling is sometimes rare. This book contains very little coverage of these areas. The only recommendation we offer is to remain sensitive to what's considered acceptable and unacceptable to your audience. When in doubt, opt for more formal language until you have a better feel for what's considered acceptable. You can adjust your tone downward from there.

Adhering to Conventions

Given the fact that most writing these days is typed, you don't need to dot your i's and cross your t's, but you still need to pay attention to *mechanics*, including the following items:

Spelling: A good spellchecker catches most typos, but it may not catch the use of wrong words, such as *their* instead of *there* and *its* (possessive of *it*) instead of *it's* (short for *it is*). You still need to proofread your prose and know how to spell and use a dictionary.

Capitalization: Capitalization is a convention that helps readers identify names, titles, headings, beginnings of sentences, and so on.

Punctuation: Knowing when to use periods, colons, semicolons, commas, dashes, quotation marks, and so on is essential to cueing your readers on when to pause and to helping them move through your writing smoothly.

Abbreviations: Abbreviations, including *e.g.* (for example), *i.e.* (that is), and *etc.* (etcetera), serve as a form of shorthand. Conventions for forming and using abbreviations ensure that readers know what each abbreviation stands for.

Numbers: Conventions regarding numbers cover everything from whether to use a comma to mark the thousands place to whether you use numerals or words for 1 (one) to 10 (ten).

Appreciating the Purpose of Rules and Conventions

People sometimes argue that grammar, usage, and mechanics don't matter as long as you're able to communicate clearly. The flaw in that argument is that clear communication requires adherence to conventions. Grammar, usage, and mechanics guidelines serve as the rules of the road. As long as everyone follows them, communication proceeds smoothly. Break the rules, and clarity suffers: readers must work harder to figure out exactly what you're trying to express, and they may simply give up or misinterpret your intended meaning.

The following sections highlight a few rules and conventions for communicating effectively in English. These sections also provide examples to show how breaking the rules can muddle communication.

Place the Subject First

In English, syntax is very flexible, but people generally expect sentences to follow certain patterns: they expect sentences to begin with a subject followed by a verb. When you stray from conventional syntax, you run counter to the listener's or reader's expectations, placing an added burden on your audience to decipher your intended meaning. Following are a few examples of sentences with syntax issues:

> Sailing he was to the shores of Iceland.
> The *Titanic* an iceberg sank.
> To Natalie my tennis racket I gave.

Reading the sentences, you probably figured out their intended meaning, but your job would have been much easier if they followed conventional subject-verb syntax:

> He was sailing to the shores of Iceland.
> An iceberg sank the *Titanic*.
> I gave Natalie my tennis racket.

On the other hand, if you're writing poetry (verse), you have much greater freedom to experiment with syntax in order to develop rhythm and rhyme, but when writing prose, stick with more conventional word order.

Practice

Rewrite the following sentences as needed:

1. Plant trees is what the Arbor Day Foundation encourages people to do.

2. Over my house the jet flew.

3. The squirrel was chased up the tree by the dog.

Answers

1. The Arbor Day Foundation encourages people to plant trees.
2. The jet flew over my house.
3. The dog chased the squirrel up the tree.

Watch Where You Place Phrases and Clauses

A misplaced phrase or clause may result in ambiguity, as in the following example:

> The couple returned from their cruise which they had thoroughly enjoyed in a limousine.

Again, you can probably figure out the intended meaning, but at first reading, it sounds as though the couple had their Caribbean cruise in a limousine. You could fix this either by moving the phrase *in a limousine* closer to the verb it describes (*returned*) or by setting off the relative clause (*which ...*) with commas:

> The couple returned in a limousine from their cruise, which they had thoroughly enjoyed.
> The couple returned from their cruise, which they had thoroughly enjoyed, in a limousine.

Read more on phrases and clauses in Chapters 9 and 10.

Practice

Rewrite the following sentences as needed:

1. Because the restaurant was so drafty patrons complained of being cold.

2. Parrots tend to nest in hollowed-out trees, which are generally not nest builders.

3. His parents returned from their honeymoon in a van.

Answers

1. Patrons complained of being cold because the restaurant was so drafty.
2. Parrots, which are not generally nest-builders, tend to nest in hollowed-out trees.
3. His parents returned in a van from their honeymoon.

Avoid Awkward Shifts in Verb Tense

Verb tense conveys an action's time zone: past, present, future, and so on. Rules that govern tense help ensure that whenever someone relates a series of events, they do so in a way that's consistent with the actual chronology of the events. Just imagine how confusing a passage would be if verb tenses were used willy-nilly:

> All employees <u>will review</u> the safety policies and procedures before the accident <u>occurred</u>, but no one at the scene of the accident <u>were following</u> procedures.

Consistent use of tense clarifies the timeline, indicating when each action occurred in relation to the other actions:

> All employees <u>had reviewed</u> the safety policies and procedures before the accident <u>occurred</u>, but no one at the scene of the accident <u>followed</u> the procedures.

Read more on verbs in Chapter 6.

Practice

Rewrite the following sentences as needed:

1. Dogs who are playful should loved the dog park.

2. I hate having move my car to the other side of the street.

3. Buzz Aldrin is the one of few men who will walk on the moon.

Answers

1. Dogs who are playful should love the dog park.
2. I hate having to move my car to the other side of the street.
3. Buzz Aldrin is one of few men who have walked on the moon.

Avoid Dangling Modifiers

A *dangling modifier* is a word or phrase that's in the wrong place. As a result, the misplaced modifier unintentionally describes the wrong word, as in the following example:

Having read the book, the movie disappointed me.

In this example, "having read the book" describes "the movie," which doesn't make sense because a movie can't read a book. By placing the modifier before the word it should describe, the sentence becomes much clearer:

Having read the book, I found the movie disappointing.

Read more on dangling modifiers in Chapter 15.

Practice

Rewrite the following sentences as needed:

1. As a tough critic, the movie disappointed me.

2. As a fan of David Foster Wallace, his books are excellent.

3. To save time, my schedule is up to date.

Answers

1. As a tough critic, I was disappointed in the movie.
2. As a fan of David Foster Wallace, I think his books are excellent.
3. To save time, I keep my schedule up to date.

Beware of Misplaced and Omitted Commas

The comma is one of the most diminutive of punctuation marks, but an omitted or misplaced comma can cause considerable confusion. Here's an example of how a comma can completely change the meaning of a sentence:

Let's bake, Grandma!
Let's bake Grandma!

A missing *serial comma* (the comma before the last item in a series) can also confuse the reader, though less dramatically. For example, suppose you're emailing a friend to say that you invited four people over for dinner—your neighbors Joe and Tammy Smith and your friends Jan and Bob. You write:

We invited the Smiths, Jan and Bob.

Without the serial comma, this could mean that you invited only Jan and Bob, whose last name is Smith, over for dinner. By using the serial comma, you clarify what you really mean:

We invited the Smiths, Jan, and Bob.

This sort of comma fun is the basis of the book *Eats, Shoots & Leaves*. Read more on commas in Chapter 17.

Practice

Rewrite the following sentences as needed:

1. The artist, Pablo Picasso, is one of my favorites.

2. The pen, which can write upside down, is my favorite.

3. I don't like those jerks, Jan, and Ian.

Answers

1. The artist Pablo Picasso is one of my favorites.
2. The pen that can write upside down is my favorite.
3. I don't like those jerks, Jan and Ian.

Use Parallel Constructions

Parallel construction results when two or more related phrases are in the same grammatical form; for example, they're all nouns, they're all verbs, or they're all *gerunds* (verbs ending in *–ing* that act as nouns). When items aren't parallel, a sentence sounds awkward, as in the following example:

> The company rewarded its employees for their hard work, expertise, and paying attention to detail.

Even to the untrained ear, something sounds a little off about that sentence. The terms *hard work* and *expertise* are standard nouns, but the last item, *paying attention to detail*, is a gerund. A list like this works much better if all the items in the list have the same form—if the items are parallel, in other words. Parallelism clarifies the meaning and improves the sound of the sentence:

> The company rewarded its employees for their hard work, expertise, and attention to detail.

Read more on parallelism in Chapter 13.

Practice

Rewrite the following sentences as needed:

1. Jill's passions included hiking, skiing, and to write.
   _____

2. My cat loves to play, to chase, and eating.
   _____

3. They say live and learn but I say make a lot of money.
   _____

Answers

1. Jill's passions included hiking, skiing, and writing.
2. My cat loves playing, chasing, and eating.
3. They say live and learn, but I say live and earn.

Chapter Review Practice

Let's review some of the basic terms. Grammar is the structure of a language according to which words are formed and arranged to build phrases, clauses, and sentences. Usage is the conventional use of a language in any given context or situation, while mechanics consist of the conventions governing spelling, capitalization, punctuation, abbreviations, and numbers. Standard informal English is acceptable and appropriate for most types of written and oral communication. The ultimate goal of learning grammar, usage, and mechanics is to be able to communicate effectively and efficiently.

Now let's practice what you learned in this chapter:

1. How many morphemes are in the following words?
   A. Second _____
   B. Indent _____
   C. Incoherent _____
   D. Unfortunately _____
2. Which of the following has a grammar problem?
   A. I count sheep when I want to fall asleep.
   B. Try to be present when talking with friends.
   C. Milk many kinds of there are.
   D. There is a premium on good writing.

3. Which of the following has a problem with mechanics?
   A. My pet rabbit is adorable.
   B. I dont like too go two work
   C. My friend Wes is mellow and kind.
   D. Working under bright lights stinks.
4. Which word accurately describes grammar?
   A. Descriptive
   B. Prescriptive
   C. Constrictive
   D. Receptive
5. Where would you be most likely to read standard English?
   A. A tweet
   B. A text message
   C. A newspaper
   D. A blog
6. Which of the following is most synonymous with grammar?
   A. Tense
   B. Predicate
   C. Style
   D. Structure
7. Which of the following is a good description of morphology?
   A. The building blocks of words
   B. The foundation of logic
   C. The philosophy of change
   D. The essence of grammar
8. Which of the following is a good example of parallelism?
   A. I haven't got much fight left in me.
   B. My cat enjoys playing with toys and tuna.
   C. A triathlon consists of running, swimming, and biking.
   D. Oh, to be young again.
9. Which of the following contains a serial comma?
   A. Joe likes to dance, and he likes to hike.
   B. Man, my rabbit can't get enough carrots.
   C. I'm used to snow, because I'm from Buffalo.
   D. Great athletes are good at running, jumping, and throwing.

10. What is the main purpose of writing?
    A. To impress people
    B. To communicate
    C. To make money
    D. To apologize

Answers

1. A. One morpheme (second)
   B. Two morphemes (in + dent)
   C. Three morphemes (in + cohere + ent)
   D. Four morphemes (un + fortune + ate + ly)
2. C
3. B
4. A and B
5. C
6. D
7. A
8. C
9. D
10. B

Beyond the Rules: Writing with Style

A parent or teacher who only says "Don't do that!" and "Cut that out!" won't be very effective. Telling people what not to do doesn't help them figure out what to do—and why. Similarly, expressing yourself effectively through language isn't only about following rules and avoiding mistakes; it also involves learning the craft of writing, so you know how to hook readers and compel them to continue reading.

While grammar, usage, and mechanics are about rules and conventions and what you should and shouldn't do, style is about what you can do. Style encompasses the infinite possibilities and potential of the English language.

Because style is about unlocking possibilities, it's more subjective than grammar. Pinning down exactly what it is and how to develop a distinctive style is difficult, if not impossible. This chapter is my attempt to bring you up to speed on style basics.

Defining Style

Style is the manner in which a writer chooses to present content to an audience in order to achieve the desired effect. While some experts define style as a writer's distinctive form of expression—or voice—style goes beyond that. A writer can change styles depending on the nature of the publication, the audience, the topic, the goal that the writer seeks to achieve, and a host of other variables. Journalists and technical writers, for example, usually make a conscious effort to keep their personality out of their writing in order to establish an objective viewpoint. Copywriters want to sell something and may try to do so by evoking an emotional response from their audience.

Style shouldn't be a mechanical structure superimposed on the content. Style should develop organically along with the content so the final written product serves whatever purpose the author has in mind. The style you use should help you convey information, describe a character, report a story, persuade readers to think or act a certain way, or achieve some other purpose.

Feel the pace shift within the following paragraph from Jack London's short story "A Piece of Steak," as the description transitions from Sandel, a spirited young boxer, to his opponent, Tom King, who's more experienced and methodical:

> Sandel was in and out, here, there, and everywhere, light-footed and eager-hearted, a living wonder of white flesh and stinging muscle that wove itself into a dazzling fabric of attack, slipping and leaping like a flying shuttle from action to action through a thousand actions, all of them centred upon the destruction of Tom King, who stood between him and fortune. And Tom King patiently endured. He knew his business, and he knew Youth now that Youth was no longer his. There was nothing to do till the other lost some of his steam, was his thought, and he grinned to himself as he deliberately ducked so as to receive a heavy blow on the top of his head. It was a wicked thing to do, yet eminently fair according to the rules of the boxing game. A man was supposed to take care of his own knuckles, and, if he insisted on hitting an opponent on the top of the head, he did so at his own peril.

While your goal may not be to write a short story or a novel, you still need to be sensitive to the subtle messages that different styles convey. If you're writing a letter of complaint to a company, for example, you want the tone to be assertive but respectful. If you were writing a letter of apology to a customer, on the other hand, you'd want to sound courteous and accommodating.

Some Different Styles

Every type of writing or genre has a certain style. Here are brief descriptions of some common writing genres and their styles:

Business writing: This includes a variety of professional writing genres, including business reports, memos, letters, and slide decks, and even job materials such as résumés. Business writing is brief and to the point. It should communicate as simply and directly as possible. (Although business writing often is full of jargon, which you'll learn more about in Chapter 12.)

News articles: These are written in an objective, presentational style by journalists. The writer tries to be invisible. This is a "just the facts" type of writing.

Column: This form of journalism expresses an opinion and is usually written in a personal style that highlights the wit of the writer. In a newspaper, you should be able to read the facts in news articles, then read someone's opinions of the facts in columns.

Editorials: Columns are sometimes called editorials, but an editorial is also a specific type of opinion piece that's usually written by the editor and represents the opinion of the entire paper. This kind of editorial usually doesn't list an author, since it is meant to represent the paper as a whole (and may be the work of a few editors). An editorial has a less personal voice than a column because it represents the periodical rather than a person.

Magazine articles: Magazine articles vary widely, but generally they are examples of in-depth reporting that dig deeply into a topic or a person's life. Magazine writers have more leeway for creativity (such as humor and extended description) than writers of news articles. Magazines also include many shorter articles.

Essay writing: This category overlaps quite a bit with magazine writing. However, essays are often more personal than magazine articles. Often, essays fall in the category of creative nonfiction, a type of writing that uses the literary devices of fiction to write about true events.

Scholarly journal articles: These are scientific articles that present and discuss research. Scholarly articles are written in all the sciences, from the hard (physical) sciences to the soft (social) sciences. This type of writing is written in an extremely objective, detached style with a meticulous eye for detail. Scholarly writing, along with newswriting, is quite impersonal.

Research papers for school: These mimic scholarly journal articles but are quite different. The main difference is that the student almost never does any original research except for reading articles, so a research paper is almost always the equivalent of a literature review (a type of writing that summarizes what has been written on a certain topic). Research papers are assigned to help students improve as writers and thinkers. They are usually written with a strong thesis statement, or a sentence that captures the argument of the paper. Without a clear thesis statement, a research paper literally doesn't have a point.

Advertising copy: This can range from a single slogan ("I'm lovin' it!") to the entire script of a commercial. One of the best examples of a clever advertising campaign was Dos Equis' "The Most Interesting Man in the World" character, perhaps the most roguish, charming beer pitchman in history. Ad copy is often humorous, and it should catch people's attention. This is writing with a simple purpose: get people to buy your product. A secondary goal would be to help people remember your product and have good associations with it. That process is known as *branding*.

Creative writing: This is a broad category that could include dramatic writing, humor writing, and advertising copy, but it most commonly refers to poetry and fiction. The simplest definitions of poetry and fiction might be that poetry expresses emotions and fiction tells stories, but those are extremely simplistic definitions that only apply in a very broad sense. Poetry and fiction are both huge categories full of variety, and you should seek out a book on either to learn more.

Theatrical writing: This includes writing for the stage, screen, or video, such as playwriting and screenwriting. Theatrical (also called dramatic) writing is just as creative as poetry and fiction, but there's a big difference: playwrights and screenwriters write for actors to perform their words. Theatrical writing also includes writing for television and internet videos, as well as dramatic forms such as the one-act play, 10-minute play, and sketch, a comedic form made famous by *Saturday Night Live*.

Comedy writing: Like ad copy, comedy writing has a simple purpose: make people laugh (and often, think). Comedy writing includes scripts for TV and movies, jokes for standup comedians and the internet, and humor pieces, which are comedic essays. One of the oldest and best sources of humor pieces is *The New Yorker*'s Shouts & Murmurs section. Another comedy institution is *The Onion*, a satirical newspaper.

Grant writing: This is a very specific type of writing aimed at securing funding from agencies and organizations that give grants (money) to businesses and individuals. Grant-writing is dry, technical, and precise (and also lucrative if you know how to do it well).

Blog post: Blog posts are as unique as the people creating them. A blog could be a series of pictures of your cat, a disconnected bunch of rants on politics, a group of posts about your vacation to Greece, or a forum for serious discussions of sociology—or any other topic. The credentials of bloggers vary wildly, too. Any person in the world can blog, from your next-door neighbor to an art professor. To judge the value of a blog, consider the quality of the writing, the purpose of the blog, and the credentials of the blogger. For your own blog, think about whether you'd like your blog to be a fun hobby or a potential asset to your career. It could be either.

Tweet: A tweet is a generally short blog post for the popular social network and microblogging service X, formerly known as Twitter, although the term is also used for other platforms such as Bluesky and Threads. Despite the seeming triviality of the form, many writers—of humor and more serious matters—have used tweeting to build an audience that has led to paying work, such as writing books or TV shows. How you tweet is entirely up to you. Reposting someone else's tweet—which is like quoting it—is retweeting.

Text message: This is probably the most informal type of writing. However, like anything else, some people take texting more seriously than others. The purpose of many texts is to pass on information, such as "I'm running late" or "My gate at the airport changed," but some people have lengthy conversations via text. How you text is up to you and your friends. But if you ever text an English professor, you might want to ease up on the emojis and tighten up the grammar.

You should also know that writing genres are not uniform types of writing: everyone writing in a genre doesn't write the same way. If you want to learn more about the style of one of these types of writing, you should pick up a book geared toward that type of writing.

When it comes to writing, there is variation within variation within variation. Each publication has its own style, but each writer also has a style. When writing in a specific genre, you should find a balance between your own style and that of the genre.

The following section is more general: it describes elements of good style that will usually help you communicate effectively and economically in words.

Practice

Identify the most likely source of the following sentences:

1. Are u ready?
2. You deserve to wear socks this cool.
3. Adams (2021) suggested that mindfulness is particularly helpful among certain populations.
4. Gwen: What do you mean by that? [Barry enters.]
5. The president made a few brief remarks to the press.

Answers

1. Text message
2. Advertising copy
3. Scholarly article or research paper
4. Theatrical writing
5. News writing

Style Guidelines

Good style is engaging, clear, and direct. Bad style is dull, muddled, and unclear. Although style varies and what constitutes a good writing style is somewhat subjective, the following guidelines can help you write with style:

Keep it simple. Writing doesn't have to be complicated to be good. It needs to be clear and direct. Unless you have a reason to do otherwise, stick with relatively short sentences and paragraphs.

Establish a smooth and logical flow. Good writing flows smoothly from word to word, sentence to sentence, and paragraph to paragraph. A smooth and logical flow is often the product of a clear idea, the right structure, and meticulous organization. When writing has a strong central idea, heavy-handed transition words—such as *although*, *therefore*, and *in conclusion*—aren't needed as much to transition from one sentence or paragraph to the next.

Make good use of repetition. You can often create subtle transitions by repeating a key word from a sentence or paragraph in the sentence or paragraph that follows it. These transitions can help your writing hold together for the reader, kind of like how I just repeated *transitions*.

Develop an attitude. Be conscious of the tone you're setting. Do you want to come across as serious or playful, intimate or detached, angry or conciliatory, tough or tender?

Start most sentences with a subject-verb combo. The subject is the person, place, or thing that's acting or being. The verb is the action or condition. Starting with a subject-verb combo helps you avoid many common flaws in style.

Vary your sentence structure. Although you should start most sentences with a subject-verb combo, you can combine sentences, add phrases and clauses, and experiment with syntax to establish an engaging rhythm and pace.

Write mostly in the active voice. Active voice makes the subject of the sentence clear. Passive voice omits or hides the subject. Check out these examples:

> **Active:** NASA launched the satellite into orbit.
> **Passive:** The satellite was launched into orbit.

Although passive voice is suitable in certain situations when you want to gloss over the subject, you should usually write in the active voice, which is much clearer and easier to read.

Write with concrete nouns and action verbs. By choosing vivid nouns and strong verbs, you won't need as many adjectives, adverbs, and phrases.

Choose precise words. You can often reduce wordiness and increase the impact of a message by taking time to choose the right words. Use a thesaurus to scope out your options and a dictionary to narrow your options to the word with just the right meaning.

Trim the fat. Terse expressions have greater impact.

Mind the meanings. Remain sensitive to a word's denotation (literal meaning) and connotation (idea or emotion that people commonly associate with the word). Certain words have a positive or negative connotation. Compare the words *miserly* and *frugal*. Both words mean to spend money sparingly, but *miserly* carries the negative connotation of being stingy, whereas *frugal* carries the positive connotation of managing money wisely.

Sharpening Your Style

One way to develop a good writing style is to consciously strive to follow the guidelines described in the previous section. The following are additional ways to develop a mastery of style:

Write with a purpose. Is your purpose to entertain, inform, instruct, persuade, or do something else? Writing with a clear purpose will help you gauge your writing's effectiveness as you draft and revise. If your writing fails to meet your objective, you have more work to do.

Don't procrastinate or be a perfectionist. Beginners often agonize about the quality of their writing so much that they're unable to get any writing done. Just start writing, even if you don't feel ready. You can always fine-tune it later, but there will be nothing to fine-tune if you don't start. Perfectionism is a double-edged sword. Don't cut yourself with it.

Write more or less in the manner you normally speak. Some writers try so hard to sound educated that the message gets lost in tortured prose. Write as you speak and then revise and reorganize as needed to make your message crystal clear.

Keep your audience in mind. When writing to an individual, keeping your audience in mind is easy. If you're writing to a larger audience, try to single out one individual and imagine yourself speaking to them.

Read good writing. You can find good writing in everything from classic novels to quality newspapers and magazines, including *Rolling Stone* magazine, *Vanity Fair*, *The Wall Street Journal*, and *The Atlantic*. Try reading a few pieces aloud to tune your ear to good writing.

Emulate a writing style you like. While you don't want to write just like someone else, exercises in emulating a certain writing style make you more conscious of style and allow that style to influence your own.

Break things up. In business, technical, and internet writing, compose short paragraphs and use headings and lists to break up the text into easily digestible snippets. This approach makes the content more accessible and easier to skim. It also reduces the need for you to transition between sentences and paragraphs.

Read your own writing aloud. If you're tripping over your own words, your readers will have an even harder time maintaining their balance. Reading aloud often reveals problems that need fixing. It might feel goofy to perform your work for an audience of just you, but the results are proven to work.

Distance yourself from what you wrote. Write a rough draft and then set it aside for a few hours or (even better) a day or two. Now read it again. This technique gives you a more objective view of the text and often reveals areas that require fine-tuning.

Seek feedback. Have someone else read what you wrote and tell you what they think. You don't have to take their feedback, but someone looking at a paper with fresh eyes can help you learn the strengths and weaknesses of your writing.

Enhancing Your Prose with Literary Devices

Literary devices are techniques that writers have developed to take language beyond its literal meaning and appeal to the senses. Literary devices are sophisticated and show skill with language beyond the basics. Although you're more likely to encounter literary devices in fictional works and poetry, you can use them in other types of writing to drive home a point, clarify an idea, or punch up your prose. The following sections cover literary devices commonly used in writing prose.

Paint a Picture with Figurative Language

Figurative language uses words to engage the senses, memories, and imagination of the reader through a variety of literary devices, including the following:

- *Simile* is a comparison using *like* or *as*: Sonny Liston jabbed like a jackhammer.
- *Metaphor* is a comparison not using *like* or *as*: The public defender was buried beneath his caseload.
- *Personification* is the attribution of human qualities to a nonhuman being or object: The tornado attacked the city like an angry mob.
- *Paradox* is the juxtaposition of two apparently contradictory ideas: A baby is a new life; for parents, it's also the end of their old life.
- *Hyperbole* is an exaggeration used to drive home a point: Marie lived life at a 100 miles an hour.
- *Allusion* is a reference to something outside of the text that the audience probably knows about: The adrenaline rush infused onlookers with Herculean strength, enabling them to lift the car off of the injured driver.
- *Idiom* is a common expression whose meaning has little or no connection with its literal meaning. For example, the phrase "keep your nose to the grindstone" doesn't literally mean to do so, it means to focus on your work. A word of caution: use idiomatic expressions sparingly, if at all, in formal writing.

Tune In to the Sounds of Language

Although this book isn't about writing poetry or song lyrics, you should still be sensitive to the way language sounds and know something about the literary devices at your disposal to produce sound effects:

- *Alliteration* is the repetition of the same first consonant sound in adjacent or nearby words: Snakes slithered softly through the grass.
- *Assonance* is the repetition of vowel sounds in nearby words: We heard the sound of pounding from the apartment down the hall.
- *Consonance* is the repetition of consonant sounds in nearby words, not necessarily at the beginning of each word: Jack mumbled dumbly.
- *Onomatopoeia* is the formation of a word that sounds like what it means; for example, *boom*, *pop*, *growl*, and *buzz*.
- *Rhythm* is any recognizable pattern of sound that helps the text flow smoothly. Sentence length and variety, word choice, and punctuation all contribute to the rhythm of a sentence. The following example contains a long sentence followed by a very short one, producing an abrupt shift in rhythm:

The show presented a magnificent array of music, dance, acrobatics, drama, and humor, all carefully choreographed and meticulously performed to engage and entertain. Unfortunately, the audience was not impressed.

Literary devices are pretty cool, but like anything in writing, don't overuse them. Indulging in too much of a good thing may distract readers from the point you're trying to make. Use literary devices sparingly and strategically to hook your readers, keep them reading, and leave a lasting impression.

Practice

In the blank, write the name of the literary device used in the sentence.

1. Following King Solomon's lead, the judge threatened to split the car in two and give each owner half. _____
2. Nothing had prepared Patty for Paul's perpetual palaver. _____
3. The homeowners were underwater on their mortgage and facing the possibility of foreclosure. _____
4. Don't loan your coat to Joan. _____
5. I'm thirsty enough to drink Niagara Falls. _____
6. After splashing water on his face, Dylan felt refreshed. _____
7. None of the senators would even utter the phrase "balanced budget," because it was such a political hot potato. _____
8. To some people, plants are like pets. _____
9. Hail smacked the metal roof like a cacophony of cats. _____
10. Earth is a doctor that heals herself. _____

Answers

1. Allusion to King Solomon
2. Alliteration—repetition of "p"
3. Metaphor—comparing the state of being behind on one's mortgage to drowning
4. Assonance—repetition of long "o" vowel sound
5. Hyperbole—nobody can actually drink Niagara Falls
6. Onomatopoeia—the word *splashing*
7. Idiom—*hot potato*
8. Simile—comparing plants to pets

9. Consonance—repetition of the hard "c" sound
10. Personification—comparing the Earth to a doctor

Chapter Review Practice

So what is style? In a nutshell, style is the manner in which a writer chooses to write. Style varies according to genre and publication, as well as individual. A good writing style uses words to engage and communicate effectively and efficiently. To hone your writing style, write with a purpose, say what you mean, and keep your audience in mind. Use figurative language, when appropriate, to engage your readers' senses. Consult style guides for grammar, usage, and mechanics guidelines, especially if you're writing or editing for publication. And most of all, keep reading good writing.

Now let's practice what you learned in this chapter:

1. Which of the following genres is written in an objective style?
    A. Poetry
    B. Fiction
    C. News articles
    D. Scholarly articles
2. Which of the following contains an allusion?
    A. My dog is as fierce as a lion.
    B. Even Hercules couldn't lift that couch.
    C. I feel cool when driving my convertible.
    D. My beard itches like a son of a gun.
3. Which of the following is an example of alliteration?
    A. Joe got arrested for the fourth time.
    B. Maury made a major mistake.
    C. Mary keeps immaculate records.
    D. Ted is a little inconsiderate.
4. Which of the following are similes, and which are metaphors?
    A. The sun was a beacon shining down.
    B. Criticisms rained down on the author.
    C. I felt like a sick dog.
    D. My dog is as quick as a rabbit.
    E. Your friendship is a gift.

5. Which of the following contains a personification?
   A. The rain fell so fast it buried the city in water.
   B. The dog slunk away.
   C. The meal sat in his stomach like a rock.
   D. The car engine purred like a happy cat.
6. Which of the following is an example of onomatopoeia?
   A. The wasps stung.
   B. The bees buzzed.
   C. The flies flew.
   D. The butterflies fluttered.
7. Which of the following is an example of assonance?
   A. Susan had to go to the hospital.
   B. Benny was a private investigator.
   C. Breaking a mirror is bad luck.
   D. The loud sounds of the proud mom resounded.
8. Which of the following is an example of consonance?
   A. Too many cooks spoil the meal.
   B. The spilt milk pooled around the cradle.
   C. The vice president adopted a rabbit.
   D. The laborer went on strike.
9. Which of the following contains hyperbole?
   A. It's hard to get any work done on Friday.
   B. My dog is fast enough to be an agility dog.
   C. This fried chicken is awfully good.
   D. My dad is a bazillion years old.
10. Which of the following is an example of paradox?
    A. Life is short but feels long.
    B. Life is a journey.
    C. Life is like a roller coaster.
    D. Life is like the ocean.

Answers

1. C and D
2. B
3. B
4. A. Metaphor
   B. Metaphor
   C. Simile
   D. Simile
   E. Metaphor
5. D
6. B
7. D
8. B
9. D
10. A

Part 2

Grammar Basics

What are the parts of speech? What is a sentence? How do the parts of a sentence work together? I'll answer these basic issues of grammar in these chapters. The meat and potatoes of this book will be served.

This section of the book is very word-oriented. I'll discuss nouns, verbs, adjectives, adverbs, prepositions, conjunctions, and interjections. Also, I'll go beyond the types of words to discuss what they can do grammatically. This is especially important when discussing how nouns become subjects and verbs become predicates. I'll include many quizzes to help you test yourself on the information.

I'll also introduce you to the types of sentences, which will be essential later when the focus shifts to style. There can be no style without grammar, and you can't use grammar without having some type of style. The twin topics of this book are always intertwined, even when one is in the spotlight.

If you have a test on grammar and style in one hour and need to cram, these are the chapters you should focus on. I'll introduce you to the terminology and concepts that will be expanded on later. These sections will lay the foundation for becoming a true student of English grammar.

Brushing Up on Parts of Speech

Parts of speech are the categories used to group words by the roles they play in sentences, kind of like how actors play lead and supporting roles on stage and in TV and movies. Some words name a thing, others express an action, some modify other words, several join words and clauses, and a few simply utter short exclamations like "Ugh!" or "Whoo!" You don't have to be able to name or define the parts of speech in order to pen punchy prose, but you do need to have a working knowledge of them, so you know what I'm talking about when I mention them in other chapters.

The good news is that the English language has only eight parts of speech: nouns, pronouns, verbs, adjectives, adverbs, conjunctions, prepositions, and interjections. The bad news is that working with some of these parts of speech can get pretty involved. This chapter brings you up to speed on the parts of speech and their nuances.

Meeting the Actors: Nouns and Pronouns

Nouns and *pronouns* represent beings: people, places, and things, including abstract things such as love and freedom. In any given sentence, they're the ones doing the action or on the receiving end of the action. The following sections explain the difference between nouns and pronouns and provide additional relevant details for dealing with them.

The Lead Actors: Nouns

Nouns conjure up images of creatures, locations, or objects—*dog, tornado, neighbor, Taylor Swift, Batman, Australia, napkin, democracy*. Anything that can act, be acted upon, or just plain *be* has a noun that names it. Nouns come in four basic types:

Common: Your average everyday nouns that represent a class of objects as opposed to a particular individual. Words such as *car, cat, toe, tree, idea,* and *location* are all common nouns.

Proper: Names of individuals and places. Proper nouns always start with a capital letter; for example, *Aunt Mary, Patrick, Bora Bora, Fido,* and the *Mississippi River*.

Compound: When two or more words represent a single being or entity, you're looking at a compound noun: *mother-in-law*, *baseball*, *toothbrush*, and *tennis shoe* are all compound nouns. Note that some are one word, some are hyphenated, and some are two or more words separated by spaces. Sometimes more than one spelling is correct, and the accepted spelling can change over time. For example, *base-ball* was once correct, but it would look weird today if you hyphenated *baseball*. Hyphens tend to disappear over time as the compound gains acceptance.

Collective: Collective nouns are those that represent a group, such as *team*, *herd*, *crew*, *flock*, *gang*, and *troupe*. Although it is representing a group, the noun itself can be treated as singular or plural.

Although they have different roles, nouns and verbs are closely related, and a verb can spawn a noun, and vice versa. Collectively referred to as *verbals*, gerunds (verb forms ending in *–ing*) and infinitives (verbs that require a "to"; for example, to jump) function as nouns; for example: *Jumping rope* is my favorite exercise.

Practice

Identify which kind of noun is used in each of the following:

1. Basketball court
2. Abraham Lincoln
3. Horde
4. Window
5. Committee

Answers

1. Compound
2. Proper
3. Collective
4. Common
5. Collective

The Supporting Cast: Pronouns

Just as nouns represent classes of objects or individual persons, places, or things, pronouns represent nouns. The English language provides you with pronouns so you don't have to keep repeating the noun, which can become quite annoying. Most pronouns have an *antecedent*—a noun that the pronoun represents, as in the following example:

> Sally always traveled with her dog.

Sally is the antecedent (a proper noun, by the way), and *her* is the pronoun that refers back to *Sally*. While nouns tend to change form only in the possessive (*Sally's* instead of *Sally*), pronouns take on many forms to reflect their function. Keep reading to find out more about the different pronoun forms.

Personal pronouns represent a specific person, place, or thing. They come in two types: subjective and objective, which play different roles in a sentence.

The following table shows the subjective personal pronouns.

	Singular	**Plural**
First person	I	we
Second person	you	you
Third person	he, she, it	they

The following table shows the objective personal pronouns.

	Singular	**Plural**
First person	me	us
Second person	you	you
Third person	him, her, it	them

For more about how subjective and objective pronouns function in a sentence, see "Changing Case" later in this chapter.

Possessive pronouns signify ownership, as shown in the following table.

	Singular	**Plural**
First person	my, mine	our, ours
Second person	your, yours	your, yours
Third person	his, hers, its	their, theirs

A word of caution: Although you typically show possession by adding *-'s* to the end of a word, *its*, the possessive form of *it* without the apostrophe before the *s* is the exception. The word *it's* is a contraction meaning "it is." Yes, English is complicated.

Reflexive pronouns reflect action performed on oneself, as shown in the following table.

	Singular	Plural
First person	myself	ourselves
Second person	yourself	yourselves
Third person	himself, herself, itself	themselves

Intensive pronouns emphasize the doer of the action. They're identical to the reflexive pronouns, but the action isn't performed on the actor. The following two examples demonstrate the difference:

Reflexive: Sally slapped herself silly.
Intensive: Sally cooked the meal herself.

Demonstrative pronouns point things out or demonstrate them. *This, that, these,* and *those* are all demonstrative pronouns.

Relative pronouns—*that, where, which, who, whom,* and *whose*—enable you to add information about the noun you just mentioned. Here are a couple examples:

The delivery truck, which was already late, slammed into the loading dock.
This summer, we're traveling to Bora Bora, where we vacationed three years ago.

Interrogative pronouns ask a lot of questions (five, to be precise): What? Which? Who? Whom? and Whose?

Indefinite pronouns can't make up their mind whom or what they refer to. The following lists some of the indefinite pronouns and distinguishes the singulars from the plurals and those that can go either way.

The Indefinite Pronouns

Singular	Plural	Singular or Plural
another	both	all
anybody	few	any

Singular	Plural	Singular or Plural
anyone	many	more
anything	several	none
each		most
either		some
everybody		
everyone		
everything		
neither		
no one		
nobody		
nothing		
one		
somebody		
someone		
something		

Reciprocal pronouns, such as *each other* and *one another*, belong to the mutual admiration society. These pronouns are used to show that two or more entities have an equal relationship. Here are a couple examples of the reciprocal pronouns in action:

> The crew members respected one another.
> Family members tend to look like each other.

Differences in Noun and Pronoun Behavior

With nouns and pronouns, you're likely to observe an inequality: pronouns come in nine flavors, but nouns have only four. Why? Because nouns change form only to become plural or possessive, whereas pronouns change to become personal, possessive, reflexive, intensive, demonstrative, and so on, all in the singular and plural.

Check it out. Regardless of the role it plays, a noun remains fairly constant:

> **Personal:** Sally drives a truck.
> **Possessive:** Sally's truck barreled past the exit.

Reflexive: Sally drove Sally to the depot. (Now you know why we have reflexive pronouns.)
Interrogative: Sally drove to the depot?

You get the idea. Now observe how versatile a pronoun is, changing form based on the role it plays:

Personal: She drives a truck.
Possessive: Her truck barreled past the exit.
Reflexive: Sally drove herself to the depot.
Interrogative: Who drove to the depot?

Changing Case

Nouns and pronouns may change *case* depending on the role they play in a sentence. English has three cases:

Subjective: The noun or pronoun serves as the subject of the sentence—the person, place, or thing doing the action or existing in some state or quality of being.

Objective: The noun or pronoun is on the receiving end of the action, typically as a *direct object* (the object being acted upon) or the *indirect object* (the object receiving the direct object). For example, if I pay *you* $25, the $25 is the direct object, because that's what I'm handing you, and you're the indirect object, because you're receiving the money.

Possessive: Nouns and pronouns in the possessive *case* own something. To show ownership, you add –'s to the end of a noun or just an apostrophe to plural nouns ending in –s. Pronouns show ownership much differently, as explained next.

Case is the form of a pronoun that reflects how the pronoun functions in a sentence. When nouns change case, you barely notice because all they do is tack on –'s to form the possessive. When pronouns change case, they morph into entirely different beings. The following table shows just a small sample for comparison purposes.

	Subjective	Objective	Possessive
Singular noun	hamster	hamster	hamster's
Pronouns:			
First person	I	me	mine, ours
Second person	you	you	yours
Third person	he, she, it	him, her, it	hers, his, its

To find out more about how pronouns change case, check out the earlier section that focuses solely on pronouns.

Practice

Fill in the blank with the correct form of the pronoun that refers to its antecedent.

1. All of us decided to visit the art museum; _____ wanted to see Picasso's painting *The Old Guitarist*.
2. The train, _____ was running ahead of schedule, showed up earlier than they had anticipated.
3. The flock of Canadian geese migrated south when _____ food supply started to run short.
4. Aurora couldn't think of _____ to buy her father for his birthday.
5. Connor _____ made the pizza from scratch.

Answers

1. we
2. which
3. its
4. anything
5. himself

Taking Action with Verbs

Verbs are words that express an action, state of being, or relationship between two things. They tell the reader what the *subject* (actor) in a sentence does or is or is being. Verbs come in three types: action, linking, and helping, as described in the following sections.

Inflection is an important aspect of verbs. Both nouns and verbs can be *inflected*; that is, you can add letters to the base of a noun or verb to change its syntactic function without changing its fundamental form. You can inflect most nouns by adding *–s* or dropping the *y* and adding *–ies* to form the plural. You can inflect a verb to change its tense or mood or make it agree with the subject of the sentence in person and number; for example, *I holler* (present tense using the verb's base) becomes *I hollered* (past tense with the base plus the inflection, *holler + ed*). To find out a whole lot more about inflecting verbs, turn to Chapter 6.

Practice

Add the correct form of –s and –ed to the following verbs:

1. Sashay
2. Crawl
3. Cry
4. Detonate
5. Spark

Answers

1. Sashays, sashayed
2. Crawls, crawled
3. Cries, cried
4. Detonates, detonated
5. Sparks, sparked

Action Verbs

Action verbs are the movers and shakers of the English language; they *build* and *demolish*, *love* and *despise*, *hope* and *despair*. They *cower* in the corner of one sentence and *emerge* triumphant at the end of another. Action verbs fuel your writing, so make them your go-to verbs instead of making them sit it out on the sidelines.

In chess, players have come up with standard relative values of the chess pieces. For example, a pawn is worth 1, bishops and knights are worth 3 apiece, a rook is worth 5, and a queen is worth 9. In writing, action verbs are queens, helping verbs are bishops, and linking verbs are pawns. Use as many queens as possible and as few pawns as necessary.

Linking Verbs

Compared to action verbs, linking verbs *are* lazy. Instead of action, they express a state or condition, connecting the subject of a sentence with a *subject complement*—a noun, pronoun, or adjective in the form of a single word or a phrase that identifies or describes the subject. Following are examples of linking verbs on the job:

> You seem terribly curious. (The adjective phrase *terribly curious* serves as the subject complement.)

Cecie is the girl with the crying-heart tattoo. (Here the linking verb identifies Cecie as the girl with the crying-heart tattoo, a noun phrase serving as the subject complement.)

Ted isn't himself when he has a migraine headache. (Here the linking verb *isn't* connects Ted to the reflexive pronoun *himself*.)

Common linking verbs are all forms of *be*, including:

am	been	was
are	being	were
be	is	

Linking verbs also include verb phrases ending in *be*, *being*, or *been*, including *can be*, *was being*, and *could have been*.

Additional linking verbs to add to your stock include the following:

appear	look	sound
become	prove	stay
feel	remain	taste
get	seem	
grow	smell	

Some of these linking verbs double as action verbs, as you can see in the following two examples:

Action verb: The chef smelled the escargot before serving it.
Linking verb: The chef smells like escargot.

To determine whether a verb is serving as an action verb or linking verb, try substituting the verb *seem*. If the sentence still sort of makes sense, you're looking at a linking verb. If the sentence sounds terrible, you're looking at an action verb; for example, something seems off in the sentence "The chef seemed the escargot before serving it."

Practice

Identify the linking verb in the following sentences:

1. The window is leaking cold air.
2. My uncle seems a little under the weather.
3. I don't feel ready for Monday.

4. The bunny appears unaware of the dog.
5. Am I being annoying?

Answers

1. is
2. seems
3. feel
4. appears
5. being

Helping Verbs

Helping verbs pitch in when other verbs need their services, as in the following examples (the helping verbs are underlined, while the main verb is italic):

> The building <u>will be</u> *demolished* later this year.
> Everyone <u>could have</u> *finished* dinner if we had arrived 30 minutes earlier.
> Crew members <u>have</u> *delighted* cruise ship passengers for years with their zany antics.

Just so you know, separating the helping verb from the main verb is okay and more effective at times, as long as the separation doesn't risk confusing the reader. Here are a few examples:

> I <u>have</u> always *preferred* cupcakes over muffins.
> I <u>am</u> not *going* to put up with this much longer.
> <u>Did</u> you *wonder* where I'd been?

Transitive and Intransitive Verbs

Grammarians also classify verbs as transitive and intransitive:

Transitive verbs require an object; for example, "The jar <u>contains</u> …." is an incomplete thought that leaves the reader wondering what the jar contains … jam, beets, lightning bugs?

Intransitive verbs, on the other hand, *don't* take a direct object; for example, in the sentence "Everyone <u>laughed</u>." the word *laughed* is intransitive. Now, if everyone *laughed off the practical joke*, the verb would be transitive.

Most verbs can function as either transitive or intransitive depending on the context:

Transitive: The accountant balanced the books.
Intransitive: The account balanced.

To find out whether a verb is transitive or intransitive or both, look it up in a dictionary. Dictionaries typically group meanings and tag each group as *v.i.* (verb intransitive) and *v.t.* (verb transitive) or *used with an object* and *used without an object*.

Practice

Which of the following sentences contain a transitive verb?

1. My girlfriend carried the groceries.
2. The computer monitor is dirty.
3. I broke the vase.
4. We ordered some takeout.
5. When the phone rang, I jumped.

Answers

1, 3, and 4

Infinitives

The *infinitive* form of a verb (see Chapter 6) is *to* + *verb*; for example, *to forgive, to forget, to imagine*. Infinitives are tricky little buggers. Although they're forms of verbs, they don't act as verbs; instead, they play the role of nouns, adjectives, and adverbs, as in these examples:

To admit my limitations would convey a lack of confidence. (Infinitive serving as a noun, the subject of the sentence.)

After careful deliberation, I decided to admit my limitations after all. (Infinitive serving as an adverb modifying the verb *decided*.)

I have a responsibility to admit my limitations to other team members. (Infinitive serving as an adjective describing the noun *responsibility*.)

Adjectives and adverbs are covered later in this chapter.

Practice

In each of the following sentences, underline the verbs. If a helping verb accompanies an action verb, be sure to underline the helping verb as well.

1. Nobody knows how many guests will be coming to the party.
2. Journalists question everything; as a rule, they are a very inquisitive bunch.
3. Now that Mark was feeling much better, his doctors agreed to release him from the hospital.
4. Patrons are not allowed to use cell phones in our restaurant.
5. You have two 15-minute breaks, during which time you are not allowed to leave the building.

Answers

1. Nobody <u>knows</u> how many guests <u>will be coming</u> to the party.
2. Journalists <u>question</u> everything; as a rule, they <u>are</u> a very inquisitive bunch.
3. Now that Mark <u>was feeling</u> much better, his doctors <u>agreed</u> to release him from the hospital. (If you underlined *to release*, that's incorrect, because <u>to release</u> serves as an adverb modifying the verb *agreed*.)
4. Patrons <u>are</u> not <u>allowed</u> to use cell phones in our restaurant. (If you underlined *to use*, that's incorrect, because <u>to use</u> serves as an adverb modifying the verb *allowed*.)
5. You <u>have</u> two 15-minute breaks during which time you <u>are</u> not <u>allowed</u> to leave the building. (Again, underlining *to leave* would be wrong, because it's an adverb modifying the verb *allowed*.)

Getting Descriptive with Adjectives and Adverbs

Adjectives and adverbs are commonly referred to as *modifiers* because they narrow the meaning of nouns, verbs, and sometimes other adjectives and adverbs. If nouns and verbs are the main actors in the play of language, then adjectives and adverbs are the set design and stage directions. The following sections introduce these descriptive words and reveal their similarities and differences.

Adjectives and Articles

Adjectives modify nouns and pronouns by answering any of the following four questions:

- **What kind?** the *nosy* neighbors, the *sparkling* jewels
- **How much?** or **How many?** *numerous* compliments, *countless* nights

- **Which one?** *this* finger, *that* house
- **Whose is it?** *my* money, *their* home, *her* child (The possessive adjectives or possessive determiners are *my, your, her, his, its, our,* and *their*.)

You usually place an adjective directly before the word it modifies, except in the following two situations:

- When using the adjective as a *predicate adjective* following a linking verb: The evening grew dark.
- When you want to have the adjective after the noun for some good reason: The players, worn out from the long trip, appeared listless on the field.

The most basic and popular adjectives are the articles: *a, an,* and *the*. If English is your first language, you instinctively choose the right article by ear. If English is your second or third language, you may need to brush up on the rules for choosing the correct article:

- Use *a* or *an* (*indefinite articles*) to introduce a nonspecific member of a group for the first time; for example, *A slug is a lousy choice for a pet*. Use *a* before words that start with a consonant sound and *an* before words that start with a vowel sound.
- Use *a* or *an* to indicate membership to a group; for example, *Barbara is a Buddhist*.
- Use *the* (*definite article*) to introduce a specific person, place, or thing or one or more specific members of a group; for example, *Ethiopia has plans to dam the Blue Nile* (a specific body of water). *Young George Washington chopped down the cherry tree* (referring to a specific cherry tree).
- Use *a* or *an* to introduce a specific instance of a specific thing; for example, you'd normally introduce *sun* with *the*, but you might use the indefinite article instead in a sentence such as *A cruel sun scorched the fields*.
- Use *the* to emphasize the importance or singularity of a person, place, or thing, as in the sentence *California is the place to go for avid surfers*.

Omit the article:

- When discussing people, places, or things in general; for example, *Movies are my favorite form of entertainment*.
- Before mass nouns when mentioning them generally. A mass noun (sometimes referred to as a noncount noun) is one that can't have a number before it; for example, coffee and electricity. Here's an example of a mass noun in a sentence: *Rice is a staple in most Asian countries*.
- When mentioning a sport, as in the sentence "Sandy loves to watch football."
- Before the names of most countries, unless they contain the words kingdom, republic, state, or union (as in the Soviet Union) or when referring to multiple areas (as in the Bahamas).

Frequently, you use an indefinite article before a noun the first time you mention it. After the reader knows which member of the group you're referring to, you use the definite article before the noun, because the noun is no longer general but specific. Here's an example:

Melissa has two pets: a gerbil and a ferret. The ferret is friendly; the gerbil is not.

For more about adjectives, head to charming Chapter 7.

Practice

1. What kind of questions do adjectives answer?
   A. What kind?
   B. How many?
   C. Which one?
   D. Whose is it?
2. What do adjectives modify?
   A. Adverbs
   B. Nouns
   C. Verbs
   D. Propositions
3. Which of the following are also adjectives?
   A. Adverbs
   B. Propositions
   C. Articles
   D. Nouns

Answers

1. All of these
2. B
3. C

Adverbs

Adverbs play several roles, modifying verbs, adjectives, and other adverbs. Most adverbs end in –*ly*; for example, *carefully*, *expeditiously*, and *scornfully*. But many don't end in –*ly*, especially the adverbs that designate a location where the action took place, such as *here*, *there*, and *everywhere*. To further complicate their usage, nouns can double as adverbs; for example, *today*, *tomorrow*, and *north*.

When modifying verbs, adverbs commonly answer the following questions:

- **How?** steps *gingerly*, dances *enthusiastically*
- **When?** arrives *early*, leaves *late*
- **Where?** travels *abroad*, tunnels *underground*
- **To what degree?** *nearly* completed, *almost* won

You may also use adverbs to modify adjectives and other adverbs, as in the following examples:

> **Adverb modifying an adjective:** *Jimbo has established himself as an incredibly talented musician.* (The adverb *incredibly* modifies the adjective *talented*.)
> **Adverb modifying another adverb:** *He will probably never sacrifice his practice time.* (The adverb *probably* modifies the adverb *never*.)

In this section, you merely dipped your big toe in the sea of adverbs. To fully immerse yourself, dive in to Chapter 7.

Practice

1. Which of the following questions do adverbs answer?
   A. How?
   B. When?
   C. Where?
   D. To what degree?
2. What do adverbs modify?
   A. Verbs
   B. Adjectives
   C. Adverbs
   D. Nouns
3. Which suffix is most associated with adverbs?
   A. –ed
   B. –ing
   C. –s
   D. –ly

Answers

1. All of these
2. A, B, and C
3. D

Making the Right Connections with Conjunctions

Conjunctions enable words and *phrases* to reach across the aisle and hold hands. English has three types of conjunctions: *coordinating*, *subordinating*, and *correlative*. To find out more about each type, read on.

Coordinating Conjunctions

A *coordinating conjunction* connects words, phrases, or clauses of pretty much equal rank. They are: *and, but, or, for, nor*. Use them to join a pair of items, several items in a series, or two or more phrases or coordinate clauses, as in the following examples:

> Stan ate Polish sausage, pierogi, and golumpki. (Connecting items in a series.)
>
> He felt full, but he decided to order dessert anyway. (Connecting two coordinate clauses.)
>
> The desserts, printed on the menu and arranged on the dessert tray, all looked delicious. (Connecting two phrases.)
>
> Stan deliberated over whether to order babka or budyn. (Connecting two items, both nouns.)

A *phrase* is a group of words functioning as a conceptual unit that doesn't qualify as a clause, because it doesn't have a subject (actor) and a predicate (action). A *clause* is sort of a sentence within a sentence, in that it has a subject and a predicate, but it's part of another sentence. Clauses come in two flavors: coordinate and subordinate. A *coordinate clause* is the same rank as the main clause and could stand alone. A *subordinate clause* embellishes the main clause and can't stand alone. A sentence is a combination of a subject and predicate that can stand on its own two feet; that is, it expresses a complete thought.

Practice

1. Which of the following is a phrase?
    A. He enjoyed
    B. Enjoyed Earl Grey tea
    C. Earl Grey tea rules
    D. Rules are important

2. Which of the following are types of clauses?
   A. Main
   B. Coordinate
   C. Subordinate
   D. Holistic

Answers

1. B
2. A, B, and C

Subordinating Conjunctions

Subordinating conjunctions introduce subordinate clauses, which might not make sense yet. After you meet the subordinating conjunctions and see them used in examples, you'll have a better idea of what they are and their purpose in life. So, without further ado, here are the most commonly used subordinating conjunctions:

after	even though	that
although	how	though
as	if	till
as long as	in order that	unless
as much as	inasmuch as	until
as soon as	now that	when
as though	provided	whenever
because	since	where
before	so that	wherever
even if	than	while

Here are some examples of subordinating conjunctions in action. Note that the entire subordinating clause is underlined and notice the position of each clause—at the beginning or end of the sentence.

<u>Provided that I receive your check this week</u>, I will send you the car's title in the mail.

<u>Wherever it ultimately decides to move</u>, the company will offer its employees jobs and relocation packages.

Please proceed to the waiting room <u>after you have completed and submitted your forms</u>.

The herd of antelope migrated north <u>because the drought had turned the grasslands to desert</u>.

Practice

1. What do subordinate conjunctions introduce?
   A. Nouns
   B. Verbs
   C. Subordinate clauses
   D. Coordinate clauses
2. Which of the following is not a subordinate conjunction?
   A. After
   B. But
   C. While
   D. Whenever

Answers

1. C
2. B

Correlative Conjunctions

Correlative conjunctions come in pairs, with the second conjunction of the pair being a coordinating conjunction, as shown in the following table.

Correlative Conjunction	Coordinating Conjunction
both …	and …
either …	or …
neither …	nor …
not only …	but (also) …
whether …	or …

To understand the function of correlative conjunctions, you need to know what *correlate* means. Basically, it means that the pair of words forming the correlative conjunction connect two equal grammatical terms, as in the following examples:

> Neither Charles nor Andrea knows about the party.
> You can either wash the windows or mop the floors.
> This project gives you not only an opportunity to experiment, but also a chance to earn some big bucks.

Correlative conjunctions are tricky when you're trying to decide whether the subject of the sentence is singular or plural (see Chapter 5) or trying to maintain parallelism (covered in Chapter 13), but don't concern yourself with those issues just yet.

Practice

1. Which is a feature of correlative conjunctions?
    A. Each is part of a pair.
    B. Each has an opposite.
    C. Each has an adverb.
    D. Each is part of a clause.
2. Which of the following is always paired with a correlative conjunction?
    A. A coordinating conjunction
    B. A subordinating conjunction
    C. Another correlative conjunction
    D. A noun phrase

Answers

1. A
2. A

Building Relationships with Prepositions

Prepositions establish a relationship between a noun or pronoun and another word in a clause. For example, if you climb under a table, the preposition *under* describes your relation to the noun *table*.

In most cases, prepositions are accompanied by other words to form a *prepositional phrase*, usually consisting of the preposition followed by an article and a noun that serves as the *object of the preposition*. The following paragraph contains two examples of prepositional phrases with the prepositional phrase in italics and the preposition underlined:

> Spelunkers climbed *down a cable ladder* lowered *into the cavern* to rescue Ms. Fitzgerald's cat. (Preposition *down* establishes the relationship between the spelunkers and the cable ladder, and *into* reveals the relationship between the cable ladder and the cavern.)

Every *prepositional phrase* includes a preposition and *object of the preposition*, which usually comes after the preposition.

Here are some commonly used single-word prepositions:

about	by	outside
above	concerning	over
across	down	past
after	during	since
against	except	than
along	excluding	through
amid	following	to
among	for	toward
around	from	under
at	in	underneath
before	inside	unlike
behind	into	until
below	like	up
beneath	near	upon
beside	of	versus
besides	off	via
between	on	with
beyond	onto	within
but (meaning "except")	opposite	without

Some prepositions are made up of two or more words:

according to	close to	instead of
ahead of	due to	near to
all over	except for	next to
as early as	in back of	on top of
as late as	in between	other than
as much/many as	in front of	out of
as of	in keeping with	similar to
as often as	in place of	up to
away from	in spite of	with regard to
because of	in view of	with respect to
close by		

Practice

In each of the following sentences, underline every prepositional phrase, including the preposition and the object of the preposition.

1. The marina was on the far side of the lake.
2. Dandelions tend to sprout along the edges of the lawn.
3. From the shore, Gary waved to his friends.
4. The writer was typing away beside the window.
5. After the movie, the young couple went out for veggie burgers.

Answers

1. The marina was <u>on the far side of the lake</u>.
2. Dandelions tend to sprout <u>along the edges of the lawn</u>.
3. <u>From the shore</u>, Gary waved <u>to his friends</u>.
4. The writer was typing away <u>beside the window</u>.
5. <u>After the movie</u>, the young couple went out <u>for veggie burgers</u>.

Dealing with Interjections: Yay!

An *interjection* is an exclamatory remark that typically expresses emotion and is grammatically unrelated to any other words in the sentence in which it appears. In fact, interjections often stand on their own, complete with their own punctuation, as in "Ouch!" Here's a short list of interjections:

ahh	gee	ouch
ahem	gosh	shoot
alas	hey	ugh
alrighty	hmmm	uh
argh	huh	whoa
awww	mmm	whoops
boo	nah	wow
darn	ooh	yay
duh	oops	yikes

Writers often use interjections in dialogue to make it sound more realistic. Just about any word can be used as an interjection or exclamation. Will Ferrell's character Ron Burgundy is a good example of this, as he has been known to exclaim virtually anything, from "Knights of Columbus!" to "Uncle Jonathan's corncob pipe!" Similarly, anything from "What!" to "Pancakes!" could be an exclamation in the right context.

Practice

1. Which of the following is not an interjection?
   A. Yow!
   B. Yipes!
   C. Yikes!
   D. Who?
2. Which punctuation mark is associated with interjections?
   A. .
   B. ,
   C. !
   D. ?

Answers

1. D
2. C

Blurring the Lines That Define Parts of Speech

Many words in the English language defy attempts to categorize them as a particular part of speech. Often, the only way to really tell which role a word or phrase plays in a sentence is to examine it carefully in context. Here are a couple examples of words functioning as different parts of speech:

Merely thinking of jogging jogged his memory. (The word *jog* is used first as a noun and then as a verb.)

With his can of oil, Ed oiled the hinges on the door, being careful not to get any on the oil painting hanging on the nearby wall. (Here, *oil* is first a noun, then a verb, and finally an adjective.)

Joe felt meh about the second season of *The Americans*. (The interjection *meh* is being used as an adjective.)

Chapter Review Practice

Although their jobs are complex, each part of speech has a specific job to do. Nouns name a person, place, or thing; pronouns usually reference a previously mentioned noun. Verbs express action or being and come in three types: action, linking, and helping. Adjectives modify nouns and pronouns; adverbs modify verbs, adjectives, and other adverbs. Coordinating conjunctions connect grammatical elements of equal rank; subordinating conjunctions introduce grammatical elements of lesser rank. Prepositions establish a relationship between a noun or pronoun and another word in a clause. Interjections are exclamatory remarks that show emotion and are unrelated, grammatically, to any other words in a sentence. All these parts work together to help us communicate.

Now let's practice what you learned in this chapter:

1. Write in the blank which is used in the following sentences, first, second, or third person:
    A. The boys were playing hockey. _____
    B. I forgot to bring my boots. _____
    C. You better go home now. _____
    D. They never listen to me. _____

2. Which of the following can adverbs not modify?
   A. Adverbs
   B. Nouns
   C. Adjectives
   D. Verbs
3. Which of the following is not commonly thought of as an interjection?
   A. Hello
   B. Ugh
   C. Problematic
   D. Meh
4. Which of the following is not a type of verb?
   A. Action
   B. Helping
   C. Linking
   D. Transitive
5. Which of the following is not an interrogative pronoun?
   A. Which
   B. Who
   C. Whom
   D. Whose
   E. What
6. What do prepositions establish?
   A. Tense
   B. Mood
   C. Voice
   D. Relationship
7. Can a preposition consist of more than one word?
8. What kind of conjunction must go with a correlative conjunction?
   A. Coordinating
   B. Subjective
   C. Objective
   D. Simple

9. Underline the verbs in the following sentences:
   A. I majored in international relations in college.
   B. Will the Buffalo Bills ever win a Super Bowl?
   C. It's been two years since my mother moved.
   D. What do you have to offer the group?
10. What do conjunctions do?
    A. Separate
    B. Connect
    C. List
    D. Abbreviate
11. Which is not one of the cases in English?
    A. Subjective
    B. Possessive
    C. Conjunctive
    D. Objective

Answers

1. A. Third
   B. First
   C. Second
   D. Third
2. B
3. C
4. D
5. They all are interrogative pronouns.
6. D
7. Yes
8. A
9. A. I <u>majored</u> in international relations in college.
   B. <u>Will</u> the Buffalo Bills ever <u>win</u> a Super Bowl?
   C. <u>It's been</u> two years since my mother <u>moved</u>.
   D. What do you <u>have</u> to offer the group?
10. B
11. C

4

Recognizing the Parts of a Sentence

Chances are you know people who have a bad habit of not finishing their sentences. They start strong and then fade out at the end, assuming you'll catch their drift. Needless to say, those incomplete sentences are annoying, especially if you have no idea what the person is trying to say.

Of course, we all kind of stumble along when we're speaking, and the standards for talking aren't nearly as strict as they are for writing. But some people bring the incompleteness and chaos of speech into writing, and that can cause problems for readers.

If you happen to be one of those people, this chapter can cure you of that foible. Here you'll discover the difference between sentences, phrases, and clauses; the various ways to end and embellish sentences; and a variety of sentence structures.

By learning more about the rules for making sentences, you'll learn something more: how to communicate as clearly as possible.

What Exactly Is a Sentence?

A *sentence* is a collection of words containing a noun (or pronoun) and a verb that expresses a complete thought, statement, question, or command. Here's an example of a sentence in its simplest form:

    Martha   paces.
    Noun   **Verb**

Grammarians use more precise language to describe the two parts of a sentence:

    Subject: The person, place, or thing that the sentence is about along with all the words that modify that person, place, or thing.
    Predicate: The verb that animates the subject and all words that modify that verb.

Although the subject usually comes first, you can invert the order, placing the predicate first. Here are a few examples of subjects and predicates forming sentences:

Natalie	chuckled.
Subject	**Predicate**
Here comes	the sun.
Predicate	**Subject**
Dylan, realizing he was late,	hurried home.
Subject	**Predicate**
At the end of the path stood	Larry.
Predicate	**Subject**

The following sections describe the subject and predicate in greater detail and give instructions on how to identify each in a sentence.

Part 1: Subject

The *subject* of a sentence can be simple or complete. A *simple subject* consists solely of a noun or pronoun. A *complete subject* consists of the noun or pronoun and any words or phrases that modify (describe) it. Here's an example:

> A premature baby with medical issues requires considerable attention and care to remain healthy.

Here, *A premature baby with medical issues* is the complete subject; *baby* is the simple subject.

Part 2: Predicate

Just as a subject can be simple or complete, so too can a *predicate*. A *simple predicate* is the main verb (or verb phrase) in a sentence. A *complete predicate* consists of the verb and any words or phrases that describe the verb, such a phrase describing how the action was performed. Here's an example:

> Management decided to offer the company's employees a cafeteria plan.

Here, *decided to offer the company's employees a cafeteria plan* is the complete predicate; *decided* is the simple predicate.

The subject of a sentence is the person, place, or thing the sentence is about. The predicate is the action that the subject performs or the subject's state of being.

Sentences with Compound Subjects and Verbs

Compound subjects consist of two or more nouns. *Compound verbs* consist of two or more verbs. When you have a sentence with a compound subject, be careful to choose the right verb form: singular if only one of the subjects performs the action or plural if two or more perform the action. For example:

> The elephant, giraffe, and hippopotamus *live* in the jungle.
> The elephant, giraffe, or hippopotamus *lives* down the street.

With a compound verb, the subject performs more than one action; for example:

> This morning, Sam scrambled the eggs and fried the bacon.

When you have a compound verb consisting of only two verbs, avoid the temptation to separate them with a comma:

> **Right:** Nancy hit a homer and circled the bases.
> **Wrong:** Nancy hit a homer, and circled the bases.

Use the comma only when separating two complete sentences—also known as independent clauses—as shown here:

> **Right:** Nancy hit a homer, and the crowd cheered.

Identifying the Subject

Knowing who or what the sentence is about is important for two reasons: First, whether the subject is singular or plural determines whether the verb needs to be singular or plural. Second, knowing what the subject is helps you write more concisely and directly using nouns and verbs instead of phrases such as *there are*, *it is*, and *here are* (more about that in a minute).

Unfortunately, picking out subjects in a sentence can be nearly as difficult as finding a lost kid at an amusement park. The following are some tricks of the trade for pinpointing subjects:

Find the action first, then ask, "Who or what is doing this?" For example, suppose the sentence is "Outside the perimeter of our fence live wild animals." The verb is *live*, so you ask "Who or what lives?" The answer: *animals*.

Ignore any prepositional phrases. For example, suppose the sentence is "Beyond the river breeds a colony of seagulls." The verb is *breeds*, so you ask "Who or what breeds?" Of course, the seagulls are actually doing the breeding, but *of seagulls* is a prepositional phrase modifying *colony*, so you must disregard it according to this rule. When you do, you discover the true subject of the sentence: *colony*.

Proceed with caution when sentences begin with *there are*, *here are*, or similar word combinations. These combos usually include a false subject (*here* or *there*). The true subject appears later in the sentence. For example, in the sentence "There are numerous options," *There* is the false subject; the true subject is *options*—the options are numerous.

Assume that *you* is the subject in commands and requests. For example, in the sentence "Forge ahead!" the subject *you* is understood, not stated. In a request, such as "Please pass the porridge," again, *you* is understood or assumed; it doesn't appear in the sentence.

To find the subject in a question, rephrase the question as a statement. For example, if the question is "When is the train scheduled to arrive?" the statement is "The train is scheduled to arrive when …." Now identifying the subject is a snap: *train*.

Keep in mind that certain forms of verbs function as nouns. *Gerunds* (verbs ending in *–ing*) and *infinitives* (*to* + *verb*) function as nouns. In the sentence "Jogging around the park reinvigorates me," the simple subject is *Jogging* (a gerund), because jogging is doing the reinvigorating, even though I'm the one doing the jogging.

Write sentences with strong nouns and verbs. Avoid starting a sentence with a wimpy word combo such as *There are* … or *It is* ….

Practice

Underline the simple subject in each of the following sentences, keeping in mind that more than one noun may comprise the subject.

1. The sky burst into color with the arrival of the butterflies.
2. There are dozens of hostels along the Pilgrim route of the Camino Santiago in Galicia, Spain.
3. Barry, along with the rest of his family, planned to arrive early to get better seats.
4. Toward the finish line sprinted Jessie.
5. On his way to work, Jerry stopped for a cappuccino.

Answers

1. The <u>sky</u> burst into color with the arrival of the butterflies.
2. There are <u>dozens</u> of hostels along the Pilgrim route of the Camino Santiago in Galicia, Spain.

3. <u>Barry</u>, along with the rest of his family, planned to arrive early to get better seats.
4. Toward the finish line sprinted <u>Jessie</u>.
5. On his way to work, <u>Jerry</u> stopped for a cappuccino.

Completing Actions with Complements

A *complement* is a noun, verb, or adjective (any of which can be a single word or a phrase) that's part of the predicate and that completes the action. Following are a few examples of complements in action (the complement is underlined):

Glenn quickly became <u>irritated</u>.
The poodle learned <u>to jump</u> through hoops.
Voters elected Obama <u>president</u>.
The bank teller handed Wanda her <u>cash</u>.

Complements come in different forms, depending on the function they perform in a sentence. The following sections describe the different forms and provide examples.

Direct and Indirect Objects

Direct and *indirect objects* are on the receiving end of the action (verb):

Direct object: The person, place, or thing that receives the action of the verb. For example, if you're launching a spaceship to Mars, *spaceship* is the direct object, because that's what's being launched.

Indirect object: The person, place, or thing *to which/whom* or *for which/whom* the action is performed. The indirect object always precedes the direct object. In the sentence "Canada sends Mali humanitarian aid," *Mali* is the indirect object, and *aid* is the direct object.

The tricky part about indirect objects is that if you put the word *to* or *for* before the object, you're no longer looking at an indirect object; you're looking at a prepositional phrase. Reword the previous example sentence as "Canada sends humanitarian aid to Mali," and now *Mali* is no longer an indirect object; it's the object of the preposition *to*. (For more about objects of prepositions, see Chapter 3.)

To sum up: A direct object is a noun or pronoun that the action touches. An indirect object is a noun or pronoun to whom or for whom the direct object has been acted upon.

Object Complements

An *object complement* is a noun or adjective that comes after a direct object and explains what the direct object has become. Once you see some examples, you'll have a better idea of what object complements are:

> The Thortons painted their house <u>yellow</u>.
> Committee members voted Halloway <u>chairperson</u>.
> The landscapers kept the branches <u>pruned back</u>.

In each of these examples, the direct object (*house*, *Halloway*, and *branches*) becomes something (*yellow*, *chairperson*, and *pruned*). What the direct object becomes is an object complement.

Why does this matter? Because proper placement of the word is important for expressing your intended meaning. For example, if instead of painting their *house yellow*, the Thortons painted their *yellow house*, you'd still be wondering what color they painted it. By moving the word *yellow* before *house* instead of placing it after *house*, you transform the word *yellow* from an object complement into an adjective, and it performs an entirely different function with a totally different meaning.

Subject Complements

A *subject complement* is a noun or adjective that follows a linking verb and describes the subject of the sentence. Subject complements come in two types:

Predicate nominative: A noun or pronoun that follows a linking verb and modifies the subject; for example:

> Michael is a licensed <u>beautician</u>.

Predicate adjective: An adjective that follows a linking verb and modifies the subject; for example:

> Our new neighbors seem <u>amicable</u> and <u>fascinating</u>.

Practice

In each of the following sentences, underline the complements and write the type of complement in the blank—use the abbreviations d.o. (direct object), i.o. (indirect object), o.c. (object complement), and s.c. (subject complement). In the case of subject complements, you can identify whether it's a predicate nominative (p.n.) or predicate adjective (p.a.) to earn extra credit.

1. Your dog seems more affectionate than mine. _____
2. Friends and family sent Michelle flowers to congratulate her on her promotion. _____
3. Readers of the newspaper overwhelmingly named Mel's Diner their favorite restaurant in Memphis. _____
4. Lilly sent Florence an email message confirming their plans. _____
5. Mel sent the cigars to me as a gift. _____

Answers

1. Your dog seems more <u>affectionate</u> than mine. (s.c., p.a.)
2. Friends and family sent <u>Michelle</u> <u>flowers</u> to congratulate her on her promotion. (i.o., d.o.)
3. Readers of the newspaper overwhelmingly named <u>Mel's Diner</u> their favorite <u>restaurant</u> in Memphis. (d.o., o.c.)
4. Lilly sent <u>Florence</u> an email <u>message</u> confirming their plans. (i.o., d.o.)
5. Mel sent the <u>cigars</u> to me as a gift. (d.o.)

Accentuating Sentences with Phrases

A *phrase* is a group of words that doesn't include a subject-verb pair that functions as a unit—a subject, verb, object, adjective, or adverb. (If the group of words were to contain a subject-verb pair, it would qualify as a clause, not a phrase.) The English language has several different kinds of phrases that vary according to their composition and function in a sentence. The following sections introduce the different kinds of phrases and show them in action.

Verb Phrases

Verb phrases, not to be confused with verbal phrases discussed later in this chapter, are typically comprised of one or more helping verbs and an action verb that together express a single action; for example:

> has investigated
> will be visiting
> had been completed

Technically speaking, these groups of words qualify as phrases, because 1) they're a group of words that act as a unit and 2) they don't have a subject-verb pair (only verbs). In this book, we prefer to treat verb phrases simply as verbs, whether the verb consists of one word or more (see Chapter 6).

Prepositional Phrases

The mother of most (not all) phrases is the *prepositional phrase*—a grammatical unit that begins with a preposition, ends with an object of the preposition, and almost always functions either as an adjective or adverb. Examples of prepositional phrases used as nouns are rare. (For more about prepositions, including a list of common prepositions, flip back to Chapter 3.) Here are a few examples of prepositional phrases with the prepositions underlined:

> <u>in</u> the yard
> <u>from</u> Nebraska
> <u>behind</u> the cemetery
> <u>inside</u> the perimeter
> <u>of</u> wombats

When working as an adjective, a prepositional phrase modifies a noun, as in these examples:

> The compost pile <u>in the yard</u> smelled rancid. (modifies *pile*)
> We met our new neighbors <u>from Nebraska</u>. (modifies *neighbors*)
> There is a woods <u>behind the cemetery</u>. (modifies *woods*)
> He passed to the guard <u>inside the perimeter</u>. (modifies *guard*)
> A noteworthy characteristic <u>of wombats</u> is their backward pouch. (modifies *characteristic*)

When filling in as an adverb, a prepositional phrase modifies a verb, adjective, or another adverb, as in these examples:

> The swim team practiced <u>in the Gulf</u>. (modifies the verb *practiced*)
> The coach seemed oblivious <u>to the risks</u>. (modifies the adjective *oblivious*)
> Jellyfish bobbed furtively <u>through the water</u>. (modifies the adverb *furtively*)

And here's something you're unlikely to bump into—a prepositional phrase functioning as a noun:

> <u>Inside of 10 minutes</u> is too little time.

Appositives

An *appositive* is a noun or pronoun (single word or phrase) that modifies another noun or pronoun and appears right after the word or just before the word it modifies. The following examples give you a glimpse of appositives at work:

> A highly venomous snake, the king cobra can deliver enough venom in a single bite to kill 20 people.
>
> Embry and Tonya, sisters and skilled equestrians, excelled in every competition.
>
> The boat, a 20-foot roundabout with a diving platform and a 150 horsepower engine, was for sale at the marina.

Beware! Not every phrase that comes before or after a noun and modifies it is an appositive. An appositive must be a noun or pronoun. For example, in the sentence "Tim, wondering who had called, checked caller ID," the phrase *wondering who had called* is a verbal phrase, not an appositive.

Verbals

A *verbal* is a verb that functions as a noun, adjective, or adverb in a sentence. A *verbal phrase* is a group of words containing a verbal that, as a unit, functions as a noun, adjective, or adverb in a sentence. Take a look at the following examples:

> Skipping rope is a great cardiovascular workout. (*Skipping* is a verb used as a noun. *Skipping rope* is the verbal phrase.)
>
> Elated, the fans jumped for joy. (The verb *elated* is used as an adjective to modify *fans*.)
>
> People take vacations to relax. (The infinitive form of the verb *relax* is used as an adverb to modify the verb *take*.)

Verbals come in four forms: gerunds, infinitives, and present and past participles.

A *gerund* is a verb form ending in *–ing* that functions as a noun; for example, "Flying is exhilarating." A gerund phrase is the gerund along with any associated words; for example, "Flying over Pittsburgh is wonderful!" Like its first cousin, the noun, a gerund can serve different roles in a sentence:

> **Subject:** Fishing is a popular sport.
> **Direct object:** I hate waiting in line.
> **Object of a preposition:** Our employees became more efficient by working smarter.
> **Subject complement:** Pat's favorite hobby is gardening.

An *infinitive* is a verb form, typically consisting of *to* + verb, that functions as a noun, adjective, or adverb; for example, in the sentence "Ellen loves to ski," *to ski* functions as a direct object. An infinitive phrase is the infinitive along with any associated words; for example, "Ellen loves to ski on lakes and rivers." Following are examples of infinitives functioning as different parts of speech:

> To sleep through the night would be a welcome relief. (*to sleep* functions as a noun, the subject of the sentence)
>
> The tourists decided to dock at Key West. (*to dock* functions as a direct object)
>
> The diver's purpose was to discover sunken treasure. (*to discover* functions as the predicate nominative describing the subject *purpose*)
>
> Dr. Miller had the foresight to patent the innovative new medical procedure. (*to patent* functions as an adjective modifying the noun *foresight*)
>
> We live to love. (*to love* functions as an adverb modifying the verb *live*)

Although the infinitive form of a verb includes the word *to*, in some cases, the *to* is dropped, creating what's commonly called a *bare infinitive*, as in these examples:

> I let her buy me a drink.
> You had better call home.
> Help them decide.

A *participle* is a verb form that, when used without a helping verb such as *is* or *has been*, functions as an adjective, as in the following examples:

> The darkening skies indicated that a storm was brewing.
> Blurred vision may be a symptom of cataracts or macular degeneration.

Participles come in two varieties:

Present participle: Like the gerund, the present participle is the verb form ending in *–ing*. (But remember that gerunds are nouns, whereas present participles are adjectives.)

Past participle: Past participles of regular verbs (see Chapter 6) end in *–ed*. Past participles of irregular verbs end in *–d*, *–e*, *–g*, *–t*, *–en*, or *–n*; for example, *paid*, *done*, *sung*, *sent*, *spoken*, and *grown*.

Beware! Don't confuse a participle that functions as an adjective with a participle that's part of a verb phrase expressing action. For example, in the sentence "The president was willing to compromise," *was willing* is a verb phrase, the predicate of the sentence, not an adjective.

Past and present participles can team up with other words to form *participial phrases*, as in the following examples:

Concerned about his growing debt, Gary consulted a financial advisor. (In this example, a past and a present participle, *concerned* and *growing*, both play a role in the participial phrase.)

The ship, sailing to Bermuda, disappeared in the area known as the Bermuda Triangle. (This example contains two participial phrases: the first starting with the present participle *sailing*, and the second with a past participle *known*.)

Practice

In each of the following sentences, a phrase is underlined. Write the phrase type in the blank: prepositional, appositive, gerund, infinitive, present participle, or past participle. If the phrase modifies another word, also write down the word it modifies.

1. Bill and Melinda Gates, well-known philanthropists, manage a multibillion dollar trust fund. _____
2. Blessed with abundant rich farmland, the United States plays a key role in combating world hunger. _____
3. To avoid problems, the hikers chose a longer route with fewer obstacles. _____
4. The crew was scheduled to reach its destination within six days. _____
5. On summer mornings, Melissa loved tending to her flower garden. _____
6. Named Employee of the Month, Stu was allowed to park in the space nearest to the front entrance. _____
7. Against all odds, the sockeye salmon survived their 900-mile trek up three rivers, climbing 6,500 feet. _____
8. To audition for the play had always been his dream. _____
9. Disillusioned by politics, Samantha decided to return to business. _____
10. The parent-teacher organization let Steve lead its fundraising efforts. _____

Answers

1. Appositive acting as a noun to modify *Bill and Melinda Gates*
2. Past participle acting as an adjective to modify *the United States*
3. Infinitive acting as an adverb to modify the verb *chose* (why they chose a longer route)
4. Prepositional acting as an adverb to modify the verb *scheduled* (when the crew was scheduled)
5. Gerund
6. Past participle serving as an adjective to describe *Stu*
7. Prepositional phrase used as an adverb to modify the verb *survived*

8. Infinitive used as a noun, the subject of the sentence
9. Past participle used as an adjective to describe *Samantha*
10. Bare infinitive

Grasping the Basics of Clauses

A *clause* is a group of words containing a subject and a predicate. Grammarians distinguish between two types of clauses: independent and dependent. Dependent clauses are further categorized according to the role they play in the sentence—noun, adjective, or adverb. For additional details, read on.

Independent Clauses

An *independent clause* can stand on its own two feet; if you pull it out of a sentence, capitalize the first letter of the first word, and stick a dot at the end, you have a sentence—probably a short sentence, but a sentence nevertheless. Following are examples of independent clauses appearing along with either independent or dependent clauses:

> Police evacuated the city as the storm approached.
> The magician performed amazing feats of prestidigitation, but the crowd was not impressed.
> Wherever they moved, good fortune followed.

When combining independent clauses in a sentence, connect them with coordinating conjunctions: *and, but, or, for, nor*. For more about coordinating conjunctions, jump back to Chapter 3.

Dependent (Subordinate) Clauses

A *dependent (subordinate)* clause has a subject and verb but doesn't express a complete thought and therefore is not a sentence. A subordinate clause almost always begins with a word or two that signals the clause's dependency and establishes a relationship between the clause and the rest of the sentence. Here are some words that clue you into the fact that you're probably looking at a subordinate clause:

after	because	provided that
although	before	since
as	even if	so that
as if	even though	than
as long as	if	though
as though	in order that	unless

until	whenever	wherever
whatever	where	whether
when	whereas	while

In a sentence, a dependent clause may play the role of a noun, adjective, or adverb.

A *noun clause* is a dependent clause that functions as a noun in a sentence. Here are a few examples:

> Whoever steps up to the challenge will receive a commendation. (subject)
> I doubt whatever he says about Larry. (direct object)
> Melinda said that we can sleep over at her house. (direct object)

An *adjective clause* is a dependent clause that modifies a noun, as in the following examples:

> My neighbor, who just won the state lottery, is my friend.
> The lake, where I do most of my fishing, is three miles from my house.
> They're the times that I love best.

An *adjective clause* often begins with a relative pronoun, such as *which*, *who* or *whoever*, *whom* or *whomever*, and *that*. In most cases, the relative pronoun refers back to an *antecedent*—a previously mentioned noun. Relative clauses can be restrictive or nonrestrictive:

Restrictive clauses contain information that's essential to the meaning of the clause, so are not separated from the main clause by a comma; for example, "The person *who has the winning ticket* receives a prize." The relative clause, in this case, restricts the person receiving the prize to only that individual who has the winning ticket.

Nonrestrictive clauses contain supplemental information that the reader doesn't need to determine the identity of the antecedent, so they're separated from the main clause by a comma; for example, "Amanda, whom the CEO appointed department head, is unlikely to micromanage her staff."

An *adverb clause* is a dependent clause that modifies a verb, adjective, or another adverb, as in the following examples:

> Amy visits her mother whenever she feels the urge. (adverb modifying *visits*)
> This dishwashing detergent is more effective than the other leading brand is. (adverb modifying the adjective *effective*)
> Geese migrate farther than ducks do. (adverb modifying another adverb, *farther*)

The *infinitive clause* straddles the line separating phrases and clauses. Technically speaking, an infinitive clause has a subject and a verb, but the verb is in the form of an infinitive, which doesn't function as a bona fide verb. The following examples shed some light on this phrase/clause phenomenon:

> The electric company expects <u>its customers to pay their bills</u>.
> I invited <u>my friends to visit me</u>.

As you can see, each of these clauses has a subject along with the infinitive form of a verb.

In an *elliptical clause*, one of the key components (the subject or the verb) is implied, not stated directly. Here are a few examples with the omitted (implied) words enclosed in brackets:

> Ben likes ice cream more than Joe [likes ice cream].
> While [she was] driving to the mall, Jen discovered a shortcut to her doctor's office.
> The massage therapist spent more time with my sister than [she spent] with me.

Practice

In each of the following sentences, a clause is underlined. Write the type of clause (independent or dependent) in the blank. For dependent clauses, specify whether the clause functions as a noun, adjective, or adverb.

1. Carolyn, <u>whose counsel is so important to me</u>, is well-known for her integrity. _____
2. Loan officers had suspected fraud all along, <u>but they failed to report it to authorities</u>. _____
3. <u>Whenever they purchased presents</u>, they donated an equal amount to charity. _____
4. Scott always maxed out his IRA contributions, <u>so that he would be able to retire in relative comfort</u>. _____
5. Jolie suspected the entire time <u>that her brother was planning a surprise birthday party for her</u>. _____
6. Tim golfs <u>whenever he has the opportunity</u>. _____
7. Although Louise has an active social life, <u>she enjoys her solitude</u>. _____
8. <u>As businesses begin to harness the marketing power of facial recognition technology</u>, consumers are becoming increasingly concerned about privacy issues. _____
9. Do you know <u>who is responsible for locking the doors</u>? _____
10. <u>When my alarm buzzes</u>, I know I need to wake up. _____

Answers

1. Dependent, adjective (modifies Carolyn)
2. Independent
3. Dependent, adverb (tells when they donated)
4. Dependent, adverb (explains why Scott maxed out his IRA contributions)
5. Dependent, noun (what Jolie suspected)
6. Dependent, adverb (specifies when Tim golfs)
7. Independent (the clause that wasn't underlined is dependent)
8. Dependent, adverb (explains why consumers are becoming concerned)
9. Dependent, noun (object of the verb *know*)
10. Dependent, adverb (indicates when I know)

Common Sentence Structures

One component of good writing is to vary the sentence structure, as explained in Chapter 14, and one way to vary sentence structure is to combine independent and dependent clauses in different arrangements to form any of the following four sentence types: simple, compound, complex, or compound-complex. The following sections describe each of these sentence types in turn and challenge you to practice forming the different sentence types.

Simple Sentences

A *simple sentence* is comprised of only one subject-predicate combination, as in the following examples:

> Stars shimmer at night.
> Qualified technicians perform all repairs on our customers' computers and related equipment.

As demonstrated in the second example, a simple sentence can be quite long, but it's made up of only one independent clause and contains no dependent clauses.

Compound Sentences

A *compound sentence* contains two or more independent clauses and no dependent clauses, as in the following examples:

> The band's performance was exceptional, but the song selection disappointed fans.
> Joan wanted to take a taxi; John preferred the subway.
> John and Joan disagreed on the mode of travel; nevertheless, they reached a compromise and decided to take a bus.

You have several options for linking the independent clauses that comprise a compound sentence:

Comma and conjunction: Use a comma followed by one of the coordinating conjunctions: *and, but, yet, or, for, nor*.

Semicolon, no conjunction: To subtly indicate that two independent clauses are related, separate them with a semicolon instead of a period.

Semicolon and conjunctive adverb: To more clearly indicate the logical or chronological relationship between two independent clauses, use a semicolon with a conjunctive adverb followed by a comma. Conjunctive adverbs include the following:

accordingly	hence	otherwise
also	however	similarly
besides	incidentally	still
certainly	likewise	then
consequently	meanwhile	therefore
finally	moreover	thus
further	nevertheless	undoubtedly
furthermore		

Complex Sentences

A *complex sentence* contains only one independent clause and one or more dependent clauses. Here are a few examples of complex sentences with the independent clauses underlined and the dependent clauses in italics:

> *Before Jessie's father would grant his permission*, she needed to present him with an itinerary for the evening.
> To generate additional revenue, Illinois raised taxes on businesses, *whereas Indiana lowered taxes to attract more businesses*.

<u>The Rocky Mountains</u>, *which were formed 50 to 100 million years ago*, <u>run from southern Colorado to the Canadian border</u>.

Compound-Complex Sentences

A *compound-complex* sentence contains at least two independent clauses and one dependent clause. Following are a couple examples of compound-complex sentences with the independent clauses underlined and the dependent clauses in italics:

<u>Darryl</u>, *who is an incredible accordion player*, <u>joined a Zydeco band; the band plays regularly at venues in and near the French Quarter</u>.
Although Reese pledged her support for the proposal, <u>she secretly doubted</u> *that it would fix the problem*; <u>the proposal failed to address some key issues</u>.

Practice

In each of the following sentences, identify the sentence type: simple, compound, complex, or compound-complex:

1. Whoever is the last person to leave the building needs to lock all the doors, because burglaries are common in this neighborhood. _____
2. Whenever we have a big storm, the water floods our basement. _____
3. Mandy invited Christy and her friends to the concert, which was scheduled for the following Friday; unfortunately, Christy already had plans. _____
4. Sam returned the defective merchandise and demanded a refund or store credit. _____
5. Danny and Scott pretended to be honest business owners, but they both knew that what they were planning was unethical, even though it happened to be legal. _____

Answers

1. Complex
2. Complex
3. Compound-complex
4. Simple
5. Compound-complex

Chapter Review Practice

To sum up, a sentence requires at least one subject-predicate pair. A complement is a noun, verb, or adjective (single word or phrase) that's part of the predicate and completes the action. A phrase is two or more words that form a grammatical unit but don't contain a subject and predicate. A verbal is a verb form that functions as another part of speech—a noun, adjective, or adverb. A clause contains a subject-verb pair that can stand alone as a sentence (independent clause) or not (dependent clause). Structurally, sentences come in four types: simple, compound, complex, and compound-complex.

Now let's practice what you learned in this chapter:

1. Underline the simple subject in the following sentences:
   A. Where is your rabbit?
   B. The bubble tea is delicious.
   C. A man, woman, and child were scurrying about.
   D. This is a sunny day.
2. Now circle the simple predicate in the same sentences (from question 1).
3. Which of the following sentences contains an appositive?
   A. My brother, a former basketball player, is tall.
   B. My brother used to play football professionally.
   C. My brother is a successful tennis player.
   D. My brother could have gone to the Olympics.
4. Which of the following sentences contains a verbal?
   A. I like hiking in the woods.
   B. Swimming is great exercise.
   C. You don't look very happy.
   D. I really don't want to work.
5. Which of the following sentences is compound-complex?
   A. Whenever I get hungry, I get angry.
   B. Something is wrong with my computer.
   C. To be honest, I don't understand the em dash; that's why I never use it in my writing, and I never will.
   D. Pole vaulting is a difficult sport that takes a great deal of strength and skill.
6. Which of the following sentences is complex?
   A. Despite the weather, I will make it to your party.
   B. I know how to speak three different languages—not to brag.

C. There's no material reason for me to care about your cause.

D. Even though the economy is terrible, I'm starting a new business.

7. Which of the following sentences is simple?

    A. Whenever it snows, we get the day off.

    B. I'm the only historian I know.

    C. Who controls the means of production?—that's what I'm trying to find out.

    D. These children selling candy make me feel bad, but I don't know what to do about it.

8. For the following, identify whether the example is a phrase or clause:

    A. Ate the potato chips _____

    B. That my friend borrowed _____

    C. Which I love _____

    D. Flew away _____

Answers

1. A. rabbit
   B. tea
   C. man, woman, child
   D. day
2. A. is
   B. is
   C. were
   D. is
3. A
4. A, B, and D
5. C
6. D
7. B
8. A. Phrase
   B. Clause
   C. Clause
   D. Phrase

Part 3
Using the Parts of Speech to Build Sentences

Now it's time to combine the building blocks of writing into larger forms you can use when making sentences. In these chapters, you'll get a closer look at the most important words of all: nouns and verbs. You'll learn how nouns form the subject and object of a sentence, naming all the people, places, things, and conditions that exist. You'll learn how verbs explain what those nouns do and are. Since a subject and verb are needed to make a grammatical sentence—or an independent clause—it's important to understand nouns and verbs thoroughly. Nouns and verbs are to grammar what hydrogen and oxygen are to water: essential, irreplaceable components. There's also a chapter on complements, which add information to subjects, predicates, and objects.

I'll also go in-depth on adjectives and adverbs, words that modify other words. Those adjectives and adverbs aren't as powerful as nouns and verbs, but you should understand and use them carefully. A well-placed adjective or adverb can make a sentence sound smooth and flowing. An unnecessary or vague adjective or adverb can make a sentence sound clichéd, annoying, or confusing.

In this part, I'll discuss phrases and clauses, which are the largest chunks of language outside of complete sentences. You'll learn the difference between a phrase and a clause and how to move both around a sentence when revising. I'll also look at the different types of phrases and clauses and how to identify them.

5

Using Nouns and Pronouns as Subjects

Thing is one of the broadest, most general words in English. In a way, everything is a thing. All those things have nouns that represent them, and just as there are varied nouns, there are diverse subjects of sentences.

Every sentence and every clause has a subject, but they don't all have the same type of subject. The subject may be a noun or a pronoun, singular or plural, stated or unstated. If a sentence begins with a pronoun, it probably has an antecedent—a noun it refers to. In addition, you can start sentences with dummy subjects, such as *it* and *there*. In other words, using nouns and pronouns as subjects is much more involved than it sounds.

This chapter takes some of the complexity out of starting sentences with nouns and pronouns and shows you how to use nouns and pronouns properly to identify the subject of the sentence—the person, place, or thing the clause or sentence is about.

Starting a Sentence with a Noun

Most sentences begin with a noun or pronoun. Starting with a noun is by far the easier of the two options because, as explained in Chapter 3, nouns change form only in the plural and possessive.

The following sections explain how to start sentences with a singular or plural *subject* and explore some variations you're certain to encounter. The subject of a sentence is the person, place, or thing the sentence is about. The rest of the sentence describes what the subject is doing or being.

Starting with a Singular Subject

A singular subject is a solitary singular noun that the sentence is about, as in the following example:

> Evan capitulates.

One person, *Evan*, performs the action—*capitulates*. Note that when a singular noun performs the action, it calls for a singular verb form, as explained in Chapter 6.

Remember from Chapter 3 that collective nouns are often treated as singular nouns, even though they represent numerous beings:

A swarm of bees chases Jenny.

Starting with a Plural Subject

A plural subject is a plural noun or two or more nouns that the sentence is about. Here are a couple examples:

Evan and Sue capitulate. (two nouns functioning as a plural subject)
The bees chase Jenny. (a plural noun functioning as a plural subject)

When a sentence is about two or more beings, the verb must be in its plural form for *subject-verb agreement*. For subject-verb agreement, the subject of a sentence must always agree with its verb in number, so singular subjects need singular verbs and plural subjects need plural verbs. This is explained more in Chapter 6.

In the second example, notice that even though bees are still chasing Jenny, *bees* is plural (unlike the collective noun *swarm*), so the subject requires the plural form of the verb *chase*.

Inserting the Subject in a Question

When composing questions, putting the subject in the correct place is more challenging, because positioning depends on the type of question:

Subject questions: In a subject question, an interrogative pronoun usually comes first, followed by the verb, and functions as the subject; for example:

Who ate my candy bar?
What happened?

Object questions: In an object question, the subject usually appears in the question sandwiched between a helping verb and an action verb or immediately after the helping verb. Here are a couple examples:

Who do you want to win the contest?
Where did you go?

To identify the subject in a question, rephrase the question as a statement. For example, if the question is "Who ate my candy bar?" reword it as "So-and-so ate my candy bar." All the words match up except for *Who* and *So-and-so*, so *Who* serves the same function as *So-and-so*—the subject of the statement. Object questions are even easier. Rephrase "Where did you go?" as the answer to the question, and you get "You went _____. *You* is the subject.

Omitting the Subject in a Command

When issuing a command, you do so in the imperative mood, as explained in Chapter 6, and typically drop the subject, *you*, because *you* is implied:

> [You] Take out the trash.
> [You] Please help me find my keys.

Using a Verbal as a Subject

As explained in Chapters 3 and 4, certain verb forms—specifically gerunds, infinitives, and participles—can function as nouns. As such, they can also function as subjects in sentences. Following are a few examples of verbals acting as subjects:

> <u>Passing</u> on the right is something drivers should never do.
> <u>To sit</u> at the hospital all day is exhausting.
> <u>Listening</u> may be the more important skill.

With verbals, you still need to watch subject-verb agreement or, in this case, verbal-verb agreement. Although a verbal is almost always singular, you could have two of them acting as a compound subject, as in this example:

> <u>Swimming</u> and <u>skiing</u> are my two favorite water sports.

Practice

Underline the subject in each of the following sentences:

1. The saplings arrived just in time for fall planting.
2. Plan to check in at least 15 minutes prior to your scheduled appointment.
3. A gaggle of Canadian geese formed a menacing flotilla.
4. Looking forward to the next game, the coach decided to formulate a new strategy.
5. Cats and dogs actually live together quite often.

Answers

1. saplings
2. you
3. gaggle
4. coach
5. cats and dogs

Starting with a Pronoun Instead of a Noun

Not all sentences start with nouns. Some begin with *pronouns*, such as *I*, *you*, *we*, or *they*. If you're starting with first- or second-person pronouns (*I*, *we*, *you* singular, or *you* plural), you're probably not going to run into any problems, as long as you remember the rule that plural nouns and pronouns require plural verbs. These pronouns are easy, because there's usually no question about who they represent.

Pronoun use becomes more complicated when starting a sentence with a third-person pronoun—*he*, *she*, or *it* (all singular) or *they* (singular or plural)—because who or what these pronouns represent must be previously established. If, out of the blue, someone tells you, "It was the best meal I ever ate," you have no idea what that person is talking about. For such a sentence to make sense, the pronoun must clearly refer back to an *antecedent*—a noun that the pronoun represents. If the person was talking about eating a steak dinner at Debbie's Diner, and then says, "It was the best meal I ever ate," now you know what *it* stands for—the steak dinner at Debbie's Diner.

In the following sections, you'll find out how to choose the correct pronoun and establish a clear connection between a pronoun and its antecedent.

Subjective Pronouns

When using a pronoun as the subject of a sentence, choose the subjective personal pronoun that most accurately refers to the antecedent or represents the speaker or the person the sentence is about. As explained in Chapter 3, the subjective personal pronouns are shown in the following table.

	Singular	Plural
First person	I	we
Second person	you	you
Third person	he, she, it, they	they

Antecedent-Pronoun Agreement

Regardless of what role a pronoun plays in a sentence, it must agree with its antecedent in person, number, and gender:

Person: The type of individual(s)—for example, whether the pronoun refers to person(s) or thing(s).

Number: The quantity of individual(s)—one (singular) or more than one (plural).

Gender: The sexual identity of the person, place, or thing. In relation to subjective personal pronouns, the three genders relate only to the third-person singular pronouns: *he* (masculine), *she* (feminine), and *it* (neuter). *I*, *we*, and *you* can be masculine or feminine; *they* can be masculine, feminine, or nongendered.

Clarifying the Antecedent-Pronoun Connection

The biggest issue you face when using subjective third-person personal pronouns is making sure the pronoun clearly refers back to the intended antecedent. An ambiguous connection leaves a sentence open to misinterpretation. Usually when an antecedent-pronoun connection is ambiguous, the ambiguity is caused by one of the following issues:

- The antecedent and pronoun are very far apart: Linda went to the movie by herself, because her friends Jackie and Stacy were both away on vacation. She loved it. (In the last sentence, the reader has to do a little work to identify what *she* refers to. Figuring out what *it* refers to [*the movie*] is even harder, because the word *vacation* is so near to *it*.
- Two or more nouns precede the antecedent and are in close proximity to one another: When Fred dropped his accordion on the coffee table, it shattered. (Did the accordion or the coffee table shatter? When reading, you should assume the pronoun refers to the closest possible candidate to be the antecedent—in this example, *table*. However, if the accordion shattered, then the ambiguity would definitely be misleading. It's best to revise a sentence so it can only be read one way.)
- *It* is used as a dummy subject: It was obvious from the look on his face that he was guilty. (This leaves the audience wondering "What was obvious?" Certainly not the antecedent. A clearer way to say this would be: Obviously, from the look on his face, he was guilty.)

To avoid pronoun-antecedent ambiguity, place the pronoun as near to the noun it modifies as possible. If ambiguity still exists, then repeat the noun, as in the following example:

> When Fred dropped his accordion on the coffee table, the accordion shattered.

Dealing with Reflexive Actions and Pronouns

You don't use reflexive pronouns to start a sentence, but they're so integral to the subject of a sentence, we thought we should mention them here. To refresh your memory, reflexive pronouns are the *self* and *selves* pronouns: myself, himself, herself, yourselves, themselves, and so on.

As explained in Chapter 3, a reflexive pronoun describes action performed on oneself. Here's another, more practical way to put it: use a reflexive pronoun after a transitive verb when the subject is the same as the direct or indirect object. Here's an example:

I	blame	myself.
Subject	**Transitive verb**	**Direct object**

You're more likely to see certain verbs teaming up with reflexive pronouns. Here are some verbs commonly used with reflexive pronouns:

apply	express	lost
behave	find	see
blame	help	teach
cut	hurt	wash
dry	introduce	
enjoy	kill	

Practice

Correct each of the following sentences to ensure pronoun-antecedent agreement and clear up ambiguous references.

1. Each of the teams will have their own captain.
   _____

2. Mia and Alyssa took the bus into town and ate lunch at Dan's Deli, because it was less expensive than taking a taxi.
   _____

3. Jayden invited Olivia to dinner to meet his mom and dad, not realizing he would be away on business.
   _____

4. Despite their ability to survive in freshwater habitats, the bull shark isn't a freshwater species.
   _____

5. Every one of the players blamed themselves for the loss.

Answers

1. Each of the teams will have its own captain.
2. Mia and Alyssa took the bus into town, because it was less expensive than taking a taxi, and ate lunch at Dan's Deli. ***Or:*** Mia and Alyssa took the bus, which was less expensive than taking a taxi, into town and ate lunch at Dan's Deli.
3. Jayden invited Olivia to dinner to meet his mom and dad, not realizing his dad would be away on business. (meaning his dad would be away on business) ***Or:*** Jayden, not realizing he would be away on business, invited Olivia to dinner to meet his mom and dad. (meaning Jayden would be away on business)
4. Despite its ability to survive in freshwater habitats, the bull shark isn't a freshwater species.
5. All the players blamed themselves for the loss. ***Or:*** Every one of the players blamed herself or himself for the loss.

Pronouns and Gender

Of all the parts of speech, pronouns have gotten the most attention in recent years, thanks to evolving ideas about gender. This change can be seen in many places, such as job application forms, which now tend to ask for your pronouns, with choices such as he/him, she/her, they/them, or something else, such as Xe, Thir, or another possibility.

As the complexity of gender becomes more accepted, varied pronoun use will likewise become standard. But the key thing to keep in mind is that a person's pronouns don't really change the grammar of how to talk about them—it's more of a vocabulary issue. So if you had been writing, "Anne and her brother went to the sea," but you learned that Anne prefers *they*, the revision is simple: "Anne and their brother went to the sea."

Beyond individual preferences, *they* and *them* are increasingly accepted as singular pronouns. Sometimes this is a person's preferred pronoun, as in, "Andy is their own worst enemy." Other times, *they* or *them* is used to avoid specifying a gender, as in, "Who's at the door? Let them in!"

The increased attention to pronouns is a classic example of language change. Language is always evolving as long as people use it, and if you don't like it, you might want to consider becoming a Latin scholar. Dead languages don't change.

Person-Centric Language

Language has changed in the most accepted way to refer to people with certain conditions. It's no longer acceptable to refer to *slaves*—the preferred term is *enslaved persons*. Similarly, avoid referring to *the homeless*. Instead, it's better to say *people experiencing homeness*.

How you refer to people is important. Due to the *thingness*, the power, of nouns, the word *slave* makes it sound like the person in question is nothing more than a slave. Person-centric language tries to reverse this by putting the person first, and it makes a lot of sense. None of us can be reduced to a single condition, and it's a positive step to make our language more reflective of reality. Person-centric language gained traction in the world of accessibility and helping people experiencing disabilities. The person-centric approach would be to say *person with autism* rather than *autistic* or *autistic person*. Again, the idea is to avoid reducing people to a single feature, especially a negative one.

However, language is complex, and person-centric language isn't a one-size-fits-all solution. Some people with autism, for example, take pride in their neurodivergence and prefer to be called *autistic*. Whenever possible, refer to people the way they want to be referred.

Using Expletive Expressions Sparingly

When you see or hear the word *expletive*, you may think *swear word*, but *expletive* also refers to a generic word that stands in place of a subject or object in anticipation of a word or phrase that defines it more clearly, as in the following examples:

>There are few people who shop for groceries on Friday nights.
>It wasn't until my 53rd birthday that I started feeling old.

Technically speaking, nothing is wrong with constructions such as these. Stylistically, however, expletives use weak verbs, make sentences wordy, and leave readers wondering what *there* or *it* refers to. Whenever you come across a sentence containing *There are … who …* or *It is … that …* or other sentences that follow that pattern, try to revise the sentence to place the true subject first followed by the verb. Following are revisions of the previous examples:

>Few people shop for groceries on Friday nights.
>Not until my 53rd birthday did I start feeling old.

Occasionally, *There is/are* ... and *Here is/are* ... constructions are okay to use, especially if they're introducing an important point or a list. Here are a couple examples:

> Here are the three clues to look for: ...
>
> There are numerous reasons to exercise. First, exercise improves cardiovascular health. ...

In general, avoid starting sentences with *It is/was* or *There are* unless you're referring to an antecedent or have some other good reason for doing so.

Practice

Reword the following sentences to remove the expletive:

1. There are about three million people who live in Chicago.

2. It is faster to ride the train than to drive.

3. There are numerous benefits to owning your own home.

4. It is a fact that a walrus can eat up to 6,000 clams in a single meal.

5. It is my favorite time of year: autumn.

Answers

1. About three million people live in Chicago.
2. Riding the train is faster than driving.
3. Owning your own home has numerous benefits.
4. A walrus can eat up to 6,000 clams in a single meal. ***Or:*** That a walrus can eat up to 6,000 clams in a single meal is a fact.
5. My favorite time of year is autumn.

Sorting Out *Who, Which,* and *That*

Choosing between *that*, *which*, and *who* can be quite a challenge. The following rules offer guidance:

- Use *who* to refer to people or named animals: for example, Rover the dog and Garfield the cat. Place a comma before *who* if the clause is nonrestrictive. (See Chapter 4 for more about the difference between restrictive and nonrestrictive clauses.)
- Use *that* or *which* without a comma before it in restrictive clauses to refer to places, things, and unnamed animals.
- Use *which* with a comma before it in nonrestrictive clauses that refer to places, things, and unnamed animals.

Following are some examples:

> The doctor who examined me is from Slovenia. (Use *who* because the doctor is a person; omit the comma because the clause is restrictive—it's required to identify the specific doctor who examined me.)
>
> My doctor, who owns a Lamborghini, is from Slovenia. (Use *who* here again, but set off the relative clause from the rest of the sentence with a pair of commas, because the clause is nonrestrictive; it's not necessary for identifying which doctor the sentence is about.)
>
> The bug that bit Jessie is either a sweat bee or a horse fly. (Use *that* or *which* with no comma before it, because the clause is restrictive; it's talking about the bug that bit Jessie and not some other bug that may have done something else.)
>
> Rhododendrons, which are highly susceptible to root rot, grow poorly, if at all, in clay soils. (Use which, but use a comma before and after the nonrestrictive clause to set it off from the rest of the sentence.)

Practice

Select the correct word in each example:

1. The mechanic (who/that) worked on my car was certified.
2. Animals (who/that) migrate usually do so to find food, reproduce, or seek out better weather.
3. *Cloud Atlas*, (which/that) didn't win an Oscar in any category, was my favorite movie of the year.

Answers

1. who
2. that
3. which

Knowing When to Use *Who* or *Whom*

No pronouns cause more confusion than *who*, *whom*, and their close cousins *whoever* and *whomever*. The following rules help you decide which to use:

Use *who* or *whoever* when the pronoun functions as a subject or predicate nominative:

> Whoever wants the last piece of pizza can have it. (*whoever* as subject)
> Nobody at the party knew who the stranger was. (*who* as predicate nominative; *the stranger* was *who*)

Use *whom* or *whomever* when the pronoun functions as an object:

> The boy whom Sally took to the dance was quite handsome. (*whom* as direct object—the person Sally asked)
> You can purchase tickets from whomever you choose. (*whomever* as the object of the preposition *from*)

Usage tip: Drop the pronoun when possible to tighten up your prose. For example, instead of writing "The dog that I adopted has fleas," say "The dog I adopted has fleas." The word *that* is often unnecessary, but also look for occurrences of *who*, *whom*, and *which* that can be cut without confusing the reader.

Practice

In each of the following sentences, circle the correct pronoun:

1. Mason, (who/whom) I gave directions to, had no trouble getting to the airport on time.
2. Bella's dog, (who/whom/which) she adopted from a shelter, is a full-bred Keeshond.
3. (Who/Whom) left the back door open?

Answers

1. whom
2. whom
3. Who

Chapter Review Practice

In this chapter, you learned some basic facts about sentences, and one of them is that a singular noun requires a singular verb and a plural noun requires a plural verb. Similarly, a pronoun must agree with its antecedent in person, number, and gender. Use expletive expressions, such as "There are …" and "It is …" sparingly if at all. Use *who* and *whom* to refer to people or named animals. Use *that* and *which* to refer to places, things, and unnamed animals. Use *who* for subjects and *whom* for objects.

Now let's practice what you learned in this chapter:

1. Identify which of the following are subject questions, and which are object questions:
   A. Where are my keys? _____
   B. Which team is your favorite? _____
   C. What kind of ice cream do you like? _____
   D. Why are you smiling? _____
2. What can be omitted in a command?
   A. The subject
   B. The verb
   C. The preposition
   D. Any adjectives
3. Which of the following sentences has a plural subject?
   A. Joe and Jane went down to the river.
   B. Joe went down to the ocean.
   C. Jane went down to the lake.
   D. Water is relaxing.
4. Which of the following is an example of a grammatical expletive?
   A. Put down the gun!
   B. If I had my way, I'd run for mayor next year.
   C. There's no wrong way to start a business.
   D. What is this crap?

5. What must a pronoun agree with?
    A. Its adjective
    B. Its adverb
    C. Its antecedent
    D. Its antonym
6. How do you decide what pronouns to use for someone?
    A. Take a guess
    B. Ask them
    C. Consult a style guide
    D. Flip a coin
7. Which of the following is correct?
    A. Do you know whom stole the tennis racket?
    B. You borrowed the gold club? From whom?
    C. Whom is your teacher, young man?
    D. I don't know whom I am anymore.

Answers

1. A. Object
   B. Subject
   C. Object
   D. Object
2. A, as in "Get out of here." (*You* is understood.)
3. A
4. C
5. C
6. B
7. B

6

Taking Action with Verbs

Verbs have power. Verbs do things. They make things happen in language. Verbs eat, jump, organize, slash, collect, explode, explain, and play. Verbs are the athletes of language, and they're definitely multi-sport.

Everyone knows that verbs express action, but they convey much more than that. They also provide subtle clues as to who or what is performing the action; when the action occurs, occurred, or will occur; the attitude of the speaker; and whether the subject of the sentence is on the giving or receiving end of the action.

Sound complicated? It is. However, this chapter breaks everything verb-related into easily digestible, bite-size morsels.

Just as there are many different verbs for consuming food—such as biting, chewing, swallowing, and digesting—there are many steps in the verb-consuming process. If you take verbs one step at a time, you'll have an easier time absorbing their lexical nutrients.

Recognizing Verb Forms

Every verb has four forms that, as shown in the following table, you use to create the various tenses—present, past, future, and so on.

Verb Forms

Present/Root	Present Participle	Past	Past Participle
live	(is) living	lived	(have) lived
work	(is) working	worked	(have) worked
swim	(is) swimming	swam	(have) swum

I added *is* and *have* to the present and past participles as a reminder that these require a helping verb; for example, instead of saying "I living in Chicago," you say "I am living in Chicago." As explained in Chapter 3, some of the helping verbs include *am, is, are, was, were, have, has, has been, had,* and *will be.*

In the following sections, I explain how to form the infinitive (easy stuff) and then show you how to form the present participle, past, and past participle of the most common verbs. Once you've mastered these basics, you're well on your way to forming verb tenses.

Forming the Infinitive

A verb's *infinitive* is the action itself without any tense or other accoutrements. To form the infinitive, you simply add *to* to the beginning of the root. So the infinitives of the verbs listed in the preceding table are *to live, to work,* and *to swim.*

You can use infinitives as nouns or parts of noun phrases (for example, "I love *to swim*"), to give a reason for performing another action (as in "I often walk *to clear* my mind"), and to express general or habitual action (as in "To grow flowers, you must plant seeds.") See Chapter 9 for more about using infinitives in phrases.

Regular Verb Forms

Creating the four verb forms of regular verbs is a snap, as shown in the following table.

Root	Verb
Root/present	verb
Present participle	verb + *–ing*
Past	verb + *–ed*
Past participle	verb + *–ed*

Following are some variations on the theme:
- If the verb ends in *e*, drop the *e* before adding *–ing* or *–ed*, as in *moving, moved.*
- For one-syllable words, double the consonant at the end of the verb before adding *–ing* or *–ed,* as in *beg, begging, begged* and *hop, hopping, hopped.* (Words ending in *w, x, y,* and *z* do not follow this rule.)
- For two-syllable words accented on the second syllable, double the consonant at the end of the verb before adding *–ing* or *–ed,* as in *admit, admitting, admitted,* and *refer, referring, referred.*

Irregular Verb Forms

Irregular verb forms are more difficult to master, because they don't follow the rules for forming the past and past participle. They might …

- Change vowels as in *shrink, shrank, shrunk.*
- Change endings as in *lose, lost, lost.*
- Completely change as in *go, went, gone.*
- Drop a vowel as in *lead, led, led.*
- Change vowels and add an ending as in *fly, flew, flown.*
- Stay the same as in *bet, bet, bet.*

The following table lists some of the most common irregular verbs along with their past and past participle forms. You still form the present participle by adding *–ing* to the base (and dropping the *e* or doubling the consonant at the end of the verb when necessary).

Irregular Verb Forms

Root	Past	Past Participle
be	was/were	been
beat	beat	beaten
become	became	become
begin	began	begun
bend	bent	bent
bet	bet	bet
bid	bid	bid
bite	bit	bitten
blow	blew	blown
break	broke	broken
bring	brought	brought
build	built	built
burn	burned/burnt	burned/burnt
burst	burst	burst
buy	bought	bought

Irregular Verb Forms …

... Irregular Verb Forms

Root	Past	Past Participle
catch	caught	caught
choose	chose	chosen
come	came	come
cost	cost	cost
cut	cut	cut
dig	dug	dug
dive	dove/dived	dived
do	did	done
draw	drew	drawn
dream	dreamed/dreamt	dreamed/dreamt
drink	drank	drunk
drive	drove	driven
eat	ate	eaten
fall	fell	fallen
feel	felt	felt
fight	fought	fought
find	found	found
fly	flew	flown
forget	forgot	forgotten
forgive	forgave	forgiven
freeze	froze	frozen
get	got	got/gotten
give	gave	given
go	went	gone
grow	grew	grown
hang	hung/hanged	hung/hanged
have	had	had
hear	heard	heard
hide	hid	hidden

Root	Past	Past Participle
hit	hit	hit
hold	held	held
hurt	hurt	hurt
keep	kept	kept
know	knew	known
lay	laid	laid
lead	led	led
learn	learned/learnt	learned/learnt
leave	left	left
lend	lent	lent
let	let	let
lie	lay	lain
lose	lost	lost
make	made	made
mean	meant	meant
meet	met	met
pay	paid	paid
prove	proved	proven/proved
put	put	put
read	read	read
ride	rode	ridden
ring	rang	rung
rise	rose	risen
run	ran	run
say	said	said
see	saw	seen
sell	sold	sold
send	sent	sent
set	set	set

Irregular Verb Forms ...

... Irregular Verb Forms

Root	Past	Past Participle
show	showed	showed/shown
shut	shut	shut
sing	sang	sung
sit	sat	sat
sleep	slept	slept
speak	spoke	spoken
spend	spent	spent
stand	stood	stood
swim	swam	swum
take	took	taken
teach	taught	taught
tear	tore	torn
tell	told	told
think	thought	thought
throw	threw	thrown
understand	understood	understood
wake (intransitive)	awoke	awoken
wake (transitive)	woke	woken
wear	wore	worn
win	won	won
write	wrote	written

Practice

1. What makes verbs irregular?
   A. Nonstandard root form
   B. Nonstandard past form
   C. Nonstandard past participle form
   D. Their etymology

2. Which of the following words is used to form the infinitive?
   A. Of
   B. From
   C. To
   D. Too
3. Which of the following is one of the four main verb forms?
   A. Present
   B. Present participle
   C. Past
   D. Past participle

Answers

1. B and C
2. C
3. All of these

Telling Time with Tenses

The verb tense provides a general indication of the action's timing—for example, past, present, or future. The following table lists the 12 tenses and briefly describes when to use each tense.

The Twelve Verb Tenses

Tense	Use to Describe	Example
Present	Current or habitual action	*I camp.*
Past	Completed action	*I camped.*
Future	Future action	*I will camp.*
Present progressive	Continuous present action	*I am camping.*
Past progressive	Continuing action completed in the past	*I was camping when the storms moved in.*
Future progressive	Continuing action that is yet to happen	*I will be camping.*

The Twelve Verb Tenses ...

... The Twelve Verb Tenses

Tense	Use to Describe	Example
Present perfect	Completed or continuing action	*I have camped in the winter.*
Past perfect	Action completed before another past action	*I had camped before I visited Mount Rushmore.*
Future perfect	Future action or condition completed before another future action or condition	*By next Sunday, I will have camped for two weeks.*
Present perfect progressive	Past action continuing into the present	*I have been camping all month.*
Past perfect progressive	Continuing past action stopped by a past event	*I had been camping for a week before the tornado sirens sounded.*
Future perfect progressive	Continuing future action completed before a future event	*By the time you read my letter, I will have been camping for at least two weeks.*

The following table gives you a bird's-eye view of the 12 tenses and how to form them using the four verb forms discussed in the previous section: root, past, present participle, and past participle.

Forming the Twelve Verb Tenses

Tense	Formation	Example
Present	Present	*walk*
Past	Past	*walked*
Future	will/shall + root	*will walk*
Present progressive	am/is/are + present participle	*is walking*
Present perfect	have/has + past participle	*has walked*
Past perfect	had + past participle	*had walked*
Future perfect	will have + past participle	*will have walked*
Past progressive	was/were + present participle	*was walking*

Tense	Formation	Example
Future progressive	will/shall + be + present participle	*will be walking*
Present perfect progressive	have/has + been + present participle	*have been walking*
Past perfect progressive	had + been + present participle	*had been walking*
Future perfect progressive	will + have + been + present participle	*will have been walking*

In the following sections I explain the 12 tenses in greater detail, along with some nuances for using each tense and common problems that arise in selecting which tense to use. But first, let's take a look at how to form the tenses of the very irregular verb *to be*.

Tensing Up with the Verb *To Be*

The weirdest verb of all irregulars is the verb that expresses being—*to be*. Since *to be* is used to form many of the other tenses, you really need to know how to *conjugate* it; that is, you need to know all of its forms in simple and perfect tenses and in person and number. Person refers to who is doing the action (for example, *I*, *you*, or *they*); number refers to singular or plural. (For example, *it* is singular and *they* is plural.)

For *to be*, the tricky tenses to conjugate are the present, past, and present perfect tenses and their continuous counterparts, as shown in the following table.

Tense	Singular	Plural
Present	I *am* you *are* he/she/they/it *is*	we *are* you *are* they *are*
Past	I *was* you *were* he/she/they/it *was*	we *were* you *were* they *were*
Present perfect	I *have been* you *have been* he/she/they/it *has been*	we *have been* you *have been* they *have been*

... Tensing Up with the Verb To Be

Tense	Singular	Plural
Present progressive	I *am being* you *are being* he/she/they/it *is being*	we *are being* you *are being* they *are being*
Present perfect progressive	I *have been being* you *have been being* he/she/they/it *has been being*	we *have been being* you *have been being* they *have been being*
Past progressive	I *was being* you *were being* he/she/they/it *was being*	we *were being* you *were being* they *were being*

For the remaining tenses, the verb form is identical regardless of person and number.

Tense	Form
Past perfect	*had been*
Future	*will be*
Future perfect	*will have been*
Past perfect progressive	*had been being*
Future progressive	*will be being*
Future perfect progressive	*will have been being*

Keeping It Simple

Present, past, and future are the so-called *simple tenses*, which aren't always as simple as people like to think, as explained in the following sections.

Simple tenses indicate only the time of the action, not whether the action has been completed or is ongoing.

Present

Use the present tense to describe action that happens right now:

> I understand your concern.
> The peaches are ripe.

The present tense is also commonly used to describe facts or habitual action, as in the following examples:

> I always call my mom on Mother's Day.
> Jennifer swims the 400-meter freestyle. Mark swims the 200-meter butterfly.

People rarely run into problems knowing when to use the present tense, except when they mix the present and past tense while referring to something that still exists in the present:

> Last week, I wrote a letter to our CEO. My letter questioned his judgment in laying off 25 percent of the company's employees.
> Last week, I watched a documentary that claimed global warming was a hoax.

In these examples, the letter, the documentary, and the topic of global warming are still in existence and always will be, so you need to describe them in the present tense:

> Last week, I wrote a letter to our CEO. My letter questions his judgment in laying off 25 percent of the company's employees.
> Last week, I watched a documentary that claims global warming is a hoax.

Past

Use the past tense to express past action that's over, done, finished:

> We ate catfish last night.
> Sally and Roger traveled to Denver for spring break.

Future

If you're like most people, you have little trouble figuring out when to use the future tense or how to form it, but you do need to be aware of the following subtleties:

In the old days, people used *shall* instead of *will* with *I* or *we*, as in "We shall overcome." This is no longer a rule, but when you're offering to help someone, you should use *shall* instead of *will*, as in "Shall I help you carry your groceries?" To avoid sounding stuffy, avoid *shall* altogether in such cases: for example, "May I help you carry your groceries?"

You can also express future action by using a form of the verb *go* with the infinitive of the action verb; for example, "I am going to discuss this with my supervisor."

You can also use the present or present progressive tense to express future action, as in "Cindy leaves for Las Vegas later today" or "Cindy is leaving for Las Vegas later today."

Recognizing the Perfect Tenses

English has three *perfect tenses* used to describe action that occurred just prior to the present, past, or future. The perfect tenses express action completed before another action occurred, occurs, or will occur. For example, the future perfect tense expresses future action that has been completed prior to another future action. The following sections explain the perfect tenses and explore their nuances.

Present Perfect

Use the present perfect to express action leading up to the present and possibly still occurring, as in the following examples:

> Patrick has often dreamed about owning his own farm. (Patrick dreamed in the past and presumably is not done dreaming about this.)
> My parents have spent every winter in Alabama since I can remember. (Action occurred in the past and continues to the present.)

A common mistake is to use present perfect to express action that happened sometime in the past and is over. For example:

> I already have responded to your email message!
> Congress has voted on the legislation and is now waiting for the president to sign it into law.

For action completed in the past, use the simple past tense:

> I already responded to your email message!
> Congress voted on the legislation and is now waiting for the president to sign it into law.

Past Perfect

Use the past perfect tense to express action completed prior to another past action, as in the following examples:

> James had called home before he left work. (Both actions occurred in the past, but had called came first.)
> The buyers signed the contract moments after the sellers had lowered their price. (Both actions occurred in the past, but had lowered came first.)

Often, people mistakenly use the past tense for all actions that occurred in the past, even when some past actions occurred before others:

> Natalie's eyes expressed her disappointment with the engagement ring her fiancé gave her. (The verb gave should be had given, because the fiancé gave the ring before Natalie's eyes expressed disappointment.)

Future Perfect

Use the future perfect tense to express action completed sometime in the future, as in the following examples:

> My father will have turned 65 years old on his next birthday. (The father's birthday will happen in the future, but he will have turned 65 years old by that time.)
> Ten days from now, most of the seeds you planted will have sprouted. (Some seeds may sprout before the ten days have passed.)

Recognizing the Progressive Tenses

The progressive tenses all use the *–ing* form of the action verb to indicate that the action is happening in the specified time frame—present, past, or future. The following sections provide guidance on when to use each of these progressive tenses.

Present Progressive

Use the present progressive tense to express action that's occurring right now, as in the following examples:

> A frog is hiding underneath this lily pad.
> Rays of sunlight are sparkling on the lake's surface.

You can also use the present progressive tense to express future action, as shown here:

> I don't know about you, but I am sleeping in tomorrow morning. (You could also use the future progressive tense, as explained later.)

Past Progressive

Use the past progressive tense to express action that was happening in the past. This tense comes in handy particularly when a past action is interrupted by another past action, as in the following examples:

> I was minding my own business when the lion attacked me.
> Jenny was crossing the street when she bumped into her neighbor.

You can also use the past progressive tense to exaggerate a habitual action:

> The professor was constantly berating his students.

Future Progressive

Use the future progressive tense to express action that will be happening sometime in the future. The future progressive tense is particularly helpful for expressing a future action leading up to or interrupted by a future event, as in the following examples:

> I will be driving home from work when the game starts.
> By the time I get there, everyone will be leaving.

The future progressive tense is also useful for expressing future action that's in progress. Note the subtle difference in meaning between the future and future progressive tenses:

> **Future:** I will install your water heater tomorrow.
> **Future progressive:** I'm sorry, tomorrow doesn't work for me. I will be installing four water heaters on the other side of town.

Noting the Perfect Progressive Tenses

The *perfect progressive tenses* express ongoing action completed in the past, present, or future. Use the perfect progressive tenses to express ongoing action completed in the past, present, or future.

Present Perfect Progressive

Use the present perfect progressive to express action that started in the past and continues in the present, as in the following example:

The auditor has been reviewing the financial records for the past three days. (The action started three days ago and is still in progress.)

You can also use the present perfect progressive to express continuous action sometime in the recent past, as in the following examples:

The elephants have been eating a little more than usual.
Have you been following the news?

Past Perfect Progressive

Use the past perfect progressive tense to express continuous action completed sometime in the past, as in the following examples:

How long had you been waiting before the airline let you board the plane?
The candle had been burning all night before someone blew it out.

The past perfect progressive also comes in handy for showing cause and effect. Here are a couple examples:

We achieved our goal because we had been working as a team.
Because he had not been showing up for work, he lost his job.

Be careful not to confuse the past progressive and the past perfect progressive. The past progressive is more about interrupting an action in the past. With the past perfect progressive, the emphasis is on duration of time. Note the subtle difference in meaning of the following sentences:

Past progressive: We were standing on the corner when the motorcade passed. (The emphasis here is on what we were doing at the very moment when the motorcade passed.)

Past perfect progressive: We had been standing on the corner for at least 45 minutes when the motorcade passed. (The emphasis here is on how long we were standing on that corner.)

Future Perfect Progressive

Use the future perfect progressive to express ongoing action in the future that's interrupted by a future action or event, as in the following examples:

The Sherpa will have been climbing for 48 hours by the time he reaches the summit.
How long will you have been working at Xenon Enterprises when you reach retirement age?

You may also use the future perfect progressive along with the simple future to show cause and effect, as shown here:

The workers will be exhausted at the end of the day because they will have been working nonstop for over 8 hours.

Again, be careful to distinguish the future progressive from the future perfect progressive. Use the future progressive to express an action that gets interrupted by another future action. Use the future perfect progressive to suggest a period of time. These examples shed light on the difference:

Future progressive: The fans will be standing at the start of the National Anthem.
Future perfect progressive: The fans will have been standing for 15 minutes prior to the playing of the National Anthem.

Sticking to Your Timeline

One of the most important rules to follow when describing action is to adhere to a consistent timeline. Choose a tense—usually present or past—and change tense only when necessary to reference time periods relative to your baseline tense. Any unnecessary or illogical shifts in tense are likely to confuse readers. Here's an example of a paragraph with awkward shifts in verb tense followed by a corrected version:

Awkward tense shifts: We received your cover letter and résumé. Although we had no openings at this time, your information is entered into our database, and you will be considered for any future openings that required your skills and expertise.

Smooth tense shifts: We received your cover letter and résumé. Although we have no openings at this time, your information has been entered into our database, and you will be considered for any future openings that require your skills and expertise.

Sorting Out *Lie* and *Lay*

People often struggle with the verbs *lie* and *lay*:

- *Lie* is an intransitive verb that means *to recline*, as in "I lie down to take a nap." (An *intransitive* verb does not require an object.)
- *Lay* is a transitive verb that means *to set down*, as in "Lay down your weapon." (*Transitive verbs* require objects; in this example, *weapon* is the object.)

So if the police show up at your home and incorrectly order you to "lie down your weapon," you could argue that you were confused as to whether you should lie down on the ground or lay down your weapon.

After you master that subtle distinction in meaning, you're only halfway home, having recognized the difference in the present tense. To master the other 11 tenses, you need to recognize how the verbs' principle forms differ.

Root	Past	Past Participle
lay	laid	laid
lie	lay	lain

As you can see, the past tense of *lie* is *lay*, which also happens to be the present tense of *lay*. Confusing, huh? So if your roommate is taking a nap, you might say something like "Tanya *lay* down to take a nap an hour ago." If you took a nap before she did, you might say, "And three hours before Tanya hit the sack, I *had lain* down to take my nap."

Practice

Write the correct verb form (tense) in each blank. Use the verb that appears in parentheses.

1. The zookeeper did not discover that the elephant _____ (escape) until she returned to work the next day.
2. By this time next year, the road crew _____ (complete) its work on the bridge.

3. The plane _____ (fly) for only 15 minutes when the pilot turned off the Fasten Seatbelts sign.
4. After his third Bahama Mama milkshake, Tom could not recall how much he _____ (drink).
5. At the same time police officers _____ (plan) their raid, the thieves were robbing another bank.
6. The locusts _____ (feast) on the crops all week [and still are].
7. Before the parents <u>lay</u> down to take a nap, they _____ (lie/lay) their baby in the crib. (Write the correct verb in its correct form in the blank.)
8. The critics raved about the film, many of them claiming it _____ (be) director Scorelli's most inspired work.
9. Upon hearing that his daughter _____ (incarcerate), John drove to the county jail to bail her out.
10. Since the beginning of the Industrial Revolution, hourly employees _____ (overwork) and _____ (underpay).

Answers

1. had escaped
2. will have completed
3. had been flying
4. had drunk
5. were planning
6. have been feasting
7. had laid
8. is
9. had been incarcerated
10. have been overworked; underpaid

Making Your Nouns and Verbs Agree

Every sentence has an actor and an action, a noun and a verb, and the noun and verb must agree in person and number. Singular subjects take singular verbs; plural subjects require plural verbs. Likewise, the verb must reflect the person performing the action: I, you (singular), he/she/it, we, you (plural), or they.

Every verb has six person/number forms—three singular persons and three plural persons. Here are the six present verb forms for the regular verb *love*.

	Singular	**Plural**
First person	I *love*	We *love*
Second person	You *love*	You *love*
Third person	He/she/they/it *loves*	They *love*

The good news is that you don't have to think about person and number when dealing with any tense other than the present, because in the other tenses, the verb form is the same regardless of which subject(s) are performing the action. For example, *I*, *you* (singular), *he*, *she*, *it*, *we*, *you* (plural), and *they* all *loved*, *will love*, *have loved*, *had loved*, and so on.

Most people have little trouble choosing the right verb form when the noun performing the action is clear and near to the verb. When other words get between the subject and the verb—making the subject of the sentence fuzzy—choosing the right form gets complicated. In the following sections, I provide guidance on how to deal with the trickiest situations.

Dealing with Compound Subjects

When a plural subject or two or more subjects—called a *compound subject*—perform an action, choose the appropriate plural verb form—the form for *we*, *you* (plural), or *they*. Obvious, right? Well, in some cases, the choice isn't so clear. Here are some guidelines to help you in a pinch:

- Two or more subjects connected by *and* are *they*, so use the third-person plural verb form: Sally and Dan dance together on Fridays.
- When two or more subjects are connected by *or* or *nor*, only one or none of the subjects is acting, so use the third-person singular verb form: Neither Sally nor Dan likes ballroom dancing.
- Likewise, if *either* or *neither* is the subject of the sentence, use a singular verb: Either of us makes a fine candidate for mayor.
- When *I* is one of two or more subjects separated by *or* or *nor*, place it last and use the first-person singular verb form: Neither Ms. Drake nor I am taking the train into town.
- When the compound subject includes a singular and a plural noun connected by *or* or *nor*, place the plural noun last and use a plural verb form: Neither Bryce nor the other anglers go fishing at noon.
- When a singular subject performs an action along with, as well as, or besides another noun, use a singular verb form: Senator Brewer, as well as Senator Ditch, supports the amendment.

Accounting for Collective Nouns

A *collective noun*, such as crowd, denotes a group of individuals. Often, a collective noun takes a singular verb form:

> The crowd roars.
> The team wins its first tournament game.

Sometimes, the collective noun is treated as plural:

> The faculty were outraged.
> The sheep run around the field.

To figure out whether a singular or plural verb form is appropriate, see if the collective noun is acting as one coherent entity or a bunch of singular entities. Either could be correct, depending on the situation.

For example, if a group is experiencing some discord—or you want to distinguish the members of the group for some other reason—use the plural verb form:

> Team members disagree on the presentation format.

Recognizing Singular Indefinite Pronouns

Further complicating the selection of singular and plural noun forms are the singular indefinite pronouns *anybody*, *each*, *everybody*, *everyone*, *every one*, *nobody*, *no one*, *somebody*, and *someone* when followed by a plural noun, as in the following examples:

> Every one of the lizards eats both plants and insects regularly.
> Everybody, especially the fans, appreciates good sportsmanship.

Interestingly, the pronoun *none* can be singular or plural depending on whether you intend it to mean "not one" (singular) or "not any" (plural). Both of the following are correct:

> None of the doctors agrees on the diagnosis. (Not one of the doctors agrees.)
> None of the doctors agree on the diagnosis. (Not any of the doctors agree.)

Maintaining Agreement with Amounts and Number of ...

When discussing portions using words such as *part of, majority of, some of, all of, none of, remainder of,* or a *percentage* or *fraction of,* look at the noun following *of* to determine whether to use a singular or plural noun form. If the noun is singular, use the singular verb form. If the noun is plural, use the plural verb form. Here are a couple examples:

Half of the island is underwater. (Use the singular verb *is* because *island* is singular.)

Half of the peaches were lost to frost. (Use the plural verb *were* because *peaches* is plural.)

When using *number of,* however, different rules apply:

- When using *the number of,* use a singular verb: The number of guests we need to feed is 150.
- When using *a number of,* use a plural verb: A number of guests have requested drinks.

Treat a dollar amount or a period of time as a singular noun and use a singular verb:

Twenty-five dollars is the price I'm asking.

Two months seems a long time to be away from home.

Practice

In the following sentences, underline the correct singular or plural verb form:

1. Neither Jerry nor his neighbors is/are happy about the new parking restrictions.
2. The finance committee have/has approved next year's budget.
3. Nobody, including the employees, was/were happy with the new benefit package.
4. Mrs. Bower's cat, along with her dog, cross/crosses the street at the intersection.
5. Over half of the islanders was/were left homeless.

Answers

1. Neither Jerry nor his neighbors are happy about the new parking restrictions.
2. The finance committee has approved next year's budget.
3. Nobody, including the employees, was happy with the new benefit package.
4. Mrs. Bower's cat, along with her dog, crosses the street at the intersection.
5. Over half of the islanders were left homeless.

Setting the Right Mood

A verb's *mood* conveys the attitude of the speaker. English verbs have three moods:

- **Indicative** states a fact: The king cobra is a menacing reptile.
- **Imperative** issues a command: Don't pet the king cobra!
- **Subjunctive** indicates the statement is not factual but likely or unlikely, hoped for, or feared: If I were a king cobra, I would be menacing.

Most people don't have trouble with the indicative or the imperative, but they have no idea of when to use the subjunctive or how to form it.

Use the subjunctive mood to express a wish, suggestion, or demand or a condition that's contrary to fact, as in the following examples:

> **Wish:** Sandy wishes she were more outgoing.
> **Suggestion:** Paul suggests we write letters to our representatives.
> **Demand:** The FDA has mandated that all over-the-counter sleep medications be pulled from the shelves.
> **Condition contrary to fact:** If I were leading the country, everyone would work a 30-hour week. (The condition is contrary to fact, because I'm not leading the country.)

Forming the present and past subjunctive is fairly straightforward. For nearly every verb, you simply use the verb's root: *ask*, *walk*, *talk*, whatever. In the case of the verb *to be*, you still use the root (be) to form the present subjunctive, but to form the past subjunctive, use *were* instead of *was*.

If the action that's contrary to fact occurs before another action that occurred in the past, use *had* + *past participle* of the verb, as in the following examples:

> Had I known of the risks, I never would have invested all that money.
> I would have filled the tank if the gas had been on sale.

Practice

In the following sentences, underline the verb that's in the subjunctive mood.

1. Our policy manual demands that all employees be/are on time.
2. If the pizza were/was here, we would break for lunch.
3. Christine requested that her boyfriend not call/calls her during work hours.

4. The tour guide recommended that everyone packs/pack bottled water and a few snacks for the day.
5. Have/Had the parents been informed of the details, they would never have given their permission.

Answers

1. Our policy manual demands that all employees be on time.
2. If the pizza were here, we would break for lunch.
3. Christine requested that her boyfriend not call her during work hours.
4. The tour guide recommended that everyone pack bottled water and a few snacks for the day.
5. Had the parents been informed of the details, they would never have given their permission.

Choosing a Voice

Voice conveys the relationship between the action or state of being and the doer or recipient of the action. In the active voice, someone or something performs the action. In the passive voice, the action is performed on someone or something. A verb's *voice* reveals or conceals the subject of the sentence.

With the *active voice*, you know from the get-go who's performing the action:

> The gecko sold far more auto insurance policies than did the walrus.
> We released the information prematurely.

With the *passive voice*, you don't find out who's performing the action until later, if at all:

> Far more auto insurance policies were sold by the gecko than by the walrus.
> The information was released prematurely.

In most cases, use the active voice, because it's clear and direct. Use the passive voice when you want to avoid taking or placing blame. In other cases, the passive voice is appropriate because you want to emphasize the action or whoever is performing the action is irrelevant, as in scientific studies.

Practice

Change each of the following sentences from passive to active voice:

1. Numerous complaints had been filed by irate customers.

2. New medications are developed each year by the pharmaceutical companies.

3. All of the cracks in the bathtub were sealed with epoxy.

4. The people who were affected by the floods were not allowed to return to their homes by the authorities.

5. A standing ovation was given to the cast and crew.

Answers

1. Irate customers had filed numerous complaints.
2. Pharmaceutical companies develop new medications each year.
3. Epoxy sealed all of the cracks in the bath tub.
4. The authorities did not allow the people who were affected by the floods to return to their homes.
5. The cast and crew received a standing ovation.

Chapter Review Practice

To form the 12 tenses, use the four verb forms—root, present participle, past, and past participle. Use the simple tenses to express action in the past, present, or future; the perfect tenses to express completed action; and the conditional (progressive) tenses to express ongoing action. Keep your eye on the timeline when shifting tense. The subject of a sentence must agree with the verb in person and number. Use the subjunctive mood to express a wish, suggestion, or demand—or a condition that's contrary to fact. The active voice generally is clearer and more direct than the passive voice. So mostly write in active voice, although there are some pesky exceptions.

Practice

Now let's practice what you learned in this chapter:

1. Using the verb *walk*, write the correct form of the verb for first-person singular for each of the following tenses:
   A. Present _____
   B. Past _____
   C. Future _____
   D. Present progressive _____
   E. Present perfect _____
   F. Past perfect _____
   G. Future perfect _____
   H. Past progressive _____
   I. Future progressive _____
   J. Present perfect progressive _____
   K. Past perfect progressive _____
   L. Future perfect progressive _____
2. Which of the following must agree?
   A. Noun and adjective
   B. Verb and adverb
   C. Noun and verb
   D. Preposition and verb
3. Which of the following is an example of the subjunctive mood?
   A. I have been learning how to drive a truck.
   B. If I could drive a truck, I'd be happy.
   C. I will soon have learned how to drive a truck.
   D. I don't know how to drive a truck.
4. Which of the following is an example of the indicative mood?
   A. Stay away from my dog, Killer.
   B. My dog, Killer, is a good boy.
   C. If my dog, Killer, got loose, that would be bad.
   D. Please don't feed my dog, Killer.

5. Which of the following is an example of the imperative mood?
   A. Please feed my cat while I'm away.
   B. Will you feed my cat while I'm away?
   C. I'll feed your cat while you're away.
   D. If you feed my cat, I'll walk your dog.
6. Which of the following is an example of the passive voice?
   A. The workers came together to discuss their problems.
   B. The magazines arrived with no warning.
   C. The weather looked ominous.
   D. The surveys were collected when finished.
7. Which of the following is an example of the active voice?
   A. The doctor was arrested for misbehavior.
   B. The nurse was hired because of her excellent résumé.
   C. The patient laid down on the table.
   D. The insurance was rejected for strange reasons.
8. Match the following verbs with the correct tense:
   A. Jump   E. Past participle
   B. Jumped   F. Present
   C. Is jumping   G. Past
   D. Have jumped   H. Present participle
9. What do the perfect tenses have in common?
   A. They involve a completed action.
   B. They involve an ongoing action.
   C. They take place in the present.
   D. They are immaculate.
10. What do the progressive tenses have in common?
    A. They involve a completed action.
    B. They involve an ongoing action.
    C. They take place in the present.
    D. They are liberal.

Answers

1. A. Walk
   B. Walked
   C. Will walk
   D. Am walking
   E. Have walked
   F. Had walked
   G. Will have walked
   H. Was walking
   I. Will be walking
   J. Have been walking
   K. Had been walking
   L. Will have been walking
2. C
3. B
4. B
5. A
6. D
7. C
8. A and F
   B and G
   C and H
   D and E
9. A
10. B

7

Describing Words: Adjectives and Adverbs

Nouns and verbs do the heavy lifting of language, but there's more to language than heavy lifting. If there were nothing but nouns and verbs, we'd all sound a little like a toddler or the Hulk. You can only say so much with sentences such as "Want toy!" and "Hulk smash!"

That's where adjectives and adverbs come in. These words modify other words, adding color, detail, and vibrancy to people, places, things, actions, and conditions.

Without adjectives and adverbs, writing would be short, simplistic, and boring. You'd never be able to talk about a stirring speech, a danceable song, a loud noise, or a diabolical villain. You couldn't say that you barely passed a test, happily married your best friend, or truthfully answered a question.

Adjectives and adverbs help us paint a picture of the world. Without them, the canvas of language would be mostly blank.

Adjectives: Describing Words

There's more to life than people, places, and things. There are tall people, exciting places, and annoying things. Without adjectives, we'd be at a loss to describe just about everything. Adjectives paint a more detailed picture of the world.

Adjectives describe everything that can be described. Some describe color:

black	lavender	purple
blue	magenta	red
brown	orange	teal
green	pink	white

Others describe size:

big	ginormous	medium
cumbersome	itty-bitty	sizable
enormous	large	small
gigantic	little	teeny-weeny

These adjectives describe the texture of an object:

coarse	gritty	rough
damp	hard	smooth
fuzzy	jagged	soft
grainy	porous	solid

Someone's personality can be described in the following ways—and many others:

angry	fearful	mellow
buoyant	happy	passive-aggressive
courageous	hilarious	quiet
depressed	jovial	weird

When the weather's hot, there are many adjectives besides *hot* you can use:

| blazing | scorching | tropical |
| hellish | sweltering | warm |

There are even adjectives to describe things that can't be described or understood:

incomprehensible	magical	unknowable
indescribable	mysterious	unspeakable
ineffable	unfathomable	unthinkable

Such lists could continue for hundreds of pages (and you can find such lists in a thesaurus). For now, you should know that there are many adjectives out there and that it's important to find the right one for your writing situation.

Types of Adjectives

There are four main types of adjectives: common, proper, compound, and indefinite. Knowing the types of adjectives will help you find the appropriate terms to describe your nouns and pronouns.

Common

A common adjective is a plain old adjective that consists of one word and is not capitalized. Common adjectives include *red*, *historical*, *fuzzy*, and *huge*.

Proper

A proper adjective, like a proper noun, is capitalized. Most proper adjectives are variations of names, as in the following example.

> *The Shield* is a Shakespearian tragedy.
> Are you familiar with Aristotelian logic?
> That story is Kafkaesque!
> The suspicious behavior of the president seems a little Nixon-y.
> Do you like Chicago-style hot dogs?

As you can see, many proper adjectives are also *eponyms*: words derived from names. Adjectives such as *Shakespearian* and *Draconian* are taken from names, but eponyms can be other parts of speech as well. Nouns such as *shrapnel* and verbs such as *boycott* are also eponyms.

Compound

In the previous section, the word *Chicago-style* was used as an example of a proper adjective: *Chicago-style* is also a compound adjective.

Compound adjectives consist of two words, and they are usually joined by a hyphen:

> Is this gizmo battery-operated?
> My son is left-handed.
> The ring-tailed lemur is cute.
> I have a part-time job.
> I like foot-long hot dogs.

For more on hyphens, see Chapter 19.

Just as other compound words can exist without a hyphen, sometimes a compound adjective has no hyphen, as in this example:

> She is my longtime friend.

Also, a compound adjective is sometimes two separate words:

> Did you go to the Pink Floyd concert?

Though many compound adjectives are hyphenated, don't get confused if you see an adverb followed by an adjective, as in these examples:

> Let's go to the highly anticipated lecture.
> I made freshly grilled hamburgers
> Let's watch the newly chosen winners.

In those sentences, the adverb modifies the adjective, so these are not compound adjectives; therefore, you don't use a hyphen. Remember, hyphens should be used to add clarity and create compound adjectives, but an adverb plus an adjective cannot be a compound adjective.

Practice

In the following sentences, underline the compound adjectives that should be hyphenated:

1. Do you like my flat top haircut?
2. That is flatly untrue.
3. The book has dog eared pages.
4. I love the smell of newly mown grass.
5. The artist specializes in ready made pieces.

Answers

1. Do you like my flat-top haircut?
2. That is flatly untrue. (No hyphen)
3. The book has dog-eared pages.
4. I love the smell of newly mown grass. (No hyphen)
5. The artist specializes in ready-made pieces.

Indefinite

As you might guess, indefinite adjectives are not as specific as adjectives such as *green* and *Orwellian*. Indefinite adjectives refer to vaguer concepts, mainly numbers—but not exact numbers. These are the most common:

all	every	most
any	few	several
each	many	some

Here are some indefinite pronouns used in sentences:

> Do you have any comic books?
> I like most Christopher Nolan films.
> I only have a few good friends.
> There are several dogs playing in the park.
> I don't have a lot of money, but I have some money.

Notice how those adjectives don't refer to exact amounts? That's how you know they're indefinite.

Practice

For the following sentences, identify whether the adjective is common, proper, compound, or indefinite:

1. My sweater is yellow. _____
2. I need to make a left-hand turn. _____
3. What is the Christian thing to do? _____
4. This is a hardwood floor. _____
5. I don't have many DVDs. _____
6. You should give a clean napkin to each customer. _____
7. Which red-bellied bird is that? _____
8. Your music is very Wagnerian. _____
9. I smell something gross. _____
10. I got hit by the spring-loaded boxing glove. _____

Answers

1. My sweater is <u>yellow</u>. (Common)
2. I need to make a <u>left-hand</u> turn. (Compound)
3. What is the <u>Christian</u> thing to do? (Proper)
4. This is a <u>hardwood</u> floor. (Compound)
5. I don't have <u>many</u> DVDs. (Indefinite)
6. You should give a <u>clean</u> napkin to each customer. (Common)
7. Which <u>red-bellied</u> bird is that? (Compound)
8. Your music is very <u>Wagnerian</u>. (Proper)
9. I smell something <u>gross</u>. (Common)
10. I got hit by the <u>spring-loaded</u> boxing glove. (Compound)

How to Use Adjectives

In English, the adjective often goes before the noun it modifies:

> a tasty chicken
> a breathtaking view
> an enormous horse
> some lazy children
> our adorable dog

Now let's put similar terms in sentences:

> I have a <u>splitting</u> headache.
> My dog has <u>white</u> fur.
> Canada is a <u>cold</u> country.
> Staples are <u>tiny</u> devices.
> I have a <u>runny</u> nose.

All those examples involve one adjective modifying one noun, but you can add more than one adjective to these sentences.

> I have a <u>horrible, splitting</u> headache.
> My dog has <u>white, wiry, thick</u> fur.

Canada is a cold, wintry, peaceful, northern country.
Staples are metal, bendy, tiny devices.
I have a runny, sore, swelling nose.

Use commas to separate the adjectives, but don't put a comma between the final adjective and the noun.

Adjectives and *To Be*

You can also use a form of *to be* with adjectives.

My pet rabbit is stinky.
Coffee is addictive.
Cupcakes are sweet.
Pizza is amazing.
September is refreshing.

Both these methods can be used in one sentence:

My mangy pet rabbit is stinky.
Strong coffee is addictive.
Chocolate cupcakes are sweet.
Spicy pizza is amazing.
Cool September is refreshing.

The longer the sentence, the more opportunities to use adjectives. Anytime you see a noun or a pronoun, you can modify it with adjectives.

Finding the Right Adjective

Think of adjectives as a box of crayons—a box of crayons that has thousands of colors. Every time you use an adjective, you should use the one that is just right for your situation.

Let's say you're trying to describe a TV show you like, such as *Veep*. Here's a sentence that includes some poorly chosen adjectives:

Veep is a good, funny comedy.

The problems start with *good*. Ironically, *good* is one of the worst words in English. It's too vague. I wouldn't say you should never use it, but if you do, you'd better follow it up with more specific words that show *why* what you're describing is good.

The second problem with this sentence is *funny*. That's more specific than *good*, but it's a little redundant next to the word *comedy*. If *Veep* is a good comedy, of course it's funny.

Off the top of my head—and without revision, I promise—here are 15 adjectives that could apply to *Veep*:

American	family	obscene
character-driven	fast-paced	political
cult	ground-breaking	quirky
deadpan	innovative	unusual
documentary-style	intricate	witty

All of these words—which include compound adjectives like *character-driven* and proper adjectives like *American*—are better than *good* and *funny*, and many could be used to write something specific and interesting about *Veep*. However, a well-chosen adjective isn't enough. The word *witty*, like *good*, makes a reader ask "Why?" You have to back up your adjectives with details and examples.

For example, if I said *Veep* is a political show, I would have to discuss some of its commentary on the office of the vice president and the electoral process. If I said it was a family show, I'd have to talk about the show's focus on Selina Meyer's family, including her estranged daughter and former husband. Examples make writing come alive.

Your writing will be vivid and clear if you back up your adjectives with examples that will make your readers see, hear, feel, smell, touch, and experience what you're writing about.

Here's another bad example:

> I hear something weird.

If you said this, someone would say, "What do you hear? Why is it weird?" If you wrote this, the reader would ask similar questions—or just stop reading out of confusion. When using a vague word like *weird*, follow it up with specifics to make the reader understand your meaning:

> I hear something weird. It sounds like a dog's bark mixed with a cat's meow.

See how much clearer that is? Now you understand why the writer thinks the sound is weird, and you can probably imagine the weird sound yourself.

Specifics make for better writing. Adjectives can help you be specific, but don't rely on them to do all the work.

Forming Comparisons: Fast, Faster, Fastest

One of the most important jobs of adjectives is in making comparisons. The suffixes *–er* and *–est* are helpful in transforming words.

> Joe was quick, but Jan was quicker.
> My dog is dumb, but he's not the dumbest dog I know.
> My sister is pretty. She's much prettier than my cousin.
> Football players are strong. Most are much stronger than basketball players. However, weightlifters are probably the strongest athletes.

Words of this type have three forms: the positive, the comparative, and the superlative, as shown in the following table.

Positive	Comparative	Superlative
deep	deeper	deepest
odd	odder	oddest
red	redder	reddest
silly	sillier	silliest
smart	smarter	smartest
tall	taller	tallest
thin	thinner	thinnest
weak	weaker	weakest

The positive is used when there's only one item:

> The bear is angry.

The comparative is used when you're discussing two items:

> The bear is angrier than the camper.

The superlative is used when you're discussing at least three items:

> Out of the bear, the camper, and the lion, the bear is angriest.

Some words have no comparative and superlative. For example, you have to write *more intelligent* and *most intelligent*.

Practice

For the following sentences, note whether the adjective is the positive, the comparative, or the superlative.

1. Birds are intelligent. _____
2. Pigs are the smartest animal in the world. _____
3. Canada is a colder country than the United States. _____
4. I love cupcakes because they're sweet. _____
5. I love cake because it's the sweetest dessert in the world. _____

Answers

1. Birds are intelligent. (Positive)
2. Pigs are the smartest animal in the world. (Superlative)
3. Canada is a colder country than the United States. (Comparative)
4. I love cupcakes because they're sweet. (Positive)
5. I love cake because it's the sweetest dessert in the world. (Superlative)

When *Not* to Use Adjectives

Adjectives have a little bit of a bad reputation. Many writers have claimed that they're soft words that don't carry the force of nouns and verbs. This advice is, like so much writing advice, a little bit true and a little bit false.

There's no question that an overload of adjectives can lead to fluffy, sloppy writing that doesn't say much. However, vague or inappropriate word choices will hurt your writing across the board, for every part of speech, not just adjectives.

Advice on adjectives is often contradictory. For example, professional linguists—such as Geoffrey Pullum—have noted that William Strunk and E. B. White's advice in *The Elements of Style* is inconsistent and not even followed by the authors. Strunk and White write, "The adjective hasn't been built that can pull a weak or inaccurate noun out of a tight place." As Pullum (chronicle.com/article/50-Years-of-Stupid-Grammar/25497) notes, this is an odd way to slam the adjective, since this sentence includes three of them.

In fact, it's hard to write without adjectives, and there's no reason not to use them. Just use adjectives that are specific and suited to your purpose, as all words you choose should be. If your adjectives are clear and appropriate, your writing will be, too.

Articles: Little Words with Big Jobs

Articles are a type of adjective with a specific purpose: they introduce nouns, but they also modify them, like all adjectives.

Definite Articles

In English, the definite article is *the*. Use *the* when you're referring to a specific thing, not one of several things.

> Please hand me the large fork.
> Did you see the World Series?
> I love the show *Better Call Saul*.
> Are you watching the TV?
> What's the big deal?

All those uses of *the* refer to a singular, specific thing. For situations that are more general, use one of the indefinite articles.

Indefinite Articles

In English, the indefinite articles are *a* and *an*. *A* comes before words that start with a consonant sound, and *an* comes before words that start with a vowel sound. So you would never refer to *a elephant* or *an table*: it's *an elephant* and *a table*. Here are more examples of indefinite articles at work:

> Please hand me a doughnut.
> Do you have a dog?
> Can you give me an example?
> Is your dad a politician?
> Is that animal an emu?

Articles can be tricky for people who are new to English, especially if their first language doesn't use articles. Remember that indefinite articles refer to a general or nonspecific entity, while the definite article is more specific.

"Do you have a dog?" doesn't refer to a specific dog. There might not even be a dog.
"Look at the dog begging!" refers to a specific dog.

Be sure to pay attention to articles as you read, as seeing articles in use will help you learn how to use them correctly yourself.

Since *an* comes before words that start with a vowel sound, sometimes this includes words that start with a consonant. For example, it's *an NBA coach*, not *a NBA coach*, because *NBA* starts with an *en* sound.

Practice

1. Which of the following is true of the phrase *the child*?
    A. There's a specific child.
    B. There's not a specific child.
    C. There's a bad child.
    D. There's a good child.
2. Which of the following are correct?
    A. A NRA member
    B. The NRA member
    C. An NRA member

Answers

1. A
2. B and C

Adverbs: Describing Verbs, Adjectives, and Other Adverbs

Adjectives have some close relatives: adverbs. Adverbs also describe, but they have the power to describe verbs, adjectives, and even other adverbs.

Transforming Adjectives into Adverbs

One of the defining traits of words is that they can be changed. Nouns become verbs. Verbs become nouns. Adjectives become adverbs, too. In fact, going from adjective to adverb is one of the easiest transitions in grammar. Let's start with some sentences with adjectives:

> After the tragedy, the president was solemn.
> The crying baby was loud.
> In the afternoon, the sun is bright.

These adjectives can become adverbs with the addition of *–ly*. Here's how they might work in new sentences:

> The president spoke solemnly about the tragedy.
> The baby cried loudly.
> In the afternoon, the sun shines brightly.

These sentences have similar meanings to the previous sentences, but the grammar is different. In the first group, *solemn* modifies *president*, *loud* modifies *baby*, and *bright* modifies *sun*: three cases of adjectives modifying nouns. In the second group of examples, *solemnly* modifies *spoke*, *loudly* modifies *cried*, and *brightly* modifies *shines*: three cases of adverbs modifying verbs.

How do you decide what's the best structure for your sentence? It depends on the situation. If it's important to describe how an action is happening, and to emphasize that action, especially the exact way someone is doing something, then adverbs are the way to go.

Most adverbs end in *–ly*, but not all. For example, *very* is an adverb, and some adjectives such as *hard* can act as adverbs, as in "I'm working hard." Also, *–ly* words can sometimes act as adjectives, such as *cowardly* and *bubbly*. The only way to know for sure if a word is an adjective or adverb is to see what kind of word it's modifying.

Using Adverbs to Describe Action

When it's important to describe an action, there are a few ways to use adverbs. Here are some examples.

Often, an adverb follows the verb it modifies, as in the following examples:

> The quarterback scrambled desperately to avoid defenders.
> Bees swarmed wildly over the picnic.
> Rain fell steadily.

Other times, an adverb comes before the verb it modifies.

> The kids quickly ran to the ice cream truck.
> The nurse carefully removed the cast.
> Snow slowly covered the lawn.

The adverb doesn't have to be right next to the verb it modifies. Sometimes they're separated by other words.

> The blind man crossed the street slowly.
> The writer composed a first draft quickly.
> Good comedians phrase their jokes expertly.

Using Adverbs to Describe Adjectives and Other Adverbs

Adjectives and adverbs are the two types of describing words, but sometimes adverbs describe adjectives, too.

> My dog is extremely annoying when he sees me eating. (The adverb *extremely* describes the adjective *annoying*.)
> The president was very soft-spoken during the speech. (The adverb *very* describes the adjective *soft-spoken*.)
> The actor's hideously contorted face grossed out the audience. (The adverb *hideously* describes the adjective *contorted*.)
> The circumstances of some people's lives are depressingly unfortunate. (The adverb *depressingly* describes the adjective *unfortunate*.)

Adverbs even have the power to describe other adverbs, often in a way that heightens them. For example:

> The spy very stealthily avoided detection. (The adverb *very* describes the adverb *stealthily*.)
> I quite angrily shouted at the guy who didn't pick up after his dog. (The adverb *quite* describes the adverb *angrily*.)
> I never really learned Spanish, even though I took three classes. (The adverb *never* describes the adverb *really*.)
> I always thoroughly clean the stove. (The adverb *always* describes the adverb *thoroughly*.)

Practice

1. Which of the following is used to create adverbs?
    A. *–ed*
    B. *–ing*
    C. *–s*
    D. *–ly*
2. Which of the following can adverbs modify?
    A. Verbs
    B. Adjectives
    C. Adverbs
    D. Nouns

Answers

1. D
2. A, B, and C

Recognizing Adverbs That Moonlight as Conjunctions

Conjunctions connect. There are a group of conjunctive adverbs that connect, too. These are some of the most common conjunctive adverbs:

accordingly	hence	nonetheless
also	however	otherwise
anyway	indeed	similarly
besides	instead	still
consequently	likewise	subsequently
conversely	meanwhile	then
finally	moreover	thereafter
further	nevertheless	therefore
furthermore	next	thus

Conjunctive adverbs join two clauses, much like conjunctions. Here they are at work in the following sentences:

I hate speeches; <u>nonetheless</u>, I'll join you for this speech.
My dog threw up on the rug. <u>Subsequently</u>, I washed it.
I like cheese. <u>Consequently</u>, I bought a dairy farm.
I'm tired; <u>still</u>, I could come to the party.
I went to the bank. <u>Next</u>, I went to the gym.

Whether the clauses take the form of one sentence or two, the conjunctive adjective comes between the clauses: it's the glue holding them together.

Chapter Review Practice

Adjectives are used to describe nouns and pronouns, and the main types of adjective are common, proper, compound, and indefinite. Definite (the) and indefinite (a, an) articles are adjectives that introduce nouns. Adverbs are mainly used to describe verbs, but they can also describe adjectives and other adverbs. Conjunctive adverbs join independent clauses.

Now let's practice what you learned in this chapter:

1. Underline the compounds that should be hyphenated in the following sentences:
    A. Your request is highly unusual.
    B. Look at the red breasted bird.
    C. This situation is totally illogical.
    D. The radio is battery operated.
2. Which indefinite adjective, *a* or *an*, goes with the following nouns?
    A. _____ evening
    B. _____ forest
    C. _____ quail
    D. _____ acorn
3. Identify which of the adjectives in the following sentences is positive, comparative, or superlative:
    A. I'm taller than my brother. _____
    B. My aunt Mary is the greatest. _____
    C. I like my chicken spicy. _____
    D. Cats are generally more independent than dogs. _____

4. What do conjunctive adverbs do?
   A. Join two clauses
   B. Join two phrases
   C. Describe adjectives
   D. Describe verbs
5. Which of the following can adverbs describe?
   A. Nouns
   B. Verbs
   C. Adjectives
   D. Adverbs
6. Which of the following is not a type of adjective?
   A. Common
   B. Proper
   C. Compound
   D. Indefinite
7. For the following sentences, identify whether the adjective is common, proper, compound, or indefinite:
   A. I love iced coffee. _____
   B. Give me one of the scratch-made English muffins. _____
   C. I don't have many dishes. _____
   D. My dad loved the Boston Red Sox. _____

Answers

1. A. highly unusual
   B. red-breasted
   C. totally illogical
   D. battery-operated
2. A. An evening
   B. A forest
   C. A quail
   D. An acorn

3. A. Comparative
   B. Superlative
   C. Positive
   D. Comparative
4. A
5. B, C, and D
6. They all are.
7. A. Common
   B. Compound
   C. Indefinite
   D. Proper

8

Wrapping Up Action with Complements

A *compliment* is a nice thing to say, like "That's a cool hat" or "You did a good job on the Penske file." A *complement* is something different: to complement something is to enhance or support it in some way. A hat could complement the rest of your outfit, which could result in your getting a compliment. Vegetables complement many meals, just as a painting can complement a room.

In grammar, complements also enhance something: the subject, verb, or object of the sentence. In this chapter, you'll learn how complements work and how to use them to make your writing clearer and more interesting to read.

Linking to a Subject Complement

The following sentences all have subject complements:

> My dog is a rat terrier.
> Children can be noisy.
> My cousin is creepy.
> This iced coffee is creamy and delicious.
> September is the best month of the year.

You can tell these are complements because the information after the verb tells you more about the subject, rather than telling you what the subject is acting upon.

Some complements are noun phrases, like the following:

> Beards are facial hair.
> The Emmys are a major event.
> My friend is a lawyer.
> That baby is a pain in the neck.
> Rabbits are adorable pets.

A complement follows a linking verb, which is often a form of *be*. When the complement is a noun phrase, it tells you new information about the subject or puts the subject in different words. In the previous examples, *beard* and *facial hair*, as well as *rabbits* and *adorable pets*, are the same things.

Don't confuse complements with objects, which are separate entities from the subject. Here are similar sentences with objects instead of complements:

> Beards disgust my sister.
> The Emmys ruined my career.
> My friend sued me.
> That baby peed on my couch.
> Rabbits eat grass.

When the complement is the same entity as the subject, you have a complement. When the object is a separate entity, you have an object.

> **Complement:** Rabbits are adorable pets.
> **Object:** Rabbits eat grass.

Complements can also be adjective phrases, like the following:

> Puppies are cute.
> My legs are tired and sore.
> Michael Jordan's performance in the NBA finals was superlative and historic.
> My dog runs so fast.
> This cake is disgusting.

As you can see, subject complements are useful when explaining or describing something. They're also helpful when evaluating. Next time you read a review of a movie, TV show, or album, look out for the subject complements.

Complementing a Direct Object: The Object Complement

Objects can have complements, too. Just as subject complements rename or add additional information about the subject, object complements rename or add additional information about the object. The object complements are underlined in the following examples:

My dog scared the mailman <u>to death</u>.
I called my brother Jimmy <u>a jerk</u>.
Some people call jean shorts <u>jorts</u>.
The comedian made the people <u>happy</u>.
I often call my dog <u>a good boy</u>.

As with subject complements, object complements can take several forms. Some are nouns or noun phrases:

I refer to my cat as <u>a little gentleman</u>.
I think of your mom as <u>my mom</u>.
We all know your brother <u>the supervillain</u>.
The company named me <u>acting president</u>.
Jerry called his girlfriend <u>schmoopie</u>.

Others consist of adjectives:

Powerful movies make people <u>sad</u>.
An accident makes traffic <u>worse</u>.
I considered your mom <u>friendly</u>.
Depression makes sufferers <u>tired</u>.
I want this room <u>clean</u>!

Sometimes the object complement can be a prepositional phrase, as in these examples:

The dog chased the squirrel <u>up the tree</u>.
My mom's voicemails drive me <u>up the wall</u>.
I learned to read novels <u>in the dark</u>.
I hid the stolen artifact <u>under my bed</u>.
The wind blew the garbage <u>into the river</u>.

Practice

In the following sentences, underline the subject or object complement and identify which type it is.

1. Joe drove Jillian to the store. _____
2. My hair is shiny and silky. _____
3. Cats are independent and quirky. _____

4. This rain will make everyone wet. _____
5. The criminals left the bank a disaster area. _____

Answers

1. to the store (Object complement)
2. shiny and silky (Subject complement)
3. independent and quirky (Subject complement)
4. wet (Object complement)
5. a disaster area (Object complement)

Remember, a direct object receives some action from the subject. Direct object complements expand on this relationship when appropriate. Sometimes you might want to write, "The dog ate the cake" and leave it at that. Other times you need more information, like "The dog ate the cake at the wedding."

Taking Action on Nouns with Verb Complements

Just as subjects and objects have complements, so do verbs. Verb complements add a little extra information, expanding on the verb, to explain exactly what the verb is doing.

Infinitives as Verb Complements

Remember how infinitives can operate as nouns and adverbs? Some of these uses are identical to an infinitive being used as a verb complement:

Jill wanted to leave.
Superman loves to help.
I'm working to save money.
My son is learning to juggle.
I like running to lose weight.

Gerunds as Verb Complements

A gerund can also be a verb complement, as in the following examples.

The girl likes <u>hunting</u>.
My dad is practicing <u>shooting a basketball</u>.
Today I will watch <u>bowling</u>.
I hate <u>jogging</u>.
You should do more <u>proofreading</u>.

This type of verb complement can also be classified as a direct object.

Don't let the fact that some verb complements are also direct objects drive you crazy. Grammar is terribly complex. Why do you think so many people struggle with it, including the grammar checkers in your computer? If grammar were simple, everyone would be a master of it.

Noun Phrases as Verb Complements

Other times, the verb complement is a noun phrase or clause.

I wonder <u>what's on TV</u>.
Did you eat <u>what was in the refrigerator</u>?
I like <u>that you don't have a computer</u>.
I never know <u>when to go to sleep</u>.
My dad says <u>that I should get a job</u>.

For more on phrases and clauses, see Chapters 9 and 10, respectively.

Practice

For the following sentences, underline the verb complement and identify what type is used: infinitive, gerund, or noun phrase.

1. John likes to grill. _____
2. Sometimes I teach swimming. _____
3. My dog loves chewing things. _____
4. I can never remember to tip. _____
5. Most cats like to scratch. _____
6. Some people think that the moon landing was faked. _____
7. The thieves are planning to rob a bank. _____
8. I want to scream! _____
9. I hate that I worry too much. _____
10. My dog chewed that shoe that I left out. _____

Answers

1. to grill (Verb complement: infinitive)
2. swimming (Verb complement: gerund)
3. chewing things (Verb complement: gerund)
4. to tip (Verb complement: infinitive)
5. to scratch (Verb complement: infinitive)
6. that the moon landing was faked (Verb complement: noun phrase)
7. to rob a bank (Verb complement: infinitive)
8. to scream (Verb complement: infinitive)
9. that I worry too much. (Verb complement: noun phrase)
10. that shoe that I left out. (Verb complement: noun phrase)

Chapter Review Practice

Complements add information to a subject, verb, or object. Subject complements rephrase or supplement the subject, as in the sentences "My sister is a teacher" and "My brother is weird." Verb complements add information to a verb and can be infinitives, gerunds, or noun phrases. Object complements work exactly like subject complements, rephrasing or describing the object, as *secure* does in the sentence "The president made the country secure."

Now let's practice what you learned in this chapter:

1. Identify which of the following sentences has an object, a complement, or neither:
    A. My cousin is a nurse. _____
    B. I enjoy country music. _____
    C. Gelato is delicious. _____
    D. The yogurt fell on the floor. _____
2. Identify which of the following has a subject complement, an object complement, or no complement:
    A. My cat is the suspicious type. _____
    B. I think my dog is part German shepherd. _____
    C. The squirrel ran up the tree. _____
    D. My dad loved baseball more than any other sport. _____

3. In the following, identify whether the verb complement is an infinitive, a gerund, or a noun phrase:
   A. My friend Neil loves to grow mushrooms. _____
   B. Today is a good day for biking. _____
   C. Time to go to the store. _____
   D. Everyone loves this time of year. _____
4. What do complements do?
   A. Add information
   B. Subtract information
   C. Add praise
   D. Clarify tense
5. What do complements add information to?
   A. Subjects
   B. Objects
   C. Verbs
   D. Prepositions

Answers

1. A. Complement
   B. Object
   C. Complement
   D. Neither
2. A. Subject complement
   B. Object complement
   C. No complement
   D. Object complement
3. A. Infinitive
   B. Gerund
   C. Infinitive
   D. Noun phrase
4. A
5. A, B, and C

9

Using Phrases

"That's a nice turn of phrase." "I don't like that phrase." "What's the phrase I'm trying to think of?" "Could you rephrase that?"

People talk about phrases and phrasing all the time, but they likely don't have a clear understanding of what a phrase is in the grammatical sense. This chapter will define phrases and introduce you to the different types of phrases. It will also distinguish phrases from clauses, which often have a similar length but always have a different form. To become a better writer, you need to be comfortable using phrases and moving them around as you revise.

The good news is that phrases give you vast choices. That's also the bad news: the flexibility of phrases gives you so many options that you might be overwhelmed. Don't be. With a little attention to the technical aspects of phrases, you'll be phrasing like a champ.

What a Phrase Is (and Isn't)

A phrase is a group of words that serves a function in a sentence but isn't a clause. Take the following sentence:

> My best friend in Maine is Joel.

This can be broken into three phrases:

> My best friend / in Maine / is Joel.

Each of those chunks of language has a distinctive meaning and purpose. Each is also a different type of phrase: a noun phrase, a prepositional phrase, and a verb phrase, respectively.

The Difference Between a Phrase and a Clause

The word *phrase* is often used very loosely to refer to almost any grouping of words, from a single term to a longer saying. However, in grammar, the word *phrase* means something specific—something that is different from, and lesser than, a clause.

As you'll learn in Chapter 10, a clause is a group of words that has a subject and a verb. An independent clause can be a grammatical sentence, but a dependent clause cannot. The following are dependent clauses:

> when I eat cake
> that I got lost
> who offended my family
> which infuriates me to this day
> because it hurt my foot

All those examples have a subject and verb: for example, in "because it hurt my foot" the subject is *it* and the verb is *hurt*. There's even an object: *foot*. However, the word *because* prevents this group of words from being an independent clause. *Because* makes the clause dependent.

On the other hand, a phrase—though it might look a lot like a clause—has a key difference: it doesn't have a subject and verb. The following are examples of phrases:

> in summer
> running down the street
> the boy in the hat
> during May
> out of my mind
> drinking a milkshake
> outside the gazebo
> at the tip of my tongue
> avenging my father
> a giant poodle

Like dependent clauses, phrases are also not complete sentences. A great way to think about phrases is that they are building blocks for sentences. They are grammatical LEGO bricks.

Another good way to think about phrases is that they are somewhere between words and clauses: a phrase is more than one word, but not quite a clause.

Practice

For the following, indicate whether each is a phrase or clause:

1. Riding the Green Line _____
2. That I will never forget _____
3. A gentleman named Jeff _____
4. How I learned to juggle _____
5. In the middle of the night _____

Answers

1. Phrase
2. Clause
3. Phrase
4. Clause
5. Phrase

Forming Prepositional Phrases

Prepositions, as you learned in Chapter 3, are connecting words that help establish relationships. You can also use prepositions to form prepositional phrases.

Can you spot the prepositional phrases in the following?

> My dad put his keys on the dresser.
> In the other room, I keep my James Bond novels.
> Who is in charge of this office?
> I've been in AA for about a year.
> I won't leave until Sunday.

Prepositional phrases begin with a preposition and then add a little more information. Here are the same sentences with the prepositional phrases underlined:

> My dad put his keys <u>on the dresser</u>.
> <u>In the other room</u>, I keep my James Bond novels.
> Who is in charge <u>of this office</u>?
> I've been <u>in AA</u> for <u>about a year</u>.
> I won't leave <u>until Sunday</u>.

Prepositional Phrases as Adjectives

Some prepositional phrases act as adjectives; they modify a noun.

> I am a friend of the president.
> I wrote a paper on racism.
> Those guys in the store look creepy.

Here are the nouns and the propositional phrases that modify them:

> friend ... of the president
> paper ... on racism
> guys ... in the store

Prepositional Phrases as Adverbs

Other prepositional phrases act as adverbs, which modify verbs, adjectives, and other adverbs. For example:

> My dog sometimes hides under the bed during a storm.
> Do you play tennis on the weekends?
> Until further notice, I won't help you with your homework.

Sometimes it's hard to tell if the prepositional phrase is modifying a noun or verb. Let's look at this sentence again:

> Do you play tennis on the weekends?

Though *on the weekends* seems like it could be modifying *tennis*, it is actually modifying play. Here's how you can tell: pull out the word *tennis*:

> Do you play on the weekends?

That sentence makes sense, so the prepositional phrase must be modifying *play*. Now let's look at the opposite:

> Do you tennis on the weekends?

Since that version doesn't make sense, *on the weekends* must not modify *tennis*.

In the above example sentences, there's also a case of a prepositional phrase modifying another prepositional phrase, which is like an adverb modifying an adverb. Read this sentence again:

My dog sometimes hides under the bed during a storm.

While *under the bed* acts as an adverb modifying hides, *during a storm* acts as an adverb modifying *under the bed*.

Practice

1. Prepositional phrases can act as which of the following?
   A. Nouns
   B. Verbs
   C. Adjectives
   D. Adverbs
2. Prepositional phrases can modify which of the following?
   A. Nouns
   B. Verbs
   C. Adjectives
   D. Adverbs
3. What do prepositions do?
   A. Connect
   B. Separate
   C. Modulate
   D. Order

Answers

1. C and D
2. A and B
3. C

Using Verbs as Adjectives, Adverbs, and Nouns

Verbs and verb phrases are all about action, but sometimes they can function as adjectives, adverbs, and nouns. Read on to learn more about the versatility of verbs and verb phrases.

Using Participles to Describe

Participles are verbs—which usually end in *–ing* or *–ed*—that are used as adjectives. In other words, an action is turned into a description. The participles are underlined in the following examples:

Look at the frolicking dog.
My uncle is a defeated man.
The fallen vase is in pieces.
Were you on the winning team?
The screaming parents and crying child were quite a combination.

Transforming a Verb into a Noun: Gerunds

The suffix *–ing* is added to a verb to form the present participle, as seen in these examples:

I love swimming in the lake.
What are you drawing?
I enjoy parenting with my wife.
Stop lying to me!
Who's that lurking around?

This form of verb can also be used as the subject of a sentence when an activity is treated as a thing. This creates a gerund. The following examples all use present participles as gerunds that function as the subject of sentences:

Swimming in the lake is fun.
Drawing is difficult.
Parenting takes love and patience.
Lying is a bad habit.
Lurking is creepy.

In other sentences, these gerunds could be objects:

I enjoy swimming.
My sister studied drawing.
I don't think I'd be good at parenting.
I hate lying.
I'm practicing my lurking.

A gerund can do anything another noun can do: it can be a subject, a direct object, an indirect object, or even a complement. Gerunds are versatile.

Getting More Mileage Out of Infinitives

Infinitives are also versatile. They can function as a noun, verb, or adjective. Here are infinitives that are working as nouns:

> To nap is wonderful.
> To eat pizza is fun.
> I hate to wake up in the morning.
> My dog loves to fetch.
> I need to write.

Note that sometimes the infinitive becomes an infinitive phrase, as in *to wake up*.

In other cases, an infinitive or infinitive phrase can be an adjective, as in these examples:

> Iron Man has the power to fly.
> Steph Curry has the will to win.
> Right now, I don't have the desire to eat.
> Do you even have the ability to love?
> I lack the resources to buy a house.

Sometimes, the infinitive acts as an adverb. In the following cases, infinitives or infinitive phrases modify verbs:

> You must interview to get the job.
> I worked hard to succeed.
> I drink to forget.
> Are you arguing to distract me?
> I fight to win.

Practice

1. Verbs can be used as which of the following?
    A. Adjectives
    B. Adverbs
    C. Nouns
    D. Prepositions
2. Which of the following sentences contains an infinitive?
    A. The unicorn delighted the children.
    B. I forgot to water my cactus.
    C. Where did the computer cord go?
    D. That pile of books looks dangerous.
3. Which of the following is a participle rather than a gerund?
    A. I love jogging by the lake.
    B. Flying a plane is quite a rush.
    C. Feeding the cats is one of my jobs.
    D. I hear screaming children.

Answers

1. A, B, and C
2. B
3. D

Elaborating on Nouns with Appositives

Your most important goal as a writer is to communicate, and to communicate you must be clear. While trying to be clear, sometimes you have to repeat or rephrase some information. An appositive is a phrase that puts your subject in different language: it rephrases a noun, usually adding some details to the sentence. The appositives are underlined in the following examples:

> I have two brothers, Bill and Joe.
> The former president and vice president, Mr. Obama and Mr. Biden, attended the funeral.
> The hospital, a major medical center, was located just off the highway.
> The sandwich, a beef on wick, was delicious.
> The comic book, a new graphic novel, was amazing.

Facebook, <u>a social network</u>, can be very annoying.

If you have a concussion, <u>a trauma to the brain</u>, you should go to the doctor.

The new tax, <u>an increase in government revenue</u>, goes into effect soon.

I love Jane, <u>my wife</u>.

My favorite pet is my dog, <u>a rat terrier</u>.

Appositives always restate the noun in different words, but there's a lot of freedom as to what kind of words. In some cases, an appositive is simply a synonym, such as *graphic novel* for *comic book*. Sometimes an appositive explains who someone is, like *my wife*. Sometimes an appositive gives extra information, like the breed of a dog (*a rat terrier*). You have a lot of freedom and possibilities when using appositives. It's a flexible form.

With all these types of phrases—not to mention clauses—available, how do you decide what kind to use? First, go with what's clearest. Second, remember the importance of sentence variety. If the form of many of your sentences in a paragraph is the same, the paragraph will feel repetitive and annoying. Adding an appositive—or taking one out—can help keep your writing fresh.

Practice

1. What do appositives restate?
    A. An adjective
    B. A verb
    C. A noun
    D. A preposition
2. Which of the following sentences does not have an appositive?
    A. The air conditioner, a Frigidaire, is brand new.
    B. The cat, a Siamese, is goofy on catnip.
    C. My sister, a lawyer, is on the phone.
    D. My brother, who owes me money, is older.

Answers

1. C
2. D

Rearranging Phrases to Clarify and Emphasize

Moving around phrases is one of the handiest ways to make clearer, stronger sentences. This is particularly easy with prepositional phrases. For example, take the following sentences:

> In the morning, I like to eat bacon.

The prepositional phrase can easily be moved if you want to emphasize the subject and downplay the time:

> I like to eat bacon in the morning.

As you revise, always leave enough time to deconstruct and reconstruct your sentences as needed. Take full advantage of the mobility of phrases.

Don't go overboard with prepositional phrases. Sentences can get a little odd-sounding if you have one prepositional phrase after another. Here's an extreme example:

> I like eating breakfast with my friends at the diner near the airport on weekends.

That's not a very long sentence, but it has four prepositional phrases. Here they are:

> with my friends
> at the diner
> near the airport
> on weekends

That's too many propositional phrases for one sentence. It's almost as bad as if you had that many one-word adverbs in a sentence:

> I like eating breakfast sloppily, hungrily, quickly, and thoughtlessly.

That's just too many adverbs. Too much of anything can annoy your readers, so remember to edit and refine your work to keep it fresh and interesting to readers.

Your prose should appear effortless to readers. Unfortunately, that takes a lot of effort on your part.

Chapter 9: Using Phrases   165

Practice

1. Which of the following is a problem?
   A. Too many prepositional phrases in a sentence
   B. Too many adverbs in a sentence
   C. Too many adjectives in a sentence
   D. Too much of anything in a sentence
2. Which of the following words describe prepositional phrases?
   A. *Flexible* and *combinatory*
   B. *Flexible* and *offensive*
   C. *Combinatory* and *verbal*
   D. *Subordinate* and *clichéd*

Answers

1. All of these
2. A

Chapter Review Practice

A phrase is a group of words that serves a function in a sentence and may have a noun or verb, but not both. Propositional phrases act as adjectives and adverbs. Verbs can be used as nouns, adjectives, and adverbs in the infinitive form. Verbs can become participles with the addition of *–ing* or *–ed*, which creates adjectives. A gerund is a verb plus *–ing* that is used as a noun, while an appositive is a phrase that adds extra information to describe a noun.

Now let's practice what you learned in this chapter:

1. Identify which of the following is a phrase and which is a clause:
   A. Building a sand castle _____
   B. That I used to know _____
   C. Running in place _____
   D. Wherever you go _____
2. What is the function of the *–ing* form in the following sentences: adjective, noun, or verb?
   A. I love a steaming hot bowl of soup. _____
   B. Swimming is probably the best exercise. _____
   C. The birds are chirping every morning. _____
   D. I have some old, fading photos. _____

3. Underline the appositive in the following sentences:
    A. My father, a postal worker, worked hard.
    B. The cousins, Emily and Erica, went everywhere together.
    C. The car, a Volkswagen, had few miles on it.
    D. The couple, Dave and Lauren, went to the town square.
4. Which questions do prepositional phrases answer?
    A. Where
    B. Why
    C. When
    D. What
    E. How
5. Which of the following is a gerund?
    A. Walked
    B. Skip
    C. Running
    D. Slept
6. Which of the following can verbs not be used as?
    A. Nouns
    B. Adjectives
    C. Adverbs
    D. Prepositions
7. Which of the following can prepositional phrases act as?
    A. Nouns
    B. Adjectives
    C. Adverbs
    D. Verbs

Answers

1. A. Phrase
   B. Clause
   C. Phrase
   D. Clause

2. A. Adjective
   B. Noun
   C. Verb
   D. Adjective
3. A. a postal worker
   B. Emily and Erica
   C. a Volkswagen
   D. Dave and Lauren
4. All of these
5. C
6. D
7. B and C

Adding Clauses

10

You can say similar things in many different ways in grammar. A complete sentence is also a complete thought. You can also call it an independent clause, which is one of the main types of clauses you'll learn about in this chapter.

The clause is one of the most important parts of grammar. Clauses are a lot like sentences, and some clauses (the independent kind) can be sentences. Learning to identify independent clauses and dependent clauses is a crucial part of becoming a skilled writer in English.

In the previous chapter, you learned about phrases, which are easy to confuse with clauses. They are quite different, with different forms and purposes, and we'll explain what distinguishes them.

If you know your clauses, you're more than halfway to knowing your grammar. Knowing clauses well separates people who know just a little about grammar from those who truly understand it.

Recognizing the Two Main Clause Types

A clause is a group of words that has a subject and a verb. Sounds like a sentence, right? Not necessarily. One kind of clause can be a sentence, but the other kind cannot.

Using clauses is one of the most basic aspects of writing. If you can't write and recognize a clause, you won't get far as a writer. Clauses are important building blocks of writing, and yes, "Clauses are important building blocks of writing" is a clause.

Read on to learn more about the two kinds of clauses: independent and dependent.

Independent Clauses

An independent clause consists of a subject and a verb. It's also a complete thought. Independent clauses can be short, as in these examples:

> Men shouted.
> The dog howled.

I'm sad.
It's raining.
Today is Sunday.

The key part is that they have a subject and a verb. Some sentences have more than one independent clause, as in the following examples, which each have two:

Canada is near Buffalo; Lake Erie is nearby, too.
I just took a nap, and now I feel refreshed.
My dog smells weird: I think he rolled in something disgusting.
Anchorman is my favorite comedy; I love Will Ferrell.
I think I'm going through a midlife crisis: I just bought a Corvette.

Practice

In the following sentences, identify the number of independent clauses:

1. There's a cat in a tree; someone should call a fireman. _____
2. I look like a police officer, but I'm actually an actor. _____
3. Let's go to the beach; it's a nice day. _____
4. My mom's corn muffins are awesome; you have to try them, and you should also try her waffles. _____
5. Try on this shirt—I think it'll fit you. _____

Answers

1. Two independent clauses
2. Two independent clauses
3. Two independent clauses
4. Three independent clauses
5. Two independent clauses

Dependent Clauses

An independent clause can stand alone, but a dependent clause cannot. Like an independent clause, a dependent clause has a subject and a verb. Here's the big difference: a dependent clause is not a complete thought. The following are examples of dependent clauses:

when I get a headache
who I later learned was a barber
that I'll never forget
after walking the dog
if I went to Australia

Words such as *when*, *if*, and *that* are a clue that you're dealing with dependent clauses. For example:

Independent clause: I went to Australia.
Dependent clause: If I went to Australia.

That *If* demands further information to make a complete sentence. It makes the reader wonder, "Well, if you went to Australia, then what?" Dependent clauses must be joined with independent clauses to form complete, grammatical sentences. Here's another example:

Independent clause: My back hurts.
Dependent clause: When my back hurts.

"My back hurts" is a complete thought, but "When my back hurts" is not. Adding *When* to "My back hurts" turns an independent clause into a dependent clause.

There are three kinds of dependent clauses, which mirror three of the main types of words: noun, adjective, and adverb. Knowing the difference among these types of dependent clauses will help you craft sentences, avoid errors, and introduce variety into your prose.

Because a dependent clause has a subject and a verb, it can feel like a complete thought—even though it is actually a sentence fragment. Writing a dependent clause as a complete sentence is one of the most common writing errors. For more on how to identify and fix this problem, jump to Chapter 15.

Practice

1. Which of the following describes an independent clause?
    A. Complete thought
    B. Incomplete thought
    C. Prepositional phrase
    D. Noun clause

2. What is a dependent clause on its own?
   A. Complete thought
   B. Sentence fragment
   C. Propositional phrase
   D. Verb clause

Answers

1. A
2. B

Noun Clauses

A noun clause can be the subject of a sentence: it can also be the object or a complement. Typically, noun clauses begin with one of the following words:

how	when	who
if	whenever	whoever
that	where	whose
what	whether	why
whatever	which	

The following are examples of noun clauses:

>where I learned to juggle
>where I grew up
>why I won't bike on the sidewalk
>whatever my dad says
>why I hate heights
>whoever took the last muffin
>who my grandmother married
>how experts do it
>that town bordering the lake
>when my sister got married

To figure out if a clause is a noun clause, you have to see if it sounds like a noun. Ask yourself: is it a person, place, or thing? If it walks like a noun and talks like a noun, it's a noun clause. By putting the above noun clauses into sentences, we can see that they do function as nouns:

That school is where I learned to juggle.
Buffalo is where I grew up.
Traffic laws and common sense are why I won't bike on the sidewalk.
I do whatever my dad says.
A childhood trauma is why I hate heights.
I'm going to murder whoever took the last muffin.
Joe is the guy who my grandmother married.
I'm new to cooking; I want to learn how experts do it.
I'd like to visit that town bordering the lake.
I remember when my sister got married.

You may sometimes see dependent clauses referred to as subordinate clauses. Don't be confused by this terminology. A dependent clause is the same thing as a subordinate clause. If you forget, remember that the words *dependent* and *subordinate* both indicate a lack of independence. Dependent people and subordinate people don't have the power to act alone: the same is true of dependent/subordinate clauses.

Adjective Clauses

Adjective clauses—also known as relative clauses—typically begin with one of the following relative pronouns:

of which	who	whomever
that	whoever	whose
which	whom	

Like adjectives themselves, adjective clauses describe nouns and pronouns. Adjective clauses are descriptive, giving extra information that adds color and vividness to your writing. The following are all adjective clauses:

that I grew up in
that I ate for breakfast
which is kind of lumpy
whose brother I know

> who loves hamburgers
> who works as a security guard
> that I need for this job
> whose wallet I found
> that upset my stomach

Here's how those clauses might fit into sentences to describe some nouns:

> Did you buy the house that I grew up in?
> Cereal is the food that I ate for breakfast.
> I like oatmeal, which is kind of lumpy.
> I just met James, whose brother I know.
> Jill is a friend who loves hamburgers.
> Greg is a guy who works as a security guard.
> A working knowledge of spreadsheets is something that I need for this job.
> Bernie Baldwin is the man whose wallet I found.
> Chili is the food that upset my stomach.

See how those clauses describe nouns? Let's look at one example:

> I like oatmeal, which is kind of lumpy.

The clause describes *oatmeal*. Of course, you could say "I like lumpy oatmeal," but that would have a different meaning. Both sentences are grammatical, so you should choose the one that best conveys your meaning.

The important thing to remember is that adjective clauses describe. Look at how they answer a reader's potential questions in these examples:

> Greg is a guy who works as a security guard. (What kind of guy is Greg? One who works as a security guard.)
> Chili is the food that upset my stomach. (What kind of food is chili? The food that upset my stomach.)
> Did you buy the house that I grew up in? (Did you buy the house? Which house? The one I grew up in.)

If the dependent clause doesn't describe, it must not be an adjective clause.

Adverb Clauses

Like an adverb, an adverb clause modifies verbs, as well as adjectives and other adverbs. Typically, an adverb clause begins with one of the following words:

after	even though	though
although	if	unless
as	since	until
as if	so that	when
because	than	whether
before	that	while

The following are examples of adverb clauses:

> when the days get shorter
> while Barack Obama was president
> since I have a headache
> although cats are more independent
> until the sun blows up
> whether you like it or not
> before the end of the month
> if that's your sort of thing
> after watching me do it first
> though I have my reservations

Adverb clauses usually say how, why, where, or when something is happening. They often state a condition. For example, the adverb clause "though I have my reservations" could be used in several sentences, such as the following:

> Though I have my reservations, I will sign the contract.
> I married her, though I have my reservations.
> Though I have my reservations, I moved to Buffalo, New York.
> Though I have my reservations, I bought a fedora.
> I decided to have children, though I have my reservations.

Here's how another adverb clause might fit in several sentences:

> You must pay the rent before the end of the month.
> Want to get a drink before the end of the month?

Please write 20 pages before the end of the month.
Before the end of the month, my wife will give birth.
I think the world will end before the end of the month.

In all those cases, "before the end of the month" answers the question "When?"

Practice

For the following examples, identify the dependent clause and note whether is an adjective, adverb, or noun clause:

1. I grew up in the house where Abraham Lincoln was born. _____
2. Whoever owns that car is my hero. _____
3. I feel happy wherever I am. _____
4. This is the money that I wanted to spend on travel. _____
5. When it rains, my knee hurts. _____

Answers

1. I grew up in the house where Abraham Lincoln was born. (Adjective clause)
2. Whoever owns that car is my hero. (Noun clause)
3. I feel happy wherever I am. (Adverb clause)
4. This is the money that I wanted to spend on travel. (Adjective clause)
5. When it rains, my knee hurts. (Adverb clause)

Rearranging Clauses to Clarify and Emphasize

As you can probably already tell, clauses are easy to move around in a sentence. Depending on what you want to emphasize, you can flip clauses around as needed. For example, let's go back to the noun clause "where I grew up."

There are many sentences that could be written with this clause. It can start sentences:

Where I grew up was chilly.
Where I grew up is now a parking lot.
Where I grew up is where my children will grow up.

The same clause can also end sentences:

> I love where I grew up.
> My parents still live where I grew up.
> Don't visit where I grew up.

In different sentences, "where I grew up" can function as an adjective or adverb phrase instead of a noun phrase:

> That's the house where I grew up.
> Where I grew up, people had manners.
> I've never loved anything as much as the town where I grew up.

Depending on the purpose of your sentence and the other sentences, you can and should move your clauses around. Don't leave them as they were in your first draft. Take advantage of the combinatory possibilities of clauses. They are a writer's friends, and they are highly mobile.

Practice

1. A phrase like "when I was young" can function as which of the following?
   A. Noun
   B. Adverb
   C. Adjective
   D. All of these
2. Clauses can create complete sentences when they are which of the following:
   A. Omitted
   B. Combined
   C. Conjugated
   D. Separated

Answers

1. D
2. B

Chapter Review Practice

Clauses come in several varieties. A dependent clause has a subject and a verb, but it's not a complete thought and it can't be a grammatical sentence on its own. Independent clauses are complete thoughts and can function as sentences on their own. Dependent clauses can be one of three types: noun, adjective, or adverb. Clauses can be rearranged in many ways, depending on what you want to emphasize in your sentence.

Now let's practice what you learned in this chapter:

1. How many independent clauses are in the following examples?
    A. I love crepes. _____
    B. My son is an astronaut, and my daughter is an engineer. _____
    C. I have too many things to do. _____
    D. My dog likes to run around, but my cat likes to stalk. _____
2. In the following sentences, identify the clauses as noun, adjective, or verb:
    A. Sometimes I miss the school where I learned to be a pilot. _____
    B. When it rains, I do a lot of cleaning. _____
    C. I love the sneakers that I go running in. _____
    D. When you're in love is a wonderful time. _____
3. Which of the following means the same as a dependent clause?
    A. Subordinate clause
    B. Reflexive clause
    C. Noun clause
    D. Adverb clause
4. What do adverb clauses modify?
    A. Adverbs
    B. Nouns
    C. Verbs
    D. Adjectives
5. What do adjective clauses describe?
    A. Nouns
    B. Pronouns
    C. Verbs
    D. Adverbs

6. What do noun clauses function as?
    A. Adjectives
    B. Nouns
    C. Verbs
    D. Phrases
7. Which of the following can definitely stand alone as a sentence?
    A. A noun clause
    B. An adjective clause
    C. An adverb clause
    D. An independent clause
8. Which is not true of a dependent clause?
    A. It has a noun and verb.
    B. It can stand alone.
    C. It can't stand alone.
    D. It can't be a sentence.

Answers

1. A. 1
   B. 2
   C. 1
   D. 2
2. A. where I learned to be a pilot (Adjective)
   B. When it rains (Adverb)
   C. that I go running in (Adjective)
   D. When you're in love (Noun)
3. A
4. A, C, and D
5. A and B
6. B
7. D
8. B

Part 4

Writing with Style

Grammar is only half the story when it comes to writing. You could have perfect grammar and still write a paper, article, or story that is terrible. These chapters will show how the rules and elements of grammar can be used to craft writing that packs a punch and tells a story. The grammar chapters are about the raw material of language. The style chapters tell you how to mold that raw material into compelling prose.

That's where the seven Cs of good writing come in. If you're feeling overwhelmed by the terminology and rules of other chapters, the seven Cs are another way to look at writing that can help you focus on the big picture.

In these chapters, you'll also learn some rules of thumb and tricks of the trade for writing with style. One of the most important aspects of style is sentence variety. You'll learn how to vary your sentences in terms of length and type—and why this is so important. I'll also discuss diction: word choice. I'll show you how to make strong word choices while (usually) avoiding clichés, euphemisms, slang, and jargon. Parallelism is another tool that helps you craft smooth, clear sentences. In another chapter, I'll review some of the most common writing errors and how to avoid them.

I'll also discuss how to keep your writing free of bias. This can be tricky when discussing gender, race, sexual orientation, and other identity issues, but there are some general guidelines that will keep you from accidentally being offensive, unfair, or inaccurate.

11

The Seven Cs of Good Writing

As discussed in Chapter 2, alliteration can be a very useful literary device. It's particularly helpful for making something memorable, and this is true of the seven Cs of good writing. These are seven words, all starting with the letter *C*, that should describe your writing. When your head is spinning from thinking about phrases, semicolons, participles, and gerunds, it can help to look at the big picture. That's where the seven Cs come in.

If you google, you'll find many versions of the seven Cs (or even another number), but the following are the most important ones for writing well:

1. Clear
2. Compelling
3. Consistent
4. Concise
5. Convincing
6. Complete
7. Correct

If you find yourself getting lost in the details and rules and guidelines of other chapters, the seven Cs can help you remember why all this is important. Think of them as rules of thumb that should guide everything you write.

Clear

Good writing is clear. Clear writing has an explicit overall purpose. Readers can understand the meaning of sentences without reading them several times or looking up many words in the dictionary. The organization helps the reader move smoothly from paragraph to paragraph. In short, clear writing is easy and enjoyable to read.

Making your writing clear isn't as simple as it sounds. What sounds clear in your head may be a muddle on paper. Here are a few tricks to help make your writing clear:

Replace vague language with specific language. Replace *bad* with *dangerous*. Replace *heavy* with *500 pounds*. Replace *some people* with *men from southern Indiana*. The more specific you are, the clearer your writing will be.

Use an outline. If your work has a logical flow of ideas and paragraphs, the overall point will be clear. Remember, it's okay to start writing and then outline your work to check and improve the organization. Making an outline after you started drafting is called a *reverse outline*. Some people prefer to outline first, and some people need to just dive in and start writing. All that matters is that the final result is organized.

Show it to someone else, especially someone who's not an expert on the subject. If someone who is unfamiliar with the subject understands what you're saying, your work must be clear. A fresh set of eyes can be a huge help in this regard.

Try explaining your writing to someone else. Are you able to sum it up quickly and concisely? Or do you end up rambling without a clear point? If you can't come up with a clear elevator pitch or thesis statement, chances are your writing is unclear, too.

Practice

1. Which of the following makes writing clearer?
   A. Vague language
   B. Scientific language
   C. Clear language
   D. Inventive language
2. When can outlining benefit a writer?
   A. Before drafting
   B. During drafting
   C. After drafting
   D. All of these
3. Clear writing is good at which of the following?
   A. Confusing
   B. Communicating
   C. Convoluting
   D. Creating

Answers

1. C
2. A and B
3. B

Compelling

You know how a really good book is hard to put down? Even if you're not writing a mystery or thriller, you want your writing to have that hard-to-put-down feeling.

Good writing is compelling. This is another way of saying you need to write in a way that makes people want to read it. Following are a few qualities that can make writing compelling.

Humor

Do you enjoy people who are always completely serious, who never crack a joke or smile? Most people don't. Just as a teacher can liven up a dull lecture with a little humor, you can use some humor to make your writing more fun to read.

Instead of thinking you have to include a lot of jokes, think of humor as an attitude. If you don't take yourself too seriously, that can add a positive element to your writing.

However, be careful when using humor. Often, the risks outweigh the rewards. Sexual or racial humor will rarely, if ever, be appropriate. A joke that might seem innocent to you could offend someone else. Use humor sparingly and cautiously.

Fresh Language

You're a unique person who sees the world in your own way. Let that uniqueness be part of your writing. Don't settle for the same tired phrases and terms everyone else is using. I discuss language to avoid, such as euphemisms, clichés, and jargon, in Chapter 12.

It's easier to turn stale language into fresh language if you're not writing in a rush. If you give yourself enough time to thoroughly revise and edit your work, you'll have more chances to edit out phrases that are dull and worn out. That extra time allows you to freshen up your writing with distinctive, vivid word choices.

Consistent

Good writing is consistent. Unfortunately, there are many aspects of writing where inconsistency can creep in. Following are some of the most common types of consistency errors that you should work to avoid.

Grammar

Grammar is one area where consistency is important. Look at the following sentences:

> The boys are playing outside. They were having fun.

Do you see the problem? First, the boys are playing outside now. Then, the boys were having fun in the past. This is likely a mistake, and it's a common one. It's important to keep your verb tenses consistent to avoid confusion. If revised for consistency, the sentences will make more sense:

> The boys are playing outside. They are having fun.

Here's another example of verb inconsistency:

> I had three brothers. They like to beat me up.

But it's easily fixed, unlike sibling dynamics:

> I have three brothers. They like to beat me up.

What about grammar checkers? Don't they do it for you? And don't they make this whole book unnecessary? Well, I hope that's not true. And I'm pretty sure it's not.

Grammar checkers such as Grammarly can be very useful. If you feel they improve your writing, use them. But they're not a substitute for having an understanding of grammar because no computer program is perfect. Grammar is so complex that even the most sophisticated checker is going to make mistakes. And if you have no sense of grammar, how will you spot those errors?

This is true of all digital writing tools, whether for spelling, references, or what have you. Most of them can help, but they all have a batting average below the level of perfection. You don't want to trust the results of any program too much—you want to be able to evaluate the results of a program and know whether they're valid.

So rest assured, learning correct grammar is important, whether you use grammar checkers or not—because you're smarter than any tool.

Pronouns

In Chapter 16, you'll read a variety of ways to handle pronouns while avoiding sexism. Whatever method you choose, be consistent. If you use *he/she* in one part of a paper, don't start using singular *they* in another part. In fact, these days, you're probably better off with singular *they* throughout your work if you don't want to spotlight someone's gender, or if *they* is their preferred pronoun.

Diction

Be consistent with terminology. Sloppiness with word choice can cause confusion. For example, let's say a supervisor is telling a subordinate about a new assignment in an email. In part of the email, the supervisor writes, "I'll expect this to be finished by next Wednesday." In another part of the email, the supervisor writes, "Remember, this is an optional assignment." What is the employee supposed to think?

There's a language problem there. If the assignment is truly optional, then the employee doesn't have to do it. If the supervisor expects the assignment to be completed by a certain date, then the employee does have to do it. Inconsistent word choices cause problems.

While varying your vocabulary can help your writing stay lively, don't sacrifice consistency for the sake of variety. Don't catch the thesaurus disease (see Chapter 12) or a similar strain of overly verbose writing. In most writing situations, consistency is more important than creativity.

Format

The main style guides are the Modern Language Association (MLA), the American Psychological Association (APA), and *The Chicago Manual of Style* (CMS).

You should be consistent in terms of the format you use. If a professor asks for a paper in APA format, don't use any elements of MLA format. This can be difficult if you're used to using MLA. Formatting takes patience and a willingness to fine-tune your work until you get it right.

Some books on writing—such as Diana Hacker's *A Writer's Reference*—provide basic information on all three major style guides. However, there's no substitute for going to the actual guidebook.

Be sure not to use an older version of APA format (or another style guide). Use the most current edition, which you can find by looking at the website for APA (apa.org), *Chicago* (chicagomanualofstyle.org), or MLA (mla.org).

Thesis Statement and Argument

If you're writing a paper, your thesis statement should be supported by the paper. A thesis statement is a sentence (sometimes two) that captures the argument of a paper. The following are examples of thesis statements:

> Until he wins at least six NBA titles, LeBron James cannot be considered a contender for the title of greatest basketball player ever.
>
> Comic book movies flourish while the comic book industry flounders because editors, writers, and artists are aiming for the wrong audience.
>
> Contrary to popular myths, texting and tweeting are actually making people better writers.

A thesis should be introduced in the beginning of a paper, supported throughout, and restated in the conclusion. Make sure to stay on point in supporting your thesis. If you contradict your own thesis, no one is going to believe your argument. Also, anything that doesn't fit within the thesis could prove distracting.

Assignment Directions or Work Guidelines

Being consistent with the directions or work guidelines you are given is also important. When doing assignments for school, make sure you read the directions carefully. If you turn in a paper that doesn't answer the question or fit the assignment, you'll probably fail—even if your work is excellent. Don't be afraid to ask the teacher for clarification before you start writing. It's extremely important that what you write is consistent with what your audience—in this case, a teacher—expects.

This same advice applies in the workplace, although we all know bosses and clients who don't seem to know what they want. But if you're asked to write something five pages long, with an objective tone, due next Thursday, you'd be making a big mistake to ignore any of those directions.

Some writers think they should memorize the rules of APA or MLA style, but this is not a good idea. Trying to remember all the guidelines is not a good use of your brain power. Looking up style rules is safer and easier. You should work to get faster at looking up material. Help yourself out by putting flags or notes in a physical copy of a manual or bookmarking internet pages. Odds are you'll use some pages over and over, so create shortcuts to those pages. With practice you will become more efficient at finding and understanding the rules.

Practice

1. Which of the following must agree?
    - A. Nouns and verbs
    - B. Nouns and pronouns
    - C. Nouns and adjectives
    - D. Nouns and prepositions
2. Which of the following should describe the argument of a paper or article?
    - A. Circuitous
    - B. Consistent
    - C. Vague
    - D. Concrete
3. Which of the following is not true of grammar checkers?
    - A. They're useful.
    - B. They're perfect.
    - C. They're fast.
    - D. They're ubiquitous.

Answers

1. A and B
2. B
3. B

Concise

Do you like it when someone has a "quick story" to tell that goes on for 20 minutes? Probably not. Writing is the same way: if you go on and on and on and on without saying much, your audience will be bored and stop reading. Say what you have to say, and finish.

Convincing

This point applies best to writing that makes an argument. If you're writing a movie review and you think the movie was horrible, you probably want to argue that people shouldn't waste their money on that movie. If you accomplish that goal, your writing is convincing.

How do you convince your readers of something? The following are several ways to help sell your point of view.

Use Concrete Facts

The more specific details you give, the more you'll persuade your readers. For example, the following is not very credible:

> A lot of people have cancer from smoking.

How many people? Who says this is true? What kinds of cancer? A more specific statement will pass muster with readers:

> According to the American Cancer Society, 30 percent of all cancer deaths are the result of cigarette smoking.

That is a convincing statement, due to the specific details that are hard to deny.

Write Clean, Error-Free Prose

If your writing is error-free, it shows you've paid attention to details and taken your work seriously. This gives you credibility, and it makes your writing more convincing.

Of course, we all make writing mistakes. Writing is one of those things that will never be perfect, but it is also one of those things where you should strive for perfection, mainly for two reasons: communication and presentation.

Communication—which could easily be one of the Cs—is the goal of writing, and writing errors get in the way of communication. Think of them as static ruining a good song on the radio.

As for presentation, everything you write is a chance to present yourself as a certain kind of person. Do you want to present yourself as careful and considerate or thoughtless and incompetent? The fewer errors you make, the better impression you make on readers.

Don't Overstate Your Case

Avoid exaggerations and generalizations. Make a strong point, but don't go overboard. It's easier to make a case that high school football should be banned than that all football should be banned. Keep your argument reasonable and don't overreach.

Complete

When you're writing an argument, completeness is important. For example, let's say your thesis statement is "Due to increasing knowledge of concussion-related brain injuries, high school football should be banned."

In that essay, you had better include thorough research on brain injuries—especially to high-school-age children. If you neglect the research on either brain damage or teens, your paper will be incomplete and your argument will be difficult to take seriously.

Similarly, a work of fiction needs to feel complete. A good way to figure that out is by asking if the work has a beginning, middle, and end.

Completeness is more subjective in other areas. If you're preparing a book of poems, how do you know when the book is complete? That's a judgment call for sure.

Correct

Most of this book is devoted to what's correct in writing. But correctness is complex and applies to many aspects of writing. The following sections explain some of the specific types of correctness.

Grammar

Grammatical correctness is obviously very important or this book wouldn't exist. See Chapter 1 for a good start on getting your grammar under control.

Agreement is perhaps the most important grammatical concept. A noun must agree with its verb, so "Children play," not "Children plays." A large percentage of correctness is really a form of agreement.

Facts

When writing, you should check and double-check your facts. If your writing spreads false information, it could be dangerous at worst and misleading at best. Take the time to research subjects thoroughly to provide the most correct and up-to-date information.

Your credibility is on the line with everything you write. Don't make yourself look foolish by ignoring, distorting, or mixing up the facts.

Format

If you're writing a paper for school, be sure you use the appropriate style guide. Don't use APA when your professor asked for MLA.

This may seem like a small point. After all, don't APA and MLA (and *The Chicago Manual of Style*, for that matter) do the same thing? What's the difference between calling the list of sources "Works Cited" or "References"?

Though the differences are, in a sense, trivial and small, they make a big impression on readers—a negative impression, if you're off-base. Just as misplacing a comma or calling someone by the wrong name can turn off the person you're writing to, using the wrong format or ignoring the rules of that format make you look like a sloppy, careless person. That's not an impression you ever want to make: not in school, not when applying for a job, and not even when writing a friend. Why make a bad impression when you could make a good one?

Also, formatting choices can have significant writing consequences. Since formats help you cite sources, bad citing could lead to accidental plagiarism.

Purpose

There are many reasons for writing: to inform, to entertain, to sell, to amuse, to argue, and to get a job are some common purposes. It's important that you understand your writing purpose and write accordingly.

For example, if your teacher or editor wants an objective research paper, don't turn in a personal essay. A research paper presents facts and makes an argument, while a personal essay tells a story and expresses emotions. If you start telling a story during a research paper, you've lost sight of your purpose.

This also applies to the workplace. If your boss asks you to write a white paper—a type of research paper produced by a business—you'd better not write something that sounds too personal. All research papers, including white papers, are impersonal and focused on the research and argument.

Unfortunately, even if your writing is top-notch, if your writing fulfills the wrong purpose, it will probably be a failure (literally in school, figuratively elsewhere). Double-check your purpose before writing and remind yourself of it frequently while drafting and revising.

Consulting Style Guides for More Direction

Style guides are your friends. I've taught a lot of writing classes, and I wish my students would spend more time with these friends. Style guides are important: they answer many specific questions of what to do in your writing situation. When in doubt, ask your teacher or editor what style guide they prefer.

Also, remember that no style guide will be perfect for every situation, since they end up being used for more situations than they were designed. For example, the APA manual is designed for formatting journal articles in psychology. However, APA format is used by many people for writing projects other than psychology papers. This can create gaps in style. For instance, students often wonder how to format a table of contents in APA. The answer is you can't. Since journal articles don't have a table of contents, that style is not included in APA. You have to figure out the format for a table of contents yourself using other sources. Sometimes a professor or editor will want your format to follow a rule that's not in APA or another manual. Should you ignore the professor and follow the manual? No. Give professors, editors, and bosses what they want—they are the people you're writing for.

Steering Clear of Plagiarism

There are three ways to present other people's ideas in your work: quoting, paraphrasing, and summarizing. If you're familiar with these three methods, you won't have to worry about accidentally plagiarizing.

Quoting

When you quote, you use the exact words of a source, and you let the reader know with quotation marks. The following are examples of quoting:

> Christian Bale growled, "I'm Batman."
> My grandpa said, "Tarnation! The pig's loose again!"
> President Clinton said, "I feel your pain."
> I said, "I don't want to know!" when my sister started another embarrassing story.
> "Can you hear me now?" used to be Verizon's catchphrase.

For more on quotation marks, see Chapter 18.

When writing, it can be tempting to use a lot of quotations. If you have a 10-page paper, using 5 pages of quotations could cut your work in half. As long as you cite the quotations correctly, there's no issue with plagiarism. So what's the problem? Why not write a paper that's quote, quote, quote?

The problem is that by using an excessive number of quotations you've made more of a collage than a paper. Quoting is easy—too easy. It results in weak writing, and it avoids the task of writing itself.

Don't give in to the temptation to overquote. It's a common symptom of weak writing that's easy for teachers, editors, and readers to spot.

Here's when you should include a quote: when something is extremely well said and supports your point. Quote sparingly so what you do quote has an impact. Most of the time you should be paraphrasing your sources, which is a lot more work but results in much better writing.

Make Quotations Blend In

You should also integrate quotations into your writing. Introduce your quotations. The following is a bad way to start a paragraph:

> "Spain is lovely this time of year" (Brice 35).

This version is better:

> As Brice said, "Spain is lovely this time of year (35)."

Paraphrasing

Paraphrasing is when you take someone else's ideas and put them in your own words. The following are examples of paraphrasing:

> My dad always said how you treat others is important.
> Smith wrote about how families in America are like cesspools.
> The key to good basketball, according to Steve Kerr, is playing as a team.

Paraphrasing integrates other people's ideas into your own words. By paraphrasing, you make the ideas flow smoothly, creating a coherent work.

Paraphrasing makes better writing, but it's not easy. In fact, it's hard work. If you don't paraphrase thoroughly, you could end up committing plagiarism. For example, let's say someone named Jennifer Walters wrote this sentence:

> Green is the color most associated with health and beauty.

Here's a bad paraphrase of that sentence:

> According to Walters, green is highly associated with health and beauty.

Though the author has cited Walter, the paraphrase is too close to the original. In fact, the words, "associated with health and beauty" are exactly the same. This is a type of plagiarism. One way to fix the problem is by using a partial quote:

> According to Walters, green is highly "associated with health and beauty."

Or you could keep working on the paraphrase until it is truly in your own words:

> According to Walters, there are healthy and beautiful connotations to the color green.

This is a better paraphrase because the structure of the sentence is different, but the ideas are about the same. Also, the paraphrase is the same length, which is important. A paraphrase should be about the same length as the original: don't paraphrase a sentence in a paragraph or vice versa. A paraphrase should retain the meaning and length of the paraphrased passage while changing the words and structure.

If this sounds like a lot of work, it is. Paraphrasing takes a persistent willingness to write and rewrite sentences, shifting phrases and words around, all the while going back to the original to make sure the meaning has not been lost.

Practice

A good way to practice paraphrasing—and writing in general—is by doing exercises that involve writing different versions of a sentence. Using the following sentence, write five other sentences that say about the same thing:

> The FBI gives colorful nicknames to bank robbers.

_____

_____

_____

_____

_____

Answers

There are no wrong answers, but here are five variations I came up with:

1. Bank robbers receive colorful nicknames given by the FBI.
2. If you rob a bank, you could end up with a nickname given by the FBI.
3. One of the FBI's oddest functions is giving nicknames to bank robbers.

4. The distinctive nicknames for bank robbers help the FBI track down bank robbers.
5. A bank robber with distinctive features could provide fodder for a colorful nickname: like the Super Sloth Bandit, who wore the word *Super* on a T-shirt and was extremely slow.

Some of these sentences move information around or add a little information. Deciding which sentence is best depends on what's happening in the rest of the paragraph and the paper. Only in grammar books will you ever deal with a sentence in isolation. However, by doing sentence-rearranging exercises, you can improve your ability to revise sentences. Just as physical exercises can improve your strength and agility, language exercises can make your writing stronger and smoother.

Summarizing

Summarizing is very similar to paraphrasing, except it does some shrinking: when you summarize, you take a longer batch of ideas and drill down to the overall or most essential idea. Summaries are shorter—sometimes much shorter—than the originals.

> Michael Adams' book claims slang is a form of poetry.
> Jennings explains the three types of Presidents in American history: the mavericks, the stewards, and the bridge salesmen.
> The teachings of Jesus were mostly about love.

You can summarize a paragraph, a page, an article, a chapter, a book, or even a series of books.

Often, you'll have to summarize your own work. For example, if you're writing a paper and someone asks what it's about, you can't recite the whole paper. You have to summarize. Being able to summarize your work is a sign that you know your purpose and project well. If you're unable to summarize what you did, that's a sign of confusion. More work needs to be done.

Citing Your Work

"Avoid plagiarism" can be phrased in a more positive way: give credit to others for their words and ideas. The way to give credit is through citing.

In most style formats, there are two parts of citing. The first are in-text citations. Here are some sentences with in-text citations using MLA style:

> Families are increasingly awful (Miller 32).
> According to Jones (22), Magellan invented chairs.
> Walters said that "Coffee is great" (22).

In MLA, in-text citations include a page number. In APA format, these citations would look a little different. Since APA is often used for scientific writing, the year is prominent, letting readers know if the research is current.

> Families are increasingly awful (Miller 2011).
> According to Jones (2002), Magellan invented chairs.
> Walters (2009) said that "Coffee is great" (p. 22).

In APA, a page number is necessary only for a direct quotation.

Citing is only the half of it: you also need a works cited (in MLA) or reference (in APA) entry. Please consult the appropriate manuals for a lot more information on proper citing format.

Quotations, paraphrases, and summaries all need to be cited. If you don't cite, you've committed plagiarism—even if you've done so by accident.

This is one of the most important aspects of writing. A teacher or editor will almost always give you a chance to fix a comma error, but you could fail a paper (or class) if you commit plagiarism. Plagiarism is a serious issue.

Cite your quotations. Cite your paraphrases. Cite your summaries. When in doubt, cite it. Always give credit to others.

Take So-Called Plagiarism Checkers with a Grain of Salt

There are a lot of programs out there—such as Turnitin.com and SafeAssign.com—that are supposed to be plagiarism-checkers. They're not. All these programs do is match text in your paper with text in the program's database (plus the internet). The program highlights matched text—whether it's cited correctly or not.

Here's the brutal truth: there is no program that can check for plagiarism for you. You have to rely on your eyeballs and brain. You have to be careful and meticulous, double-checking your sources, quotations, paraphrases, summaries, and style guide.

Technology can do a lot of amazing things, but making your writing plagiarism-proof isn't one of them.

Chapter Review Practice

The seven Cs are a terrific guide for writing. Your writing should be clear, concise, and easy to understand. Make your writing compelling with humor, fresh language, and clear organization. Make your writing convincing by using credible facts, writing error-free prose, and being thorough and complete. Don't skip important information. Your writing should be correct in terms of grammar, facts, format, and purpose. Consult style guides for help and always cite your work. Quotations, paraphrases, and summaries must be cited.

Now let's practice what you learned in this chapter:

1. Which of the following is most concise?
    A. The rain ruined my plans.
    B. The weather was an atrocity—I hate rain
    C. Why does it always rain when I have stuff to do?
    D. I forget my umbrella every time it rains.
2. Where would you go to improve the correctness of your citations?
    A. A thesaurus
    B. A dictionary
    C. *The Chicago Manual of Style*
    D. The internet
3. What does compelling writing do?
    A. Make you want to read
    B. Make you confused
    C. Save time
    D. Explain complex issues
4. What does convincing writing do?
    A. Explicate
    B. Persuade
    C. Entertain
    D. Amuse
5. Which of the following is a double-edged sword in writing?
    A. Citations
    B. Humor
    C. Clarity
    D. Euphemisms
6. Which of the following phrases is the most concrete?
    A. A mammal
    B. A canine
    C. A labradoodle
    D. An animal

7. Which of the following is the least concise?
    A. The butterfly landed on my head.
    B. The butterfly was quite beautiful.
    C. The butterfly was a good omen.
    D. The beautiful butterfly, which landed on my head, was surely a good omen.
8. Which of the following is the best tool to prevent plagiarism?
    A. A style guide
    B. A dictionary
    C. A plagiarism checker
    D. Your eyeballs
9. Which of the following is a means of giving credit to others?
    A. Quoting
    B. Paraphrasing
    C. Summarizing
    D. All of them
10. What do you have to give credit to others for?
    A. Their exact words
    B. Their ideas
    C. Common knowledge
    D. Clichés

Answers

1. A
2. C
3. A
4. B
5. B
6. C
7. D
8. D
9. D
10. A and B

12

Choosing the Right Words: Diction

People often feel choice fatigue when buying a cup of coffee. There are so many sizes, lattes, sugar substitutes, and flavors that it's hard to know what you want. Choice fatigue is much worse with words. Words are your friends, but they are numerous friends who can be overwhelming. Writing can feel like being at a party with a million people.

When you flip through a thesaurus or dictionary, you might feel even worse. How do you use these tools without feeling used by them? How do you know the right word for the right situation? And what does the meaning of a word really mean anyway?

This chapter will help you feel more confident about these issues. You'll learn more about the tools and rules of thumb for choosing words. It's often difficult to choose between words, but you'll need to get comfortable making those choices. This chapter will help you make better decisions.

Word Books: Dictionaries and Thesauruses

Writing can be a daunting task, but you're not alone. In addition to grammar books like the one you're holding now, there are two main types of word books: dictionaries and thesauruses.

Different Types of Dictionaries

Though people speak about looking up a word in "the dictionary," there are actually many types of dictionaries. For example, some dictionaries are geared toward specific professions, like medical and legal dictionaries. There are slang dictionaries—like the online *Green's Dictionary of Slang*—that collect words that are irreverent and informal. If you're writing a song or poem, you should look at a rhyming dictionary, which groups words together by sound.

For the history of a word, try a historical dictionary; the biggest and best is the *Oxford English Dictionary*. Historical dictionaries not only define words, they offer example citations of the word being used over time, so you can see how it is used and has evolved. Another historical dictionary is the *Dictionary of American Regional English*, a huge project that collects terms that are used regionally in the United States, but not across the entire country.

202　Part 4: Writing with Style

For most purposes, you'll be well served by a general-use dictionary such as the *New Oxford American Dictionary* or the *Merriam-Webster Unabridged Dictionary*. The online version of *Merriam-Webster* (merriam-webster.com) has become the most authoritative general-use dictionary, and it's a good bet you'll find what you need there.

Practice

Look up the following words in a dictionary, and note their definitions:

1. defenestrate _____
2. septuagenarian _____
3. synecdoche _____
4. cognomen _____
5. indefatigable _____

Using a Thesaurus

A different type of word book is called a *thesaurus*. A thesaurus groups together words with similar meanings, which can help you find words you might not have considered otherwise. Words with the same meaning are called *synonyms*.

For example, let's say you're looking for another word that means nonsense. A thesaurus will turn up terms such as *rubbish*, *fiddle-faddle*, *balderdash*, *rot*, *twaddle*, *flapdoodle*, *tommyrot*, *hooey*, *malarkey*, *horsefeathers*, *hokum*, and *mumbo-jumbo* (plus a few words we can't print here).

The key to employing a thesaurus is to use it alongside a dictionary. Let's say you decided you liked the sound of *mumbo-jumbo*. By looking it up in a dictionary, you can see if *mumbo-jumbo* is the right type of nonsense for you.

Practice

Look up the following words in a thesaurus, and write down one synonym and one antonym:

1. antediluvian _____
2. controlling _____
3. hairy _____
4. schmaltzy _____
5. abased _____

Finding the Right Word

Flipping through a dictionary can feel overwhelming. There are so many words, and so many of them look or sound similar. It's a challenge for writers at all levels to find the right word for the right situation.

For example, let's say I'm in a romantic relationship with a woman. What's the right way to introduce her? There are many choices.

> This is my wife, Gwen.
> This is my girlfriend, Gwen.
> This is my main squeeze, Gwen.
> This is my significant other, Gwen.
> This is my partner, Gwen.

How do you choose? Whether or not to use *wife* (or *spouse*) is easy: it only applies to people who are married.

The word *partner* can also apply to a married couple, or at least a couple that is very stable and perhaps living together.

Girlfriend and *boyfriend* are common words for people who are only dating but have made some level of commitment to each other. However, they sound a little goofy when the couple in question is older. *Significant other* would sound right for many couples, but might be a little serious for couples that haven't been dating long. There are many other possible words for a sweetheart (like *sweetheart*, *honey bunch*, and other sugary terms).

There isn't always a 100 percent correct answer, but a dictionary can help you figure out your options.

Checking a Word's Meaning as You Read

The best habit a writer can have is to read a lot. Read everything you can find: novels, newspapers, blogs, magazines, nonfiction books—everything. Absorbing the language and seeing how it's used will teach you how to use it yourself. Reading is the best writing teacher.

Another habit you should develop is to always look up unfamiliar words in a dictionary when reading. While you may be able to figure out part of the word's meaning from context, you'll likely miss out on something. If you read a lot and use the dictionary a lot, you'll be constantly improving your writing and vocabulary.

Denotation vs. Connotation

Denotation and connotation have to do with the meaning of a word. Denotation is the literal meaning of a word: the strict sense. Connotation is the flavor of a word. You can also think of it as the baggage a word carries from past associations.

For example, take the word *champagne*. The denotation is simple: champagne is a specific type of sparkling wine, one that is made from grapes in Champagne, France. Denotation—what a term denotes—is cut and dried.

However, *champagne* has connotations, too. Mostly, it is associated with success. If you've ever watched a sports team celebrating a championship in their locker room, you've probably seen the players pouring champagne on each other and spraying it into the air. After any success, it's appropriate to say "Let's break out some champagne!" Whether you're serious about actually drinking some champagne or not, the word *champagne* is shorthand for success. Champagne is also associated with other celebrations, such as New Year's Eve, when the champagne tends to flow.

Every word has denotation and connotation. The connotations may take time (and reading) to pick up, but they are important to consider. Using a word with a negative or inappropriate connotation can ruin a piece of writing and make a bad impression.

The Dangers of Careless Thesaurus Use

A thesaurus can be a useful tool, but it can also be dangerous, like a sharp knife. Careless thesaurus use can make your writing sound weird and inaccurate instead of smooth and clear.

Thesaurus problems often start when writers mistakenly think the goal of writing is to sound smart and clever, and the way to sound smart and clever is to dig into a thesaurus for big, fancy words. This rarely works out well.

For example, I once heard about a student in a creative writing class who described a glass as *fraught* with wine. That's a very emotional glass. Presumably, the student meant the glass was *full* of wine but thought *full* was too boring a word and went diving into the thesaurus headfirst. True, *fraught* does mean full—but only of emotion. By not investigating further, the student made an embarrassing mistake.

Should you throw out your thesaurus? Not necessarily. Use it, but use it cautiously. Specifically, you should use it for reminders of words you already know rather than as a source of brand-new words.

Avoiding the Double Negative

Good writing is consistent, and the double negative violates this principle. Here are some correctly worded negative statements:

> I have no wine.
> That isn't my car.
> We don't know each other.

A double negative would add confusion:

> I don't have no wine.
> No way that isn't my car.
> We don't not know each other.

Since two negatives equal a positive, these sentences are saying the opposite of what they should. You should avoid double negatives in almost all situations.

The exception—and there is almost always an exception when it comes to writing—is in fiction. If you're writing a character who is folksy, they might use a double negative because it's the way they talk. But (most) writing should be different from talking.

Practice

Reword the following double negatives:

1. I don't know nobody there. _____
2. I wouldn't say you aren't my friend. _____
3. I'm not not sorry. _____
4. We didn't not go there. _____
5. That's not not true. _____

Answers

1. I don't know anybody there.
2. I would say you are my friend.
3. I'm sorry.
4. We didn't go there.
5. That's true.

Avoiding Vague or Stale Language

When writing, you should strive for fresh, clear, strong, original language. That means you should avoid certain writing traps, and especially clichés and euphemisms.

Steering Clear of Clichés

Do you like taking it to another level, playing as hard as you work, and living life to the fullest? If so, good for you, but you should avoid those phrases when writing. Why? Because they're clichés. Like a pair of jeans with holes in the knees, clichés are worn out. Language that has been repeated over and over and over again becomes a cliché. Clichés are a sign of unoriginal, stale writing. Writers resort to clichés when their creativity and imagination fail them.

A cliché can be a single term (like *the bottom line*) or a whole sentence (like *It is what it is*.). Not everyone agrees on which words and phrases are clichés, but if you've heard an expression a lot—and it makes you groan a little—it's probably a cliché.

Here are some very well-known clichés:

- all in a day's work
- at the end of my rope
- at the end of the day
- avoid like the plague
- beacon of hope
- better safe than sorry
- better the devil you know than the devil you don't
- bird in the hand
- birds of a feather
- bite the dust
- bored to tears
- by hook or by crook
- can't cut the mustard
- champing at the bit
- close only counts in horseshoes and hand grenades
- down and dirty
- fool me once, shame on you
- for the birds
- good as gold

green with envy
hold your tongue
justice is blind
kiss and tell
light in the darkness
like trying to herd cats
lost his marbles
nip it in the bud
once bitten, twice shy
pain in the neck
pass the buck
raise one's game
silent but deadly
so close you can taste it
take it to the next level
the early bird catches the worm
thick as thieves
think outside the box
throw someone under the bus
till the fat lady sings
wild goose chase
work hard, play hard
worst nightmare

Some animals have a whole lexicon of clichés about them, such as dogs:

can't teach an old dog new tricks
dog days
every dog has its day
every dog is brave in his own yard
happy as a dog with two tails
let sleeping dogs lie
sick as a dog
work like a dog

Besides the repetition factor, there's another reason to avoid clichés: they're often vague. Saying "You can't change horses in midstream" will probably not be as helpful to someone as specific advice.

However, you can make a cliché sound fresh. One writing technique that's often successful is to play with a cliché. For example, "It's not what you know, it's who you know" is too old and tired to use as is, but you could write, "It's not what you know, it's who you marry" in an article on successful couples. This would allow you to take advantage of readers' knowledge of a cliché without repeating one mindlessly.

Practice

Put the following clichés into fresh language, translating them into your own words:

1. Beacon of hope _____
2. Better safe than sorry _____
3. Better the devil you know than the devil you don't _____
4. Birds of a feather _____
5. Bored to tears _____

Avoiding Euphemisms—Most of the Time

Euphemisms have a bad reputation that is mostly deserved. Whenever a company talks about *downsizing* (firing employees), the government refers to *collateral damage* (civilian deaths), or a celebrity is hospitalized for *exhaustion* (drug problems), you can tell the truth is being smoothed over and obscured. Since clarity is one of the most important elements of writing, this alone is a great reason to avoid euphemisms. Also, many euphemisms tend to be clichés too—so they're both vague and worn out.

Comedian George Carlin loved talking about euphemisms and how he thought they were harmful. In one routine, he talked about how the term *shellshock*—which once described the horrible toll of war on soldiers—was eventually renamed *battle fatigue*, then *post-traumatic stress disorder*. Each renaming added syllables while moving farther away from the grim reality of the condition, which hardly helped those who had the condition.

I'm sure you can think of many more euphemisms yourself. Hint: there are many surrounding the topic of going to the bathroom, including "going to the bathroom" itself. Euphemisms gather around taboos such as sex, death, drugs, and money.

However, euphemisms aren't all bad. *Passed away* isn't as direct as *died*, but someone dealing with the death of a loved one deserves kinder and gentler words. Use euphemisms when you want to spare someone's feelings or just be tasteful.

For example, if someone suffered a horrible injury in a war (or anywhere for that matter) you might not want to draw attention to the specific nature of the injuries. Sometimes, being euphemistic is the right thing to do.

Practice

Write the real meaning of the following euphemisms:

1. Assessment
2. Challenges
3. Having financial issues
4. Indulge
5. With child

Answers

1. Test
2. Disabilities
3. In debt
4. Overeat
5. Pregnant

Slang

Slang is difficult to define, but you can usually spot it when you see it, dude. In that sentence, *dude* is an example of slang.

Slang has a few qualities that distinguish it from other types of language. It tends to be humorous and informal. One of the best books on slang—Michael Adams' *Slang: The People's Poetry*—focuses on the wild, creative, poetic aspects of slang.

Besides being creative, slang is social. It develops in specific groups. Teenagers—who are prolific generators of slang—don't use the same slang as adults or younger children. Different groups have their own slang, and slang is part of what makes them a group. If you speak the same way I do, it reinforces our connection.

For example, the difficult and deadly conditions of war have long made soldier slang a large language category. In the US Civil War, to *skedaddle* was to retreat. Back in World War I, a *basket case* was a soldier who had lost all four limbs and needed to be carried in a basket. (Later, the term took on its current meaning, which refers to an extremely nervous person.)

More recent wars have also produced slang. In the Iraq War, *Mortaritaville* was any base that was constantly attacked; the name plays on the Jimmy Buffet song "Margaritaville," and the mortar is bombs. *Pope glass* referred to makeshift protection attached to a vehicle that looked like the windshield of the Popemobile. A *fobbit* was someone stationed at a forward operating base, also known as a FOB. *Fobbit* is a play on J. R. R. Tolkien's hobbits in more than just sound. The fobbits were thought to have it easier than soldiers who ventured away from the FOB, so fobbits were like hobbits, safe in the shire.

Jargon: Language Gets Professional

Jargon is slang's sibling who is all business.

The main meaning of *jargon* is the language of a profession. All professions have jargon, language that may be utterly meaningless to people outside the profession. For example, the term *triangle offense*—employed to great success by Coach Phil Jackson with the Chicago Bulls and Los Angeles Lakers—is part of the jargon of basketball. Another part of basketball jargon is calling player positions the 1, 2, 3, 4, and 5 (the point guard, shooting guard, small forward, power forward, and center, respectively). If you talked about how your 2 is making a play against the other team's 3 within the triangle, you'd better be talking to someone who knows their basketball. Otherwise, you'll mystify your audience.

There's a fine line between slang and jargon. Both create unity within groups, but since jargon is rooted to a profession, it has more practical uses. For example, some jargon consists of abbreviations that allow information to be relayed quickly. This can be helpful in professions that are dangerous (like being a police officer) or where speed is simply desirable (like being a waiter). The police term *APB* (all-points bulletin) is an example.

Be cautious when using slang and jargon in writing. Slang is most appropriate in speech, especially when talking to other members of the group that shares that slang. Some slang may also be okay in certain kinds of writing that are humorous or informal. However, if you use slang in a formal situation, such as most types of business writing, it could make a terrible impression.

Jargon poses different risks. While slang could be offensive to some people, jargon could just confuse them. Since the goal of writing is to communicate, you don't want to risk befuddling your readers (or listeners). Unless your audience is people who share the same jargon, you should put your ideas into words that are more likely to be understood. Assess your writing situation and use the most appropriate language.

There's another side to jargon. Often, the word *jargon* is used to mean language that is incomprehensible and also euphemistic. Business terms are notorious for this kind of odd, vague language. The TV show *30 Rock* made a brilliant spoof of business jargon when General Electric executive Jack Donaghy said he needed to *synergize backwards overflow*. That absurd, meaningless phrase has the same flavor of many real-life terms that are used to hide meaning rather than convey it.

Eggcorns: Mistakes That Make Sense

Do you feel bad about misspelling words? You really shouldn't. It happens to everyone sometimes, and making a mistake sometimes shows you're on the right track. Take the case of eggcorns.

An eggcorn is a linguistics term first discussed in 2003 on the popular linguistics blog *Language Log*. Simply put, an eggcorn is a spelling mistake that makes sense. For example, the word *eggcorn* itself came from a misspelling *of acorn*. If you didn't know how to spell *acorn*, but you knew what it was, *eggcorn* might seem right.

Eggcorns are wrong, but they make a lot of sense. It's logical to think a mind-boggling event could be mind-bottling, because when your mind is boggled, it can feel like it's been thrown in a bottle and swished around. A moot point doesn't matter, so it might as well be mute. Since chords produce music, why shouldn't we speak with vocal chords instead of vocal cords? The logic of the mistakes is why they occur.

Over time, some eggcorns become accepted variations or even replace the original word. For example, a chaise longue is a French type of chair, but generations of English speakers who know what a lounge is (but not a longue) have transformed the term into *chaise lounge*. The term *free rein* produced the eggcorn *free reign*, which makes sense because more people are familiar with a king's reign than a horse's reins. Both versions are found in print frequently, and *free reign* will probably be acceptable to everyone before long.

Language keeps changing, so make sure you consult a current dictionary, such as *Merriam-Webster*, to find the most accepted spelling of a word. It can also help to google a word. The spelling with the most hits isn't necessarily correct, but it will tell you something about how the word is being used.

The following are 12 commonly confused groups of words that sound exactly or almost exactly alike. If you're not sure which one you mean, pull out your dictionary. It's better to look a word up now than (not then) look foolish later.

accept/except	conscience/conscious	than/then
advice/advise	exasperate/exacerbate	there/their/they're
affect/effect	farther/further	we're/were/where
assure/ensure/insure	presence/presents	you're/your

Practice

Write the correct spelling of the following eggcorns:

1. For all intensive purposes, my brother is a tall man. _____
3. I won't pay these exuberant prices. _____
4. Without further adieu, I must leave. _____
5. That's interesting, but it's a mute point. _____
6. Be proactive and cease the opportunity. _____

Answers

1. all intents and purposes
2. exorbitant prices
3. further ado
4. moot point
5. seize the opportunity

Chapter Review Practice

Word books are vital tools for a writer. Use a dictionary and thesaurus while writing to ensure you're using the appropriate words. Denotation is the strict meaning of a word, while connotation is the flavor or implication of a word. Be careful when using a thesaurus. This tool can lead to bizarre word choices if you don't use it alongside a dictionary. Slang is informal language that binds social groups, while jargon is the language of a profession. Both should be used with caution in your writing. Euphemisms hide or obscure meaning and should generally be avoided—except when you have a good reason to be vague. Eggcorns are spelling errors that make some sense, such as "for all intensive purposes."

Now let's practice what you learned in this chapter:
1. Find and identify the kind of diction mistake in each of the following sentences, whether euphemism, slang, jargon, or eggcorn:
   A. This coffee creamer is hella good. _____
   B. I hope my manuscript submission passes mustard. _____
   C. The political scene is prone to hyperpolarization. _____
   D. The WNBA is hurdling toward greater success. _____
2. Identify whether the following is part of the word's connotation or denotation:
   A. candle = romance _____
   B. desk = work _____
   C. pen = writing instrument _____
   D. painting = work of art _____
3. Which of the following are clichés?
   A. Birds of a feather
   B. Raining cats and dogs
   C. Silly as a goose
   D. Smart as a chicken
4. Identify whether the following are true or false:
   A. A dictionary lists synonyms. _____
   B. A thesaurus lists the meanings of words. _____
   C. An eggcorn is a spelling mistake that makes some sense. _____
   D. Jargon can be hard to understand. _____
5. Which of the following is not true about an eggcorn?
   A. It's an example of usage.
   B. It makes sense.
   C. It's incorrect.
   D. It's standard English.
6. Which of the following does not describe euphemisms?
   A. Vague
   B. Soft
   C. Explicit
   D. Evasive

7. Which of the following does not differentiate jargon from slang?
   A. Jargon is technical.
   B. Jargon is used by a group.
   C. Jargon is professional.
   D. Jargon is specific.
8. Where would you find lists of synonyms?
   A. A dictionary
   B. A thesaurus
   C. An encyclopedia
   D. Wikipedia
9. What does *diction* mean?
   A. Word choice
   B. Verb tense
   C. Grammar checker
   D. Style guide
10. Which is the most authoritative general-use dictionary?
    A. *The Chicago Manual of Style*
    B. *Merriam-Webster*
    C. *Green's Dictionary of Slang*
    D. *Oxford English Dictionary*

Answers

1. A. Slang (hella)
   B. Eggcorn (*passes mustard* for *passes muster*)
   C. Jargon (hyperpolarization)
   D. Eggcorn (*hurdling* for *hurtling*)
2. A. Connotation
   B. Connotation
   C. Denotation
   D. Denotation
3. A, B, and C

4. A. False
   B. False
   C. True
   D. True
5. D
6. C
7. B
8. B
9. A
10. B

13

Maintaining Parallel Structure

There are many ways to make your writing sound smooth and polished. You can read your work aloud. You can spend sufficient time editing. You can use appropriate word choices and strong verbs. As this chapter discusses, you can also use parallelism.

Parallelism is a way of structuring your sentences that makes them sound clean and clear. Notice that I didn't write, "Parallelism is a way of structuring your sentences that makes them sound clean and clearly." The combination "clean and clear" is parallel, since they are both the same type of word. Parallelism is all about using words with the same form and function to make the reading experience smooth and enjoyable.

Using parallel structure separates polished writers from casual writers. Once you learn the beauty of parallelism, you'll never want to write without it. You'll become addicted to writing strong sentences, pleasing phrases, and well-chosen words.

Understanding Parallel Structure

A good sentence should make sense, read well, and be clear. One way to accomplish this goal is by using parallel structure, which I did in the previous sentence.

In math, parallel lines go in the same direction and do not touch; they're next to each other but not intersecting. In grammar, a parallel sentence consists of phrases or words that have the same form, whether it's two halves of the sentence or the components of a series. Parallel structure is one of the easiest and most effective ways to make your writing sound clear and pleasant.

Writing a Series

One of the most frequent uses for parallelism is when writing a list or series. As discussed briefly in Chapter 1, all the items in a list should have the same form, like in these examples:

> I enjoy swimming, boating, and camping.
> Your father is a saint and a gentleman.

> My dog is quick, smart, and short-haired.
> My favorite TV shows ever are *Seinfeld*, *30 Rock*, *The Shield*, and *Breaking Bad*.
> The president has shown wisdom in foreign policy, environmental issues, and civil rights.

All those sentences sound smooth—or at least not jarring—because they use parallelism. The following are examples that lack parallelism:

> I enjoy swimming, boating, and to eat fish.
> Your father is a saint and has great manners.
> My dog is quick, smart, and a rat terrier.
> My favorite TV shows ever are *Seinfeld*, *30 Rock*, *The Shield*, and reality shows.
> The president has shown wisdom in foreign policy, environmental issues, and debating issues.

Those sentences sound a little off because the items are not all the same form. Good writers avoid this mistake.

Sometimes the forms may look very similar but aren't actually the same, which can fool you into thinking a nonparallel sentence is parallel. For example:

> Dan hates jogging, juggling, and going swimming.

The sentence should read:

> Dan hates jogging, juggling, and swimming.

To write a parallel series, you need all the items to have the same form, but they don't need to be the same length. For example, the following is clearly parallel:

> My uncle likes running, biking, and reading.

This sentence is also parallel:

> My uncle likes running, biking, and reading mysteries.

It's not as perfectly parallel as the first example, but it still sounds much better than a nonparallel series. If you wanted to even out the phrases, you could write something like the following:

> My uncle likes running long distances, biking competitively, and reading mysteries.

How parallel you like your parallelism is up to you.

Parallelism and Prepositional Phrases

Watch out for prepositions when writing a series. Sometimes the preposition can carry over the whole list, like this:

> Today I need to go to the beach, the hairdresser, and the bank.

You could also write that in the following slightly more dramatic-sounding sentence:

> Today I need to go to the beach, to the hairdresser, and to the bank.

Just make sure that you keep it consistent. The following would be a bad example:

> Today I need to go to the beach, the hairdresser, and to the bank.

Prepositional phrases are also commonly used in parallel sentences.

> I went to the store and for a walk.
> My cat likes to sit on the couch, on the bed, and in a box.
> Have you looked under the bed and in the drawer for your keys?
> I enjoy swimming in the river and in pools.
> My favorite times of day are after lunch and before bedtime.

As with other examples, those sentences would sound terrible if the parallelism were removed, as in these poor examples:

> I went to the store and walking.
> My cat likes to sit on the couch, on the bed, and cross-legged.
> Have you looked under the bed and northwest for your keys?
> I enjoy swimming in the river and the backstroke.
> My favorite times of day are after lunch and 10:00 p.m.

Parallelism is one of the easiest ways to make your sentences smooth and easy to read. Use it.

Practice

Look at the following sentences and indicate which ones use parallel construction. If they're not parallel, revise them accordingly.

1. Reading comics and listening to music are fun.
   _____

2. The thief robs liquor stores, banks, and mugs people.
   _____

3. I like coffee because it's hot, roasty, and wakes me up.
   _____

4. Al, Joe, and Brent are my friends.
   _____

5. Have you looked under the table, in the drawer, and on the floor?
   _____

Answers

1. Reading comics and listening to music are fun. (Parallel: both items are gerunds.)
2. The thief robs liquor stores, banks, and mugs people. (Not parallel: "mugs people" is a verb phrase while the other items are nouns.) Correct: The thief robs liquor stores, banks, and people.
3. I like coffee because it's hot, roasty, and wakes me up. (Not parallel: *wakes me up* is a verb phrase while the other items are adjectives.) Correct: I like coffee because it's hot, roasty, and stimulating.
4. Al, Joe, and Brent are my friends. (Parallel: all three items are nouns.)
5. Have you looked under the table, in the drawer, and on the floor? (Parallel: all three items are prepositional phrases.)

Parallelism and Résumés

Parallelism does more than make your sentences sound smoother: it can help you get a job. On a résumé, you will usually have to list a serious of duties performed at a job, and it's important to use parallelism. Here's a bad example:

Summer Camp Counselor, 1998–2004

- Led activities
- Cared for disabled children
- I was a supervisor
- Arts and crafts

Here's a better example, using parallelism:

Summer Camp Counselor, 1998–2004

- Led activities
- Cared for disabled children
- Supervised other counselors
- Taught arts and crafts

By putting your duties in parallel form, you make them easier to read. When you're applying for a job, you need every edge you can get, so don't forget this basic of writing.

Using Coordinating Conjunctions

Parallelism helps you make a series sound smooth and clear, but it is also very useful when writing all sorts of sentences. Like a list, these examples use the coordinating conjunction *and*:

Eating and drinking are popular.
Ted and Nancy are my friends.
Spring and autumn are the mildest seasons.
Star Trek and *Star Wars* are both popular.
My mom and dad are nice people.

All of those sentences would sound weird if the material joined by *and* weren't parallel, as in these examples:

Eating and beer are popular.
Ted and that woman are my friends.
Spring and September are the mildest times of year.
Star Trek and the movies of George Lucas are both popular.
My mom and Frank are nice people.

Comparing and Contrasting Items

When you're comparing and contrasting two things, parallel construction is very handy—and easy—to use. The following examples all make comparisons while using parallelism:

> Cat people are quirky; dog people are not.
> Summer is blazing hot; winter is freezing cold.
> Chickens are beautiful creatures. Turkeys are disgusting beasts.
> Coffee wakes you up; beer puts you to sleep.
> Friends come and go. Family stays and helps.
> A famous book used this exact type of phrasing: *Men Are from Mars, Women Are from Venus.*

Using Correlative Conjunctions

Parallel structure gets a little trickier when it comes to correlative conjunctions. These involve words pairs such as:

> both … and
> either … or
> neither … nor
> not only … but also

Since correlative conjunctions are used to compare and contrast, you should use parallelism to make sure the items are in the same form. The following examples use parallelism:

> Summer makes me both happy and sweaty.
> My family is neither rich nor famous.
> I am not only a bounty hunter, but also an interior decorator.
> I would like either the steak or the chicken.

If the items were not the same form, these sentences would sound weird. Read the following examples that don't use parallelism:

> Summer makes me both happy and I feel sweaty.
> My family is neither rich nor celebrities.
> I am not only a bounty hunter, but also I decorate homes.
> I would like either the steak or I'll try the chicken.

Those sentences sound odd, right? They are jarring and distracting to readers. Avoid making your own readers uncomfortable by using parallelism whenever possible.

Practice

Identify which of the following sentences use or do not use parallelism correctly along with correlative conjunctions.

1. Being a standup comic is neither easy nor rewarding.
2. I avoid both people who yell on their cell phones and being hungry.
3. My dog will roll either on grass or on the sidewalk.
4. I enjoy both math and writing essays.
5. In the morning, I enjoy both pancakes and waffles.

Answers

1. Parallel: *Easy* and *rewarding* are both adjectives.
2. Not parallel: *People who yell on their cell phones* is a noun phase, and *about being hungry* is a verb phrase.
3. Parallel: *On grass* and *on the sidewalk* are both prepositional phrases.
4. Not parallel: *Math* is a noun and *writing essays* is a verb phrase.
5. Parallel: *Pancakes* and *waffles* are both nouns.

Chapter Review Practice

Parallelism helps you write clear, readable sentences. When writing a list or series, use parallelism; in other words, make the items all the same form. Parallelism can help you phrase many sentences; it is particularly effective in crafting memorable statements. Parallelism should be used when listing jobs and duties on a résumé. Parallelism is useful when comparing things. Use parallelism along with correlative conjunctions such as both … and.

Now let's practice what you learned in this chapter:

1. Which of the following sentences are good examples of parallelism?
   A. My cat enjoys playing and to scratch.
   B. At summer camp, we spend many days hiking, swimming, and camping.
   C. I enjoy stories about double agents and comedies.
   D. I spend a lot of time with my cousins, coworkers, and neighbors.

2. What is parallelism a feature of?
   A. Good writing
   B. Bad writing
   C. Math
   D. Politics
3. Which of the following are often parallel?
   A. Jokes
   B. Insults
   C. Famous quotations
   D. Job titles
4. Who would most benefit from parallelism?
   A. A writing student
   B. A fiction writer
   C. A speechwriter
   D. A screenwriter
5. Which of the following can be parallel?
   A. Prepositional phrases
   B. Nouns
   C. Verbs
   D. All of these

Answers

1. A. No
   B. Yes
   C. No
   D. Yes
2. A
3. C
4. All of these
5. D

14

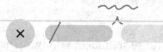

Varying Sentence Structure

Obviously, grammar is important. If it wasn't important, this book and other grammar books wouldn't exist. If grammar didn't matter, you could throw down words in any order at all. But here's a little secret: grammatically perfect writing can still be terrible. Grammar is an essential element of good writing, but it's only the first step. You could even think of it as a prerequisite for good writing. Your writing won't be good if you have grammar problems, but you can't be satisfied with your writing being grammatical and doing nothing else.

Why? Because good grammar will make your writing readable, but it won't make it interesting. Beyond grammar lies style. Good writers do more than make their nouns and verbs agree: they write intriguing sentences, flowing paragraphs, and crisp prose that make you want to keep reading. This chapter will share some tips on how to make your writing more stylish and enjoyable to read.

Rearranging Words and Phrases: Syntax

Syntax is the arrangement of words in a language. There are many, many ways you can rearrange a sentence. For example, here's a simple thought:

> My dog has a Napoleon complex.

Here are several other ways you could say about the same thing:

> My dog Wrigley has a Napoleon complex.
> A Napoleon complex is something my dog has.
> My dog has a Napoleon complex, so he's often barking at bigger dogs.
> My dog is a feisty little guy.
> You know who has a Napoleon complex? My dog.
> My dog, who has a Napoleon complex, is often barking at bigger dogs.
> I should've named my dog Napoleon instead of Wrigley.
> Wrigley, why are you barking at that big dog?

Some of those sentences add information, such as the name of the dog, specific dog behaviors, or details of the Napoleon complex. Some of them move information around the sentence. Some use commas to set off information. The last example turns the sentence into a question.

This is a small sample of the options you have for rearranging sentences. As you learn the possibilities of English syntax, you'll get better at exploiting its infinite, LEGO-like possibilities. Like LEGO bricks, the elements of English syntax are flexible, combinable, and sturdy; you can make many sentences out of the same building blocks.

Combining Short Sentences

Writers who are new to a language—or just a little inexperienced—often write a lot of short sentences. There's nothing wrong with short sentences per se, but too many of them can make your writing choppy. Read these sentences aloud and you might notice something wrong:

> The sky is dark. It looks like rain. Can you feel the humidity? It's cloudy. That's a bummer.

Those sentences are fine from a grammatical standpoint, but from a style standpoint, there's a problem. All those short sentences are causing a lack of flow. In the following section, you'll learn some ways of combining sentences.

Using a Conjunction

One of the easiest ways to combine sentences is with a conjunction. Take the following:

> The sky is dark. It looks like rain.

To combine them, add a comma and conjunction:

> The sky is dark, and it looks like rain.

When two sentences—also known, grammatically, as independent clauses—are joined with a conjunction, a comma should precede the conjunction. Here are some other examples.

> I like cats. I'm allergic to them.
> I like cats, but I'm allergic to them.
> The con man sold bridges. The police were on his trail.
> The con man sold bridges, so the police were on his trail.
> I want to go on a date. I'm so nervous.
> I want to go on a date, but I'm so nervous.

Using a Semicolon

Instead of a comma and a conjunction, you can join sentences with a semicolon.

> The detective had a hunch. The killer was the bartender.
> The detective had a hunch; the killer was the bartender.
> The Buffalo Bills lost four Super Bowls in a row. That's a record.
> The Buffalo Bills lost four Super Bowls in a row; that's a record.
> Everyone loves Johnny Cash. His music appeals to young and old.
> Everyone loves Johnny Cash; his music appeals to young and old.

For more on semicolons, see Chapter 17.

Using a Colon

A colon can also be used to bring together short sentences. When a colon is used, the second element is usually a response or follow-up to the first.

> I love robots. I want one that can do my laundry.
> I love robots: I want one that can do my laundry.
> The moon landing was a fake. It was staged by Hollywood.
> The moon landing was a fake: it was staged by Hollywood.
> My birthday is always fun. I eat my weight in cake.
> My birthday is always fun: I eat my weight in cake.

For more on colons, see Chapter 17.

Using a Pronoun

As you see, short sentences can be joined by punctuation. However, that's not always enough. Consider the following sentences, which have been combined by a semicolon:

> Jim is a jerk. Jim stole my motorcycle.
> Jim is a jerk; Jim stole my motorcycle.

Even after combining the sentences, the second example doesn't sound much better than the first. Why not? Well, the repetition of *Jim* is a bit annoying. Writing *Jim* twice in the first five words is just too much. Thankfully, pronouns can solve this problem.

> Jim is a jerk; he stole my motorcycle.

Pronouns are a useful way of avoiding repetition when joining sentences—or even if you're not joining them. Just by replacing a proper noun with a pronoun, your writing will sound better.

> When Jack visits, I go out. I try to avoid Jack.
> When Jack visits, I go out. I try to avoid him.
> Jennifer bought me lunch. I think Jennifer likes me.
> Jennifer bought me lunch. I think she likes me.
> My dad is an astronaut. Once, my dad traveled to Mars.
> My dad is an astronaut. Once, he traveled to Mars.

When working with pronouns, make sure it's clear who they're referring to at all times. The following is fine.

> Claudia likes cupcakes. She eats one every day.

The reverse doesn't work:

> She likes cupcakes. Claudia eats one every day.

After reading that first sentence, the reader will think "Who? Who likes cupcakes?" Even though they might be able to figure it out from the next sentence, don't risk creating even a moment's confusion in readers. Here's an even worse example:

> Claudia and Beth like cupcakes. She eats one every day.

It's unclear who the second sentence is referring to: Who is *she*? It could be Claudia or Beth. Your pronouns should always have clear referents; if they don't, your writing will be unclear. When there's a pronoun-reference problem, revise until the problem is fixed or simply replace the pronoun with a noun.

Practice

1. What must pronouns clearly have?
   A. A referent
   B. A predicate
   C. A phrase
   D. A clause

2. What can a semicolon join?
    A. Two nouns
    B. Two verbs
    C. Two phrases
    D. Two independent clauses
3. Which should describe the sentences in your writing?
    A. Intelligent
    B. Long
    C. Short
    D. Varied

Answers

1. A
2. D
3. D

Giving Long Sentences a Break

There isn't anything inherently bad about a long sentence. There isn't anything inherently good, either. While long sentences—if well-constructed and clear—can take the reader on an enjoyable ride, they can also lose the reader in a confusing tangle of words. For example, read the following:

> Long sentences are a huge problem, I mean, a really huge problem that can befuddle and confuse readers because the sentence just keeps going on and on; make sure to keep your sentences to a decent length or your readers will have trouble keeping up with your thoughts: this is a very important rule, and it should never be broken unless you have a very good reason, like if you were trying to write a bad example (this sentence, in case you didn't notice, is an absolutely terrible example that you should not imitate, okay?).

That's an absurd example; you probably wouldn't write such an enormous sentence naturally, but sometimes you might end up writing sentences that are longer than they should be.

Why do people write sentences that are too long? Sometimes it just happens as you draft and try to get your thoughts on paper. That's not a big problem: you can fix it as you revise. Hint: reading your work aloud is a great way to spot lengthy sentences, and by hearing your sentences aloud, it can help you figure out where to trim them.

Other people just have a tendency to write long sentences. If this is one of your habits, make a mental (or real) note to break up sentences when you get to the editing stage of writing.

Unfortunately, sometimes people write long sentences for the same reason they think they should use long words: they're trying to sound smart. This is a terrible idea. Your goal should be to communicate, not make yourself look smart. Focus on communicating in the smoothest and most direct way possible.

Don't try to look smart. Just try to communicate clearly, which *is* smart.

Trimming the Fat

Just as you have many options for bringing short sentences together, you have many options for pulling long sentences apart. In fact, let's work with a slightly longer sentence you just read:

> Just as you have many options for bringing short sentences together, you have many options for pulling long sentences apart.

You could make two sentences:

> You have many options for bringing short sentences together. You also have many options for pulling long sentences apart.

You could use different language that is also more concise:

> There are many ways to combine and separate sentences.

Often, you can trim sentences by identifying unnecessary words. How do you know which words are unnecessary? See if some are repeating the same information. Here's another example.

> I hate going to baseball games; they're so boring that I have a terrible time.

In that sentence, *hate* and *terrible time* are very similar ideas, since terrible times are hated by everyone. *Boring* is different information, since it's a reason why this person dislikes baseball. This sentence could be trimmed (or rewritten) in a few ways that eliminate redundant information:

> I hate going to baseball games; they're so boring.
> Baseball is so boring that I have a terrible time.
> I can't stand the boring game of baseball.

Varying Sentence Types

If you vary the length of sentences, your writing should have good sentence variety. However, there is a more technical way to look at this issue: you should vary the sentence types in your writing. As discussed in Chapter 1, there are four basic sentence types: simple, compound, complex, and compound-complex.

The following are simple sentences, which consist of only independent clauses:

>The dog is sick.
>I love eating pizza.
>Politics is a snake pit.

Compound sentences have two independent clauses:

>The dog is sick; he barfed on the rug.
>I love eating pizza, but I hate eating mushrooms.
>Politics is a snake pit; it attracts sociopaths.

In complex sentences, there is one independent clause along with a dependent clause.

>The dog is sick, which has ruined my plans for the day.
>I love eating pizza with anybody except my sister.
>Politics is a snake pit that has ruined America.

To make a compound-complex sentence, you need two independent clauses and at least one subordinate clause.

>The dog is sick, which has ruined my plans for the day; I had to cancel everything.
>I love eating pizza with anybody except my sister; she is a terrible person.
>Politics is a snake pit that has ruined America, and there has to be a better way.

If your writing sounds repetitive, vary the types as well as the lengths of sentences.

Varying Sentence Beginnings

There's more to sentence variety than just length and type of sentence: how sentences begin is important, too. For example, take this paragraph about an author named Swinnea:

> Swinnea's work is a remarkable commentary on the chicken industry. Swinnea shows the inner workings of chicken farms, as well as the politics of chicken-based restaurants. Swinnea's writing style is humorous, though it always has a strong sense of purpose. Swinnea has become the leading authority on chickens and other barnyard fowl.

Notice anything wrong? Every sentence starts with Swinnea: Swinnea, Swinnea, Swinnea, Swinnea. Starting too many sentences the same way is sure to annoy readers. When you notice that too many sentences are beginning the same way, revise to add variety:

> Swinnea's work is a remarkable commentary on the chicken industry. He shows the inner workings of chicken farms, as well as the politics of chicken-based restaurants. In "Chicken-ology," Swinnea's writing style is humorous, though it always has a strong sense of purpose. Through his impressive work on the subject, Swinnea has become the leading authority on chickens and other barnyard fowl.

Swinnea is still a huge part of the paragraph, but his name isn't the beginning of every sentence like before. Now the paragraph is a better read.

You should make sure that every paragraph of a paper doesn't start in the same way. Beginning every paragraph (or many paragraphs) with the same word or type of phrase shows a lack of creativity—and can drive your readers bonkers.

Practice

1. What aspects of your sentences should be varied?
    A. The length
    D. The type
    C. The beginning
    D. All of these
2. How can you deal with too-long sentences in your writing?
    A. Trim them
    B. Turn them into a few sentences
    C. Read them aloud to help editing
    D. All of these

Answers

1. D
2. D

The Virtues of Variety

You may ask yourself: Why am I rearranging all these sentences anyway? Why can't I just write a sentence and leave it be? Sorry, writing doesn't work like that. First drafts are rarely good enough: writing is mostly revising. Most elements of your work will change as you revise, edit, and proofread. The structure of your sentences is one of the aspects of writing that is easiest—and most important—to change.

Let's say you have a short paragraph about your cat.

> Mr. Pinkerton is a good cat. I got him at the pound. He is a calico. He sleeps with me. He hates my brother. The feeling is mutual. My brother is allergic.

Notice anything wrong? While the sentences are all grammatical, they're also painfully short. A short sentence is fine, but seven short sentences in a row is a style problem. You need to mix it up. Here's a second draft with some sentences combined:

> Mr. Pinkerton is a good cat. I got him at the pound. He is a calico who sleeps with me. He hates my brother, and the feeling is mutual. My brother is allergic to cats.

In that paragraph, some of the short sentences have been combined, and a little detail (about the cat allergy) has been added. Still, this is not a great paragraph. Most of the sentences are still very short and choppy. Let's try adding detail and length to more of the sentences:

> Mr. Pinkerton is a good cat—the best cat I've ever had. I got him at the pound six years ago, and my life hasn't been the same since. Mr. Pinkerton is a calico who sleeps with me. He hates my brother, and the feeling is mutual. My brother is allergic to cats.

The paragraph is starting to improve. There's more sentence variety, and only the last sentence is extremely short. Now that this tiny sentence follows some longer sentences, it's effective rather than repetitive.

However, the paragraph still jumps around. How did we get from this great cat to the conflict with the brother? That's an abrupt transition. This should probably be two paragraphs, since every paragraph should develop one idea and one idea only. It's time to revise again, adding details and depth:

> Mr. Pinkerton is a good cat—the best cat I've ever had. I got him at the pound six years ago, and my life hasn't been the same since. This beautiful calico sleeps with me and follows me around my apartment, almost like a dog. We're inseparable.
>
> There's only one problem—Mr. Pinkerton hates my brother. When my brother Jim stops by, Mr. Pinkerton hisses and tries to scratch him. Other times, Mr. Pinkerton hides until Jim goes away. Since Jim is allergic to cats, the dislike is mutual; this situation is straining my relationship with my brother.

Now we're getting somewhere. The separate ideas about the cat and the conflict have been given their own paragraphs and developed further. Both paragraphs have sentence variety: we're a long way from those teeny-weeny sentences.

This is just the beginning of the process for these paragraphs. If they're part of a personal essay, school paper, letter, or work of fiction, they could end up changing many more times, depending on what's appropriate for the larger piece of writing. They might also be cut if the writer realizes they're not necessary.

This is an important lesson for writers: don't get too attached to what you write. You'll always have to make changes, and you'll often have to cut. However, there is a bright side: words are cheap, and you can always write more.

Chapter Review Practice

Too many short sentences will make your writing choppy and annoying to read; combine them with conjunctions, semicolons, and colons. Use pronouns to avoid repeating the name of the subject in sentences. Long sentences are also a problem: they can be difficult to read and can confuse readers. Communicate your ideas clearly. Your writing will have variety with a mix of sentence types: simple, compound, complex, and compound-complex. Revising sentences is a part of writing well, so leave yourself enough time to proofread and revise your work.

Now let's practice what you learned in this chapter:

1. Sentence variety makes writing more what?
    A. Boring
    B. Confusing
    C. Lively
    D. Academic

2. Which of the following passages has the best sentence variety?
   A. My dog, Louise, loves rabbits. She gets very excited. The rabbits flee in a panic.
   B. The current job market is soft for a variety of reasons, including the reluctance of many companies to invest in high-paying jobs for talent that has a wealth of options. Job-seekers may find themselves frustrated. But the good news is that the job market is expected to improve in the next quarter.
   C. Too many moves are sequels. This is frustrating for consumers. What happened to new ideas?
   D. Any job that involves serving the public takes a wealth of skills. Besides upset customers, there are numerous difficulties. All public-facing jobs require certain problem-solving skills.
3. What is the key to sentence variety?
   A. Inspiration
   B. Collaboration
   C. Revision
   D. Indecision
4. What aspects of sentences should be varied in a paragraph?
   A. Sentence beginnings
   B. Vocabulary
   C. Sentence structure
   D. All of these
5. What is writing without sentence variety like?
   A. Exciting
   B. Strange
   C. Entertaining
   D. Boring

Answers

1. C
2. B
3. C
4. D
5. D

15

Avoiding and Fixing Common Errors

Nobody's perfect, especially when it comes to language. We all make mistakes when writing, and there are a lot of types of writing errors: spelling problems, agreement problems, improper capitalization, and so on. Fortunately, some mistakes happen a lot more often than others.

Why "fortunately"? Well, imagine if there were no consistency to writing errors. Imagine if the 200 most common errors all occurred with the same frequency. This would be a nightmare. How could you work on 200 problems that are all equally important? You can't.

The good news is that there are definitely writing errors that happen more often than others, and your writing will benefit from knowing them. Awareness of the most common errors will give you a better a chance of avoiding them.

Awareness is the first step to addressing any problem, and once you get a handle of these common writing problems, your writing will improve.

Repairing Broken Sentences

There are many ways to write a good sentence. Unfortunately, there are also many ways a sentence can go wrong. In this chapter, I'll discuss a few of the most common grammatical mistakes and how to fix them.

Defragmenting a Fragmented Sentence

A complete sentence (or independent clause) has a subject and verb and expresses a complete thought. If a sentence doesn't have a subject and verb—and, therefore, doesn't convey a complete thought—it's a sentence fragment. The following are typical examples of sentence fragments that often appear in inexperienced writers' papers:

> Which meant the movie was terrible.
> The man who I saw in the alley.

Running across the tarmac.
In the dresser beside the fancy-looking bed.
Who I later learned was my father.

Some of those sentences are dependent clauses: for example, "Who I later learned was my father" has a subject and a verb—like all clauses—but it doesn't express a complete thought. Others, like—"Running across the tarmac"—don't have a subject and verb (it's a verb phrase). Either way, when you treat a phrase or dependent clause as a sentence, you end up with a sentence fragment.

The main problem with sentence fragments is that they leave the reader hanging in some way. They raise questions. Here are those fragments again, with some of the questions they raise:

Which meant the movie was terrible. (What exactly meant the movie was terrible?)
The man who I saw in the alley. (What about him?)
Running across the tarmac. (Who was running? Why?)
In the dresser beside the fancy-looking bed. (What's in the dresser? Also, why should I care?)
Who I later learned was my father. (Who is this man? Again, why should I care?)

This is the opposite effect you want to have on your readers. Don't make your readers ask questions; make everything clear.

The Positive Side of Sentence Fragments

Writing is all about exceptions, and you'll probably notice that published writers use sentence fragments a lot. Quite a lot, actually. In fact, I just used one in the previous sentence.

There's no need to entirely avoid sentence fragments, but here are a couple things to remember about using them:

Always be aware of what's a sentence fragment. If you don't know you're using a fragment, chances are it will not work well in your writing.

Use fragments sparingly. Writers who are skilled enough to use a sentence fragment intentionally also know a little goes a long way. Don't get fragment-happy. Okay?

Make sure the fragment doesn't cause confusion. If the fragment puzzles readers, it's a mistake. Only use an intentional fragment if you're sure it will be clear and understandable to readers.

Practice

For the following examples, note whether each group of words is a fragment or a complete sentence/thought. Hint: Don't be fooled by the length of the sentence or fragment.

1. The bird chirped. _____
2. Zebras ran. _____
3. Which went against everything he believed in since he was a boy. _____
4. The coffee shop is busy. _____
5. The restaurant by the side of the road, near the hotel. _____

Answers

1. Complete sentence.
2. Complete sentence.
3. Fragment: This is only a dependent clause.
4. Complete sentence.
5. Fragment: This is only a noun phrase.

Repairing a Run-On Sentence

The run-on sentence is a common problem and a relatively easy one to fix. Here's an example of a run-on sentence:

> The dog barked the cat ran.

Are you surprised that such a short sentence is a run-on? Run-on sentences don't have to be long, even though many are. To be a run-on sentence, all you need are two or more independent clauses smashed together ungrammatically, without a conjunction or proper punctuation to connect them. Just as a fragment can be long, a run-on can be short.

Fixing a Comma Splice

The comma splice is another common error—and also a comma error. It happens when two independent clauses are linked with a comma, as in the following examples:

> I ran, the cops followed.
> The grass is green, the sky is blue.
> Weather is unpredictable, watching the Weather Channel is silly.

Those are all examples of comma splices. They can be fixed by replacing the commas with semicolons, like so:

I ran; the cops followed.
The grass is green; the sky is blue.
Weather is unpredictable; watching the Weather Channel is silly.

They can also be fixed by making the independent clauses into separate sentences. Though this option could make your writing a little choppy, it can also give it a punchy, dramatic effect when used sparingly.

I ran. The cops followed.
The grass is green. The sky is blue.
Weather is unpredictable. Watching the Weather Channel is silly.

You could also add a coordinating conjunction that makes sense in the sentence:

I ran, and the cops followed.
The grass is green, and the sky is blue.
Weather is unpredictable, so watching the Weather Channel is silly.

Practice

For the following sentences, identify the comma splice or run-on sentence and then fix the problem.

1. Concussions are a huge problem in football too many players are suffering.

2. Soccer is the popular sport in the world, it's especially beloved in Europe.

3. Mixed martial arts is very popular, people love it.

4. Softball is a major summer sport my sister plays it.

5. I'm terrible at ping pong I'm better at pinball.

Answers

1. Run-on sentence. Change to "Concussions are a huge problem in football. Too many players are suffering."

2. Comma splice. Change to "Soccer is the popular sport in the world—it's especially beloved in Europe."
3. Comma splice. Change to "Mixed martial arts is very popular; people love it."
4. Run-on sentence. Change to "Softball is a major summer sport. My sister plays it."
5. Run-on sentence. Change to "I'm terrible at ping pong. I'm better at pinball."

Clarifying the Relationship Between Ideas

There are two main ways that ideas are linked in writing: coordination and subordination. You can think of coordination as a marriage of equals and subordination as a boss and an employee. It's important not to confuse the two.

Coordination

Coordination involves linking two things together in a sentence. Coordination usually involves a coordinating conjunction, and it often occurs with the word *and*: one of the most useful, common words in English. Coordination can also occur with punctuation such as the semicolon or colon. The following are examples of coordination:

> The lady wept, and the gentleman bowed.
> I'm tired; I need a nap.
> Hold my hand; I'm depressed.
> The sky is blue, and there's a refreshing breeze.
> Tomorrow is my birthday, but I'm having my favorite meal (tuna steak) today.

You should also note that coordination links independent clauses. Coordination brings together grammatical equals who could stand on their own.

Subordination

In *subordination*, there are not two grammatical equals: there are an independent clause and a subordinate clause. The following sentences, which use subordination, consist of one dependent clause and one independent clause. The dependent clauses are underlined:

> <u>When I was younger</u>, I was quite an athlete.
> I hate <u>that I get nervous when driving</u>.
> <u>Because it's raining</u>, the baseball game is canceled.
> I respect the man <u>who I thought was my father</u>.

See how what's not underlined is still a complete thought? The combination of that independent clause plus a dependent clause is what makes subordination work.

Coordination brings together two independent clauses to make a sentence. Subordination brings together an independent clause and a dependent clause to make a sentence.

Practice

In the following sentences, note whether coordination or subordination is used.

1. There's no one I love more than the girl I met in 1986. _____
2. In spring, I go hiking, and in fall, I go hiking, too. _____
3. I like ice cream; I also like gelato. _____
4. I sprained my ankle, and I scraped my knee. _____
5. When I get a chance, I will go see your play. _____

Answers

1. Subordination
2. Coordination
3. Coordination
4. Coordination
5. Subordination

Clarifying Pronoun References

As mentioned in Chapter 5, pronoun antecedents are an important part of writing. Always make sure your pronouns have clear antecedents.

Incorrect: He is a banker. He makes a lot of money.
Correct: Mike is my friend. He's a banker.

In the incorrect example, it's unclear who *he* is. You have to make this clear through revision. Here's another pair:

Incorrect: Jill is funny. Jane is serious. She is also an actor.
Correct: Jill is funny. Jane is serious. Jane is also an actor.

In the incorrect example, you might guess that Jane is the actor, because *Jane* is closer to *she* than *Jill*, but this isn't totally clear.

Don't make your reader wonder, "Who does the pronoun refer to?" Make it obvious.

Fixing Misplaced and Dangling Modifiers

A dangling modifier is a phrase that begins a sentence but does not clearly refer to the subject of the sentence. Dangling modifiers create confusion. These are some examples:

> Slowly cooling off, I took a sip of the coffee.
> Trudging through the snow, the weather got worse and worse.
> Cowering behind the couch, the fireworks terrified my dog.

See the problem? In the second example, the sentence starts with "Trudging through the snow," which must refer to a person. However, the subject of the sentence is "the weather." This mismatch is a classic dangling modifier. The following are revisions of those sentences that are clearer:

> As the coffee slowly cooled off, I took a sip.
> The weather got worse and worse as I trudged through the snow.
> Cowering behind the couch, my dog was terrified of the fireworks.

As you can see, you have many options for how to rearrange a sentence. Look at Chapter 9 for more information on phrases and how they can be moved around grammatically.

Avoiding Shifts in Subject and Verb Forms

Remember the seven Cs? Consistency was one of them. A common inconsistency in writing is when the subject or verb shifts in a piece of writing. As discussed in Chapter 1, it's very important for verbs to stay consistent, particularly in terms of tense. If you're writing about the past, stay in the past. Don't be a time traveler when writing unless absolutely necessary.

It's also important for your subjects to remain consistent. For instance, you need to use two hands when shooting a basketball. If you don't use two hands, your shot will miss the mark. See how confusing that was? After pages and pages of giving writing advice, I suddenly gave advice on how to shoot a basketball. That's jarring and off-putting.

You also need to be aware of smaller, subtler shifts in your subject that can startle readers. Often this has to do with the purpose of a piece of writing. If you're supposed to be analyzing a topic and suddenly start giving the reader advice, that's a problem. You need to stay on point and maintain a consistent point of view and purpose.

Chapter Review Practice

Sentence fragments are not complete sentences; they are either incomplete thoughts or they lack a subject and/or verb. A run-on sentence is two or more independent clauses jammed together improperly, with no conjunction or appropriate punctuation connecting them. A comma splice is two independent clauses linked with a comma instead of a period, a semicolon, or a comma and conjunction. Make sure your pronouns have clear antecedents—don't make the reader struggle to figure them out. Keep your subjects and verbs in agreement, and keep your verb tenses consistent.

Now let's practice what you learned in this chapter:

1. Which of the following word pairs are commonly confused?
   A. Than/then
   B. Lose/loose
   C. Their/they're
   D. Accept/except
2. Which of the following is an example of a comma splice?
   A. What are you even talking about? I'm confused.
   B. The sun was beating down, the heat was unbearable.
   C. I saw Sebadoh at the Aragon—it was awesome.
   D. My boss is being a jerk; he's so frustrating.
3. Which of the following is a run-on sentence?
   A. This beer is delicious it's so fresh.
   B. Too many employers neglect the importance of proper training.
   C. Would you like anything to drink today, such as a wine cooler?
   D. Politics is so broken, the country is in trouble.
4. Which of the following is a sentence fragment?
   A. Who is a hero you look up to?
   B. From now on, I will remember to file the proper paperwork.
   C. Which made a mess on the carpet.
   D. An iguana is a large and unusual pet.

5. Which of the following has pronoun problems?
   A. Jim is the assistant manager you've been dreaming of.
   B. Jennifer is even better at her job than Gwen; she's just terrific.
   C. Who left a mess at the table?
   D. Ludwig was a philosopher; he was brilliant.
6. Which of the following words is not possessive?
   A. His
   B. Her
   C. Their
   D. It's
7. Which of the following is an example of coordination?
   A. I love fried chicken, except when it's too spicy.
   B. Whenever it's sunny, I like to sit outside.
   C. In too many cases, I sleep late.
   D. I like to watch old movies, but I dislike old books.

Answers

1. All of these
2. B
3. A
4. C
5. B
6. D
7. D

16

Avoiding Sexism and Other Biases

There are many different types of people in this world, and it's important to address them respectfully. Since language is always changing, and terms for different groups of people also change, it's important to be careful and vigilant when referring to someone's gender, race, religion, or other status.

If you can remember a time when someone insulted you, deliberately or accidentally, you'll get a sense for how people feel when they're described with offensive language. The offense is much greater when someone is part of a group that has been discriminated against for years.

You must choose your words carefully when writing about a controversial topic or referring to specific groups of people. You don't want to inadvertently offend a reader by describing them in language that's out of date or insensitive.

In other words, you need to write in a way that's inoffensive. In this chapter, you'll learn how to write without bias.

Maintaining Sex and Gender Equality

Women have long fought for equality, and this ongoing battle isn't restricted to achieving equal opportunities, equal pay, and mutual respect in the real world. Understandably, women also demand equal treatment in language. After all, how we talk about men and women influences how we treat them, and we want to treat everyone with respect.

Unfortunately, the English language provides no quick and easy solution for formulating sex- and gender-neutral expressions, especially when it comes to choosing pronouns. The old-school approach of using the pronoun *he* exclusively to refer back to a noun that has no specific sex or gender, such as *customer* or *technician*, is sexist. However, using *he or she* and *him or her* throughout a passage is tedious and annoys the reader. So what's a writer to do?

The goal is to maintain sex and gender equality without calling attention to the fact that you're doing so. To achieve this goal, you need to think creatively and employ a mix of several different strategies, as explained in the following sections.

What's the difference between sex and gender? *Sex* refers to biology—whether an individual is physically a man or a woman. *Gender*, on the other hand, refers to certain traits commonly associated with one of the sexes. Think of the difference in terms of woman/man (sex) versus feminine/masculine (gender).

Increased awareness of trans people has necessitated that even more attention be given to the issue of gender in language. Everyone, man or woman, trans or cis, deserves to be discussed in respectful, accurate language.

Choosing Ungendered Nouns

The first and most obvious way to maintain sex and gender neutrality in your writing is to choose nouns that convey no sex or gender identity; for example, instead of using *policeman*, use *police officer*. The following table provides a list of gender-specific terms followed by their non-gender-specific alternatives.

Nonsexist Noun Substitutes

Sexist Noun	Nonsexist Substitute
actress	actor
businessman or businesswoman	business person/people, executive, manager, merchant, entrepreneur, people in business
cameraman, camerawoman	photographer or videographer
chairman, chairwoman	chairperson or chair
congressman, congresswoman	representative, congressional representative, member of congress, or congressperson
craftsman	craftsperson or artisan
fireman	firefighter
hostess	host
manmade	synthetic
newsman, newswoman	newscaster; reporter
policeman, policewoman	police officer or law enforcement officer

Sexist Noun	Nonsexist Substitute
salesman or saleswoman	salesperson or sales representative
stewardess	flight attendant
waiter, waitress	server
weatherman	weather forecaster

If you're having trouble coming up with a suitable substitute, consult a thesaurus. You can find one online at thesaurus.com.

Dealing with the He/She Dilemma

One of the most frustrating issues writers deal with on a daily basis involves covering the two sexes fairly when using the pronouns *he*, *she*, *her*, *him*, and so on. Writing something like "A doctor generally prescribes what he believes is the most effective medication" is sexist. After all, the medical profession has plenty of female doctors.

So what's the solution? Well, you have several options. One option, not necessarily the most attractive one, is to use both the masculine and feminine pronouns:

A doctor often chooses what <u>he or she</u> believes is the most effective medication.

This solution has two drawbacks:

Wordiness: The repetition of *he or she* results in extra words that burden the reader, especially if dual pronouns are used frequently.

Favoritism: Whichever gender you mention first gets preferential treatment. To counter this, you must flip the order of the pronouns half the time.

To overcome these issues, someone came up with the notion of dividing the two pronouns with a slash (*he/she*) or using the unisex pronoun *s/he*. Neither of these solutions has caught on, thank goodness.

One of the easiest ways around the sexist pronoun dilemma is to make everyone plural:

<u>Doctors</u> generally prescribe what <u>they</u> believe are the most effective <u>medications</u>.

By making everyone plural, you can then refer to them using the gender-neutral pronouns *they*, *them*, and *their*. Problem solved. Unfortunately, this isn't always a viable option.

Sometimes, you can simply drop the pronoun:

> A doctor generally prescribes ~~what he believes is~~ the most effective medication.

In this particular example, dropping the pronoun also results in dropping the verb *believes*, which alters the meaning. Here's an example in which dropping the pronoun doesn't change the meaning:

> **Sexist:** Every student determines the most efficient way she can study.
> **Neutral:** Every student determines the most efficient way to study.

Another way to avoid sexism in pronoun use is to replace the pronoun with an article. Here are a couple examples:

> **Sexist:** A police officer may choose whether to arrest his suspect.
> **Neutral:** A police officer may choose whether to arrest the suspect.
> **Sexist:** Every weather forecaster knows to check her current weather map prior to broadcast.
> **Neutral:** Every weather forecaster knows to check a current weather map prior to broadcast.

Sometimes, writers simply repeat the noun, which, by definition, gets repetitive; for example:

> A doctor generally prescribes what the doctor believes is the most effective medication.

Keep repeating that noun over and over again, and you'll need that medicine yourself.

A quick and easy way to avoid gender-specific pronouns is to address the reader as *you*. Here's an example:

> **Sexist:** A police officer may choose whether to arrest his suspect.
> **Neutral:** As a police officer, you may choose whether to arrest a suspect.

Of course, this approach is rarely an option. If you're writing a how-to manual for police officers, addressing the reader directly is appropriate. However, if you're writing an article about police procedures for a general audience, you need to explore other options.

Sometimes, you can revise your way out of a potentially sexist statement, usually with the use of a relative pronoun. Here's an example:

> **Sexist:** When an employee passes the certification test, he is eligible for a promotion.
> **Neutral:** An employee who passes the certification test is eligible for a promotion.

One relatively common practice is to alternate the use of pronouns. If you're writing a nonfiction book, for example, you could use *he* and *she* in alternating chapters or in alternating sections within each chapter. This approach has two drawbacks:

You must keep score. The goal is to include equal coverage, so ideally, your text should include an equal number of references to male and female roles. Achieving this goal is pretty easy in a paragraph, but when you're dealing with long articles or book-length works, it is nearly impossible.

You must still avoid bias. If you end up referring to most managers as *he* and most employees as *she* or to most police officers as *she* and most criminals as *he*, you have a problem. You need to provide balanced coverage.

Fortunately, there's a better solution to English's gender pronoun problems: *they*. Though *they* is most commonly used as a plural pronoun, it can also be used as a gender-neutral pronoun. Here's an example:

> **Sexist:** When an employee passes the certification test, he is eligible for a promotion.
> **Neutral:** When an employee passes the certification test, they are eligible for a promotion.

Some people dislike this usage, since it takes a plural pronoun and makes it singular. However, using *they* as singular is nothing new. The *Oxford English Dictionary* has examples of *they* used as a singular pronoun going back to the 1500s. Since this usage is established in the language and solves a huge problem, you should go ahead and use *they*, *them*, and *their* as singular. This usage has gained more acceptance in recent years, and the dissenting voices have faded. Singular *they* is here to stay.

Practice

Revise the following sentences, using the specified approach along with choosing sexless nouns, when necessary, to make each statement gender neutral:

1. Each stewardess must wash her hands before serving drinks to passengers. (pluralize pronoun)

2. Every policeman should alternate his time between desk work and patrol. (drop pronoun)

3. Whenever a student misses class, she should obtain makeup work from her teachers. (use both)

4. Whenever a driver receives three moving violations, she must complete the operator retraining program. (rewrite)

5. Each manager should treat his employees with respect. (address reader)

6. A student should always respect his elders. (use plural pronoun as singular)

Answers

1. Flight attendants must wash their hands before serving drinks to passengers.
2. Every police officer should alternate time between desk work and patrol.
3. Whenever a student misses class, he or she should obtain makeup work from his or her teachers.
4. A (or Any) driver who receives three moving violations must complete the operator retraining program.
5. As a manager, you should treat your employees with respect.
6. A student should always respect their elders.

Calling People What They Want to Be Called

Few people would want to use ethnic or racial slurs to intentionally demean individuals or groups. But if you're not very careful, you could write in an offensive way by choosing the wrong terminology to describe an individual or a group. Referring to someone over 65 as *elderly*, for example, might offend that person even if you meant no harm. Here are the five most important rules to follow to avoid biased language:

Make distinctions only when necessary. If you can convey the same meaning without mentioning that the person was a gay male, a Japanese businessman, or one of the older managers, omit such details.

Call people what they want to be called. If you're unsure what the preferred term is, look it up. If you're still unsure, ask a few members of the group you're describing which terms they deem most acceptable.

Be specific. Specificity keeps you out of trouble. For example, you're better off describing someone from Japan as *Japanese* than using the more general term *Asian*. Likewise, indicating a specific age or range is preferable to using a general term, such as *adolescent* or *older person*.

Avoid inaccurate generalizations … and almost all generalizations are inaccurate. Don't ascribe certain traits or behaviors to certain groups unless *every single person* in the group exhibits those traits and behaviors. See "Avoiding Generalizations and Absolutes" later in this chapter for details.

Be careful when grouping people. Here's a dangerous sentence: "We need to keep guns out of the hands of dangerous people, including convicted felons and people with severe mental illness." That sentence implies that all people with severe mental illness are dangerous, which clearly isn't the case. Don't let a sloppy sentence slander a whole group of people; revise till your writing is fair.

In the following sections, I go into a little more detail on how to avoid bias when you have to distinguish people by race, ethnicity, age, sexual identity or orientation, or medical or physical conditions.

The term *politically correct* (PC) is often used to describe language that likely won't offend anyone; language that isn't loaded. Ironically, the term has become loaded itself and is often used insultingly for terms that go too far in softening language; many see the term as encouraging euphemistic, dishonest language. It's fine to abandon the term *politically correct* altogether and stick with more specific terms, such as *fair* and *unbiased*. If you're fair and unbiased, you don't have to worry about political correctness at all.

Avoiding Racial and Ethnic Bias

Choosing the best terms to describe people by race and ethnicity is difficult, especially given the fact that so many people, particularly in the United States, are of more than one race and/or ethnicity. Here are a few guidelines to follow:

If you mention one person's race or ethnicity, mention everyone's. For example, instead of writing "Of the 250 students, only 25 were Black," you might write, "Of the 250 students, 25 were Black, 175 were white, and 50 were Latino."

The terms *Black* and *African American* are both generally acceptable, with the preference varying depending on your audience. The term *people of color* is acceptable in most circles to describe all people who aren't Caucasian.

People of Latin American descent may prefer to think of themselves as Hispanic, Latina/Latino, or Chicana/Chicano, depending on where they live. Using *Latino* to describe all people who hail from Latin America is usually acceptable unless you're addressing or describing members of a specific community. Again, the more specific you can be, the better: for example, *Cuban* or *Argentinian*.

Asian or *Asian American* is preferred over *Oriental*. Better yet, use labels based on the country of origin, such as *Korean* or *Chinese*.

The terms *American Indian* and *Native American* both have their detractors. If possible, use the name of the specific tribe, preferably in the group's native tongue, such as *Diné* instead of *Navajo* and *Lenape* instead of *Delaware*. Many of the native people of Canada and Alaska prefer the term *Inuit* over *Eskimo*.

Use parallel terms when describing different groups; for example, *Blacks and whites* and *Asian Americans and African Americans* are acceptable phrases. Don't describe one group using color and the other using a country or region. For example, don't describe one group as *Caucasians* and the other as *Blacks*.

Steering Clear of Ageism

Ageism is any prejudice or discrimination against a person based on the person's age, regardless of whether the person is young or old. In other words, don't depict young people as being irresponsible or foolish or old people as feeble or uncool. Don't put people in boxes. Here are a few guidelines to follow:

Be careful with the terms *boy* and *girl*. Although some grammarians advise to restrict those terms to high-school-age people and younger, I recommend grade school or younger (specifically 12 years old and younger). You're usually safe referring to a teenager as *young man* or *adolescent male* and *young woman* or *adolescent female*. Refer to people 18 years and older as *men* and *women*.

When people chat, they often refer to men and women as *guys* and *girls*. There isn't any problem with the word *guy* (from a bias point of view, anyway) but *girl* can be controversial. If you refer to a grown woman as a girl, it could easily be construed as insulting and patronizing. The solution is simple: When you're writing about a woman, call her a woman.

When referring to older people, avoid terms such as *the elderly* and *old geezers*. *Senior citizens* and *seniors* are usually acceptable, but you're better off with something specific, such as *people over 65*, *septuagenarians*, or an individual's actual age.

The Right Words for Gender Identity and Sexual Orientation

Some people are uncomfortable talking about sex, but if you find yourself in a situation in which you need to discuss gender identity and sexual orientation, knowing which words to use and how to string them together can boost your confidence and keep you out of trouble. Here are a few things to keep in mind:

The term *gender identity* refers to whether a person sees himself or herself as a male or female, regardless of the person's biological sex at birth.

Sexual orientation refers to a person's preference in sexual partners—*homosexual* (attracted to members of the same sex), *heterosexual* (attracted to members of the opposite sex), and *bisexual* (attracted to members of both sexes).

The word *transgender* is an adjective used to describe people born one sex who identify themselves as being of the other sex; for example, someone who describes herself as "a woman in the body of a man." Even though this person is biologically a man, she sees herself as a woman, and you should refer to her as *she*. Always use *transgender* as an adjective and never as a noun.

The word *transsexual* describes individuals who live or want to live as members of the other sex; for example, a person who is biologically a man but is living or wants to live as a woman. Transsexuals may undergo *sex reassignment* (don't call it a *sex change*), through surgery and hormone treatments, to become members of the other sex.

Use the term *sexual orientation* instead of *sexual preference*, which implies that people are free to choose whether they're sexually attracted to members of the same or the other sex.

Avoid referring to people as *homosexuals* or *bisexuals*. The preferred terms are *lesbians*, *gay men*, *bisexual men*, and *bisexual women*. Also keep in mind that *gay* refers to both males and females in the homosexual community, so if you're talking about men, use *gay men*, and if you're talking about women, use *lesbians* or *gay women*.

Remember to use parallel terms; for example *homosexual and heterosexual couples*. Using nonparallel terminology, such as *married and same-sex couples* implies that marriage is suitable only for a biological man and woman. While that may be what the law says or what some people think, try to accommodate different beliefs and values.

In some circles and in certain publications, referring to homosexual people as *queers* is acceptable, but be careful; you usually need to be a member of the community in order to use terms traditionally considered offensive.

Gender identities and sexual orientations don't necessarily fall into neat little either/or categories. Gender identity can be hazy and flexible. People who identify themselves as heterosexual may have times when they're sexually attracted to members of the same sex. This is one reason why avoiding labels is usually best.

Unless you absolutely must mention a person's gender identity or sexual orientation, ditch the labels. Whether a person is transgender or transsexual, for example, doesn't really matter. What matters is only what that person thinks. If a person who's biologically a woman identifies himself as a man, treat him and refer to him as a man, not as a female-to-male transgender person even though that particular phrase is considered acceptable. Of course, if you're publishing a study on transgender men and women, that might be an important detail to mention.

Avoiding Bias Against People with Medical Conditions and Disabilities

People with medical conditions and disabilities have enough problems to deal with without having to carry the added burden of stigma. One way you can help fight stigma is to use the right words and phrases when you have to mention a particular condition or disability. Here are some guidelines to follow:

Put people first. Instead of saying *autistic children*, for example, say *children with autism*. Putting people first avoids reducing people to a condition.

Use *has* and *have* instead of *is* and *are*. Nobody *is* a condition, such as bipolar disorder or dementia, but people can have such conditions.

Put people before conditions. Calling someone an AIDS victim or saying that the person suffers from mental illness implies that the medical condition has power over that person. It's better to prioritize the person over the disease. For example, instead of referring to someone as an *AIDS victim*, you might consider using the phrase *person with AIDS*. Instead of saying that a person *suffers from depression*, you might say that the person is *living with depression*.

Avoid the terms *patient* and *case*. Unless you're referring to a patient in a hospital, refer to people by their names or as *people* or *participants* (in a study).

Steer clear of euphemisms. Euphemisms, such as *differently challenged* and *handicapable*, are condescending. See more on euphemisms in Chapter 12.

For additional details on bias-free expressions, consult the *Publication Manual of the American Psychological Association* or visit apastyle.org.

Practice

Rewrite the following sentences to eliminate bias. (There is usually more than one acceptable answer.)

1. We polled 150 homosexuals to find out more about their sexual preferences.

2. People who suffer with depression tend to need considerably more sleep than do normal people.

3. Native Americans and Orientals comprise about 75 percent of the town's population.

4. The man and his wife watched an educational video about the mentally ill.

5. Despite their age, senior citizens descended on Washington to protest the plan to raise the retirement age.

Answers

1. We polled 150 gay men and women to find out more about their sexual orientation.
2. People with depression tend to need considerably more sleep than do others (or than do people without depression).
3. Native Americans and Asians comprise about 75 percent of the town's population.
4. The husband and his wife watched an educational video about people with mental illness.
5. Citizens descended on Washington to protest the plan to raise the retirement age.

Maintaining an Objective Viewpoint

Maintaining an objective viewpoint and avoiding bias aren't only about choosing the right nouns, pronouns, and adjectives. You also need to think logically, express yourself clearly, and support with evidence any claims you make. In the following sections, I offer some guidance in how to write more objectively.

Never Say *Never*: Avoiding Generalizations and Absolutes

Even if it happens to be fiction, good writing is honest and reveals what is true. Bad writing, on the other hand, obscures the truth and misleads people. For example, claiming that all politicians are corrupt probably isn't true. At least a few politicians, somewhere in the world, are doing what they believe is best and do not allow money to influence their decisions. An easy way to avoid the most blatant overgeneralizations is to proceed with caution whenever one of these absolute terms pops into your head:

all	must	nothing
always	never	only
everybody	nobody	should
everyone	no one	
everything	none	

The trouble with claims that begin with absolutes is that they're rarely correct and they make the claim vulnerable to an easy rebuttal. Someone needs to provide only a single piece of evidence that counters your claim in order to prove you wrong. For example, if I ask my son, "Why do I always have to remind you to take out the trash?" and he points out correctly that three months ago, on May 13, he did, in fact, take out the trash without my reminding him, he wins, and I have to backpedal.

Unfortunately, absolute statements don't always begin with a word that makes them easy to identify. For example, a statement that "Conservatives support a pro-life platform" implies that all conservatives support a pro-life platform, which I know isn't true. I know several people who consider themselves conservatives but pro-choice.

When you see the words *always* or *never*, you should be a little suspicious. Writing rarely works that way and neither does the world.

To avoid making overgeneralizations, qualify statements with words such as *most*, *many*, *almost*, *rarely*, and *nearly*. Better yet, be specific; for example, instead of saying *several*, give an exact number, such as *3* or *7* or *258*. Instead of saying "most people favor …," give a percentage; for example, "53 percent of the 3,025 people polled favor the proposed school voucher program." Instead of saying, "In the past …," specify the exact time; for example, "Fifty years ago, researchers believed …." Specifics make writing strong.

A word of caution: Qualifications are important, but avoid the temptation to qualify everything you write. Too many qualifications can drain the vigor from your writing. Find a balance between saying too much and too little.

Support Any Claims with Evidence

Whenever you state something as fact, back it up with evidence from a reliable source. For example, instead of merely claiming that "the number of children with food allergies has risen dramatically in just the past few years," add the facts and figures and cite your source:

> According to the Centers for Disease Control and Prevention (CDC), food allergy prevalence among children younger than 18 rose from 3.4 to 5.1 percent between 1997 and 2011.

As you can see, the evidence not only cites a reliable source, but it also clears up a lot of ambiguity. It explains what is meant by *children* (younger than 18), *dramatic increase* (from 3.4 to 5.1 percent), and past few years (1997 to 2011). By adding specific evidence, you make your argument stronger and more credible.

Be Careful When Making Value Judgments

A value judgment is a subjective assessment of the value, quality, or goodness of someone or something. Whenever you make a value judgment, you're sizing up someone or something based on your own standards. For example, you may consider someone who doesn't mow and edge his or her lawn twice a week lazy or someone whose home is impeccably clean an overachiever. However, not everyone shares your standards and beliefs.

Instead of using subjective assessments to describe people, places, and things, you should objectively describe characteristics or behaviors and let the audience draw its own conclusions. Instead of describing a manager as overbearing, for example, you might mention that the manager demanded daily progress reports from everyone in the department and visited every employee's cubicle twice a day to observe. If you do go ahead and make the value judgment, be sure to back it up with specifics to define more precisely the standard you're using to make that judgment.

Practice

Choose the more objective sentence in each of the following sentence pairs:

1. Life, as we know it, does not exist on any planet outside of our solar system. *Or:* Scientists have yet to discover signs of life on planets other than Earth.
2. Several people at the party mentioned that the cheese dip was particularly delicious. *Or:* Everyone at the party enjoyed the cheese dip.
3. According to the CDC, 51.5 percent of adults 18 years and older have had at least 12 alcoholic drinks over the course of the past year. *Or:* Most adults 18 years and older report that they are regular drinkers; that is, they drink at least 12 alcoholic beverages annually.
4. Public opinion has little influence over gun control legislation. *Or:* Although a recent poll showed 83 percent of the electorate favoring stricter gun control laws, the Senate voted against expanding background checks.
5. Researchers concluded that chronic stress impairs a person's problem-solving performance, because they had no time to engage in self-affirmation activities. *Or:* Participants who were operating under high levels of chronic stress solved half as many problems as the unstressed participants.

Answers

1. Scientists have yet to discover signs of life on planets other than Earth.
2. Several people at the party mentioned that the cheese dip was particularly delicious.
3. According to the CDC, 51.5 percent of adults 18 years and older have had at least 12 drinks over the course of the past year.
4. Although a recent poll showed 83 percent of the electorate favoring stricter gun control laws, the Senate voted against expanding background checks.
5. Participants who were operating under high levels of chronic stress solved half as many problems as the unstressed participants.

Chapter Review Practice

To avoid gender bias, choose gender-neutral nouns and try to work around using the pronouns *he* and *she*. Singular *they* can be very helpful. Don't make distinctions based on gender, race, ethnicity, medical conditions, or disabilities unless such information is relevant. Avoid terms such as *elderly* and *senior citizen* to describe older people; a specific age or range is preferable. The word *gay* refers to both males and females; to draw a distinction, use *gay men and women*. When referring to people with medical conditions or disabilities, use person-first language; for example, *children with ADHD* instead of *ADHD children*.

Now let's practice what you learned in this chapter:

1. Which of the following is an example of person-first language?
    A. Deaf people
    B. Autistic people
    C. Blind people
    D. People with disabilities
2. Which of the following pronouns is the best choice to avoid calling out someone's gender?
    A. He
    B. She
    C. He/she
    D. They
3. Which of the following is the best example of gender-neutral language?
    A. Flight attendant
    B. Stewardess
    C. Fireman
    D. Barista

Answers

1. D
2. D
3. A

Part 5
Fine-Tuning the Mechanics

Now that you've spent some time on the big-picture aspects of writing, it's time to get small again, and take a look at those tiny tools of writing called punctuation marks.

Some little things have big jobs, and that's certainly true of the punctuation marks that end sentences: periods, question marks, and exclamation marks. I'll also discuss some punctuation marks that are often misused: commas, colons, and semicolons.

Don't feel bad if you've misused a comma or two in your day; commas have so many jobs that it's no wonder people get confused. On the other hand, semicolons don't have many jobs at all—just two—so you have no excuse not to learn those jobs by heart. I'll cover less frustrating punctuation marks as well: quotation marks, hyphens, dashes, parentheses, and brackets.

This part will also include tips for capitalizing words and navigating the minefield that is English spelling. I'll mention many of the general rules for English spelling, as well as the numerous exceptions.

Punctuation, spelling, and capitalization may seem like small issues, but they make a big impression on readers. If you use them correctly, you'll look like a smart, careful writer. If you misuse them, you'll look inexperienced or sloppy. In writing, there really are no little things.

17

Basic Punctuation

In writing, the little things matter—especially the little things known as punctuation marks. Without punctuation, sentences would be confusing messes. With improperly used punctuation, sentences are hard to understand and annoying to readers who know the rules.

Every punctuation mark has its own use or uses. Some have only one use (the question mark) or two uses (the semicolon), making them fairly easy to learn. Others, such as the comma, have many uses. Even worse, some of the uses are judgment calls rather than hard rules. That makes the comma particularly challenging to use.

It's worth taking some time to focus on punctuation, which is connected to grammar and style but really its own category. Sometimes punctuation is the difference between a grammatical sentence and an ungrammatical sentence. Sometimes punctuation is the difference between a boring sentence and an interesting sentence.

This chapter will help you get a handle on all of this and more.

Putting an End to Your Sentences

Like all good things, sentences have to end. Following are the three punctuation marks you can use to end a sentence.

The End, Period.

The most common way to end a sentence—as you can see in the sentence you're reading right now—is the period. This tiny dot is powerful: it says, "You're done." Long and short sentences can both be ended by a period.

> The mailman wept.
> There's a bug in your hair.
> I like to play pinball with my friend Neil.

When summer comes, it fills me with longing for the days when my beloved Valerie used to throw peanuts to squirrels in the park.

The vast majority of sentences in English end with a period.

How many spaces go after a period? One or two? Back in the days of typewriters, it was common to skip two spaces after a period. These days, skipping one space is far more common. You're better off in almost every situation allowing just one space. However, there are exceptions. The most recent edition of the APA manual brought back the practice of skipping two spaces. For some reason, this out-of-date practice just won't die.

Ending with a Question Mark?

The question mark is probably the best-named punctuation mark, since it only has one function: ending a question. Questions come in many sizes and types in English.

> Where's the train station?
> What do you think of the philosophy of Wittgenstein?
> Huh?
> Have you ever been in love, so deeply in love, that you feel like you're losing your mind?

When you use a question mark, make sure the sentence really is a question. The best tip-off is a word such as *who*, *what*, *where*, *when*, *why*, or *how*. *Did* and *do* also begin many questions. It can help you recognize a question if you read it aloud and feel your voice inflecting upward at the end of the sentence.

Don't forget the question mark when you write a question. Some writers accidentally write sentences like this:

> How do we know vampires don't exist.

Since that sentence is asking something, it's a question and needs a question mark:

> How do we know vampires don't exist?

If you really don't want to write a question, rephrase the idea as a statement:

> We don't know for sure whether or not vampires exist.

That's not a question because it states something rather than asks something.

End Already! The Exclamation Point

The third way to end a sentence ends with a bang! The exclamation point is used for sentences that end with strong emphasis. This punctuation mark brings high energy: you could think of it as raising your voice or banging your fist on the table.

> There's a fire in the kitchen!
> I can't believe you forgot my birthday!
> I lost my keys!
> Ow!
> You have disappointed your parents and disgraced your ancestors!

As you can tell from these examples, the exclamation mark is best used in situations that are informal. Using exclamation marks in an email, tweet, or text message is fine. An exclamation mark could also be acceptable in a personal essay, if used sparingly. If you're writing fiction, exclamation marks could be helpful in writing dialogue. Many advertisements use exclamation marks to convey energy and enthusiasm.

However, in formal writing situations, you should avoid exclamation marks. If you're writing a résumé, cover letter, research paper, or anything with a serious purpose, don't use exclamation marks. They set the wrong tone, and they'll make you sound silly (and loud).

Practice

Add final punctuation to the following sentences:

1. How many times do I have to tell you I hate pea soup
2. My name is Henry; I eat a lot of plums
3. I am so angry right now
4. When I watch *Mad Men*, I'm glad I wasn't around in the 1960s
5. Where the heck are my keys

Answers

1. How many times do I have to tell you I hate pea soup?
2. My name is Henry; I eat a lot of plums.
3. I am so angry right now! (This sentence could also end with a period. In fact, a period often has better effect than an exclamation mark, which often feels forced and overblown.)

4. When I watch *Mad Men*, I'm glad I wasn't around in the 1960s. (Despite starting with *when*, this is a statement, not a question, so it ends with a period.)
5. Where the heck are my keys?

Knowing When to Use Commas

Commas are one of the most helpful punctuation marks—and one of the most confusing. This situation is ironic, since the main purpose of the comma is to avoid confusion.

Why are commas an issue for many writers? Well, some comma rules are strict and universally accepted; other rules are flexible and extremely subjective. You have a lot of company if you've ever misplaced a comma, but with a review of the types of comma use, you should be ready to use commas like a pro.

Separating Items in a Series

A politician, a nun, and a sailor walk into a bar. I'm not sure what they did there, but it would be hard to tell jokes like that—or write any kind of list—without commas. Separating items in a list is one of the main uses of the comma. For example:

> Cupcakes, brownies, potato chips, and pizza ruined my diet.

Without commas, this would be a smooshed-together mess that's difficult to read:

> Cupcakes brownies potato chips and pizza ruined my diet.

Not everyone agrees on whether there should be a comma after the second-to-last item in a list. Some publications (especially newspapers) omit that final comma—called a *serial comma*—like so:

> The politician kissed a baby, told a lie and ate a hamburger.

The comma that comes after the second-to-last item in a series is often referred to as a *serial comma* or *Oxford comma*, so named because it's preferred by Oxford University Press. Many—including the author of this book—prefer using the Oxford comma because it doesn't hurt and does sometimes help eliminate ambiguity in sentences.

Separating Two or More Adjectives

If you're writing about a dapper, classy, well-dressed dude, you need commas to separate the adjectives. This rule applies even when dealing with only two adjectives:

> My dog is a well-behaved, fluffy poodle.

Don't get comma-happy, though: resist the temptation to put a comma between *fluffy* and *poodle*; that is, don't separate the last adjective in the series from the noun it modifies. The commas should only separate adjectives; a comma before the noun will create confusion.

Joining Two Independent Clauses

An independent clause is a complete thought that could be a grammatical sentence. Independent clauses can be very short, as in these examples:

> Cats ran.
> Dogs howled.

When joining independent clauses, you have a few options. You can join them using a semicolon:

> Cats ran; dogs howled.

You can join them using a comma and a conjunction:

> Cats ran, and dogs howled.

That comma is needed only if the sentence joins two independent clauses. The following sentence doesn't need a comma:

> The bird sang and fluttered around the apartment.

Why no comma after *and*? Because you only have one subject (the bird) performing two actions (singing and fluttering). You're not joining two separate, complete sentences.

A common mistake—the comma splice—occurs when two independent clauses are joined by a comma with no conjunction, like so:

> My dad is an astronaut, my mom is a teacher.

Fortunately, this is an easy mistake to fix:

> My dad is an astronaut, and my mom is a teacher.

You can also fix the problem with a semicolon:

> My dad is an astronaut; my mom is a teacher.

For more on joining independent clauses, see Chapter 4.

Setting Off Nonessential Clauses and Phrases

In language and in life, some things are essential and others are nonessential. Commas are used to set off nonessential clauses and phrases from the rest of a sentence.

For example, here's an essential element:

> The president asked for an advisor who is an expert in foreign affairs.

That whole phrase—*an advisor who is an expert in foreign affairs*—is essential. An advisor who doesn't know foreign affairs from Foghorn Leghorn wouldn't do. Here's a similar sentence with a nonessential element:

> The president summoned Congressman Wilson, who is a football fan.

The sentence structure is almost exactly the same, but the meaning is different. The fact that Congressman Wilson is a football fan is probably not the reason for the president's summons, so the information is nonessential. For this kind of nonessential clause, use a comma.

Sometimes these clauses or phrases appear in the middle of the sentence:

> The book, written three years ago, won six awards.

Often, determining whether a clause or phrase is essential or nonessential is a tough call. Depending on the rest of the paragraph, this punctuation might be fine, too:

> The book written three years ago won six awards.

Pausing After an Introductory Element

After getting a good night's sleep, you'll probably write better. You'll also remember comma rules better, as in that sentence about sleeping and writing. Introductory words and phrases are usually followed by commas, especially when a comma makes the sentence easier to read, as in these examples:

> Last winter, I lost my toboggan.
> Usually, my cousin works out at the gym.
> When I get bored and restless, I walk on the beach.
> After contemplating the events of that fateful Thursday afternoon, I napped.

If those introductory elements were removed, you'd still have grammatical sentences:

> I lost my toboggan.
> My cousin works out at the gym.
> I walk on the beach.
> I napped.

Introductory elements modify the sentence in some way, adding information that tells you where, when, or how the actions of the sentence are happening. These introductory elements act as adverbs, and single adverbs are often introductory elements themselves, as in the following sentences:

> Gradually, I learned how to speak Russian.
> Politically, the scandal is a minefield for the president.
> Brazenly, my cousin asked to borrow money.
> Lately, I've been getting weird pains in my side.

Sometimes an introductory word or phrase can exist without a comma, and it's up to you as a writer to decide if the comma is necessary or not. For example, in this sentence, the comma after "For example" is helpful, but in the previous sentence, a comma after "Sometimes" isn't really needed.

Hopefully is one of the most controversial words in English. It has long been used in sentences like, "The puppy gazed hopefully at his owner's dinner plate." However, many writers object to hopefully being used as a modifier for an entire sentence, meaning "it is hoped." The following are examples of the controversial usage:

> Hopefully, the Buffalo Bills will win the Super Bowl someday.
> Hopefully, I'll find true love.
> Hopefully, the sun won't blow up anytime soon.

Despite the dislike some feel for this usage, it's very common in speech, and it's becoming more commonly accepted in writing. Use *hopefully* to modify sentences in informal writing, but avoid it in formal writing. When in doubt, it's better to err on the side of not annoying people.

Pausing for Interruptions in a Sentence

Sometimes you use a comma just because it sounds right, you know?

For example, in the preceding sentence, placing a comma right before addressing the reader makes the sentence easier to read and understand. Other times, a comma might be used to create a pause, as in this headline from *Entertainment Weekly*:

> "Networks Embrace the Miniseries, Again"

That comma puts extra emphasis on the last word. This type of comma is closely related to how we speak, and it's most appropriate in writing that's a little informal.

Other Uses for Commas

If that's not enough, commas have even more uses. You need them to write dates, places, addresses, and numbers:

> I was born on April 4, 2009.
> My mom is from Memphis, Tennessee.
> My friend Joe lives at 14 Blake Street, Apartment 765.
> My brother says he scored 144,500 points at *Ms. Pac-Man*.

You also use commas to introduce direct quotations:

> My brother said, "I scored 144,500 points at *Ms. Pac-Man*!"

You don't need a comma for a similar sentence that doesn't include a direct quote:

> My brother said he scored a lot of points at *Ms. Pac-Man*.

No wonder so many people make comma mistakes—no other punctuation mark is so versatile. Despite the potential for confusion and mistakes, though, don't let commas discourage you. As you write and read more, you'll get a handle on the problems commas can and can't solve. You'll also get better at using them properly. Well-placed commas will make your writing clear, smooth, and flowing—in other words, enjoyable to read.

Practice

1. What is another name for the Oxford comma?
   A. The Harvard comma
   B. The antecedent comma
   C. The serial comma
   D. The coordinating comma
2. What do commas create?
   A. Interruptions
   B. Pauses
   C. Tenses
   D. Clauses
3. Which of the following can be used to join independent clauses?
   A. A semicolon
   B. A comma and a conjunction
   C. A comma and a preposition
   D. A colon

Answers

1. C
2. B
3. A, B, and D

Using a Semicolon to Join Items

After the comma, the semicolon might be the most commonly misused punctuation mark. Even native English speakers frequently make semicolon mistakes. Yet the semicolon is a useful weapon in a writer's arsenal, and you can avoid confusion if you remember that it only has two uses.

Joining Independent Clauses

The first use of the semicolon is to join two independent clauses; I used it for that purpose in this sentence. As we learned earlier, an independent clause is a complete thought that could be a grammatical sentence in its own right. The following are examples of independent clauses joined by a semicolon:

> Geese flew; ducks swam.
> The king ordered an execution; the prince gasped in horror.
> In spring, dogs play at the park; squirrels must be vigilant.

The semicolon is not the only option when dealing with two independent clauses. Sometimes, the best thing to do is let the independent clauses be separate sentences:

> I have a crick in my neck. Do you know a good chiropractor?

Sometimes the independent clauses are best joined by a comma and coordinating conjunction.

> Cats are more independent than dogs, and that's why I love them.

When the flow and logic of the sentence suggest a quick sequence of thoughts, the semicolon is an elegant way of joining them.

> There's nothing I enjoy more than basketball; the players' athleticism is breathtaking.

The choice is up to you as a writer, based on your ear for language and your purpose for writing. Just make sure you don't throw in a semicolon when you need a colon. The following is a common mistake, but a mistake all the same:

> These are my favorite superheroes; Batman, Daredevil, and the Punisher.

A semicolon cannot introduce a list: that job belongs to the colon. The semicolon has two jobs; introducing lists isn't one of them.

Practice

For the following sentences, insert the proper punctuation:

1. I have a stomachache it feels like I ate a fireball.
2. There are two things I hate about tests studying and worrying.
3. I like to relax by listening to music jazz is especially soothing.

Answers

1. I have a stomachache; it feels like I ate a fireball.
2. There are two things I hate about tests: studying and worrying.
3. I like to relax by listening to music: jazz is especially soothing. (A semicolon would also work here.)

Separating Items in a Series

The other use of a semicolon involves items in a series. As discussed in the section on commas, a sentence containing a series should look like this:

> I'm on Facebook, X, LinkedIn, and Pinterest.

That's easy enough. But what if one of the items in your list has a comma in it? The following would look odd because of comma overload:

> I've lived in Buffalo, New York, Chicago, Illinois, and Santa Fe, New Mexico.
> I like women with long, flowing hair, thriving, lucrative careers, and stylish, fashionable wardrobes.
> The keys to a good TV drama are a powerful, charismatic lead actor, a smart, adaptable showrunner, and a cool, interesting premise.

When an item in a series has a comma in it, separate the items using semicolons:

> I've lived in Buffalo, New York; Chicago, Illinois; and Santa Fe, New Mexico.
> I like women with long, flowing hair; thriving, lucrative careers; and stylish, fashionable wardrobes.
> The keys to a good TV drama are a powerful, charismatic lead actor; a smart, adaptable showrunner; and a cool, interesting premise.

Practice

Add commas to the following sentences as needed:

1. Excuse me can I help you?
2. I enjoy salty barbecued snacks.
3. I'm passionate about SEO.
4. Too many emojis can come across as frivolous silly and unprofessional.
5. To make her point she walked out of the meeting.

Answers

1. Excuse me, can I help you?
2. I enjoy salty, barbecued snacks.
3. I'm passionate about SEO.

4. Too many emojis can come across as frivolous, silly, and unprofessional.
5. To make her point, she walked out of the meeting.

Brushing Up on Colon Usage

Like a handshake, a colon is used for introductions. A colon tends to set up forthcoming information: read on and learn the types of language that can follow a colon.

Introducing a List

The most common use for the colon is in introducing a list.

> My dog likes four things: chasing, fetching, eating, and sleeping.
> These are the ingredients: flour, sugar, gluten, peanuts, and cilantro.
> The president has made progress in several areas: foreign policy, health care, and business growth.

You don't need a colon when there isn't a pause before introducing the list. With a little revision, those sentences no longer need a colon:

> My dog likes chasing, fetching, eating, and sleeping.
> The ingredients are flour, sugar, gluten, peanuts, and cilantro.
> The president has made progress in foreign policy, health care, and business growth.

Introducing a Formal Statement or Long Quotation

The colon is also used for introducing phrases or formal statements.

> The strange man had this to say to his critics: "I am not a bounty hunter."
> I hate going to the mall: it is a nightmare.
> Let me come right out and admit it: I've been having an affair.

Separating Independent Clauses

Remember the passage earlier about how semicolons separate independent clauses? Colons can do that job, too. When you have two independent clauses that are closely linked—too closely to make separate sentences—you can join them with a colon.

The general had a plan: he would hide the chickens before his secretary came in.

Too many dog owners forget something important: dogs are allergic to chocolate.

Daniel Day-Lewis seems to win an Oscar for every movie he's in: it's that predictable.

Using a colon to separate independent clauses is a judgment call, but it's most appropriate when the first clause is asking a question that the second one answers.

More Uses for Colons

You can also use a colon in sentences that consist of an independent clause and a phrase. This use is very similar to the above cases where a colon joins two independent clauses.

I've never been sure how to use *whom*: that pesky word.

My dad is a postal worker: so was his dad.

The robin's breast is red: a bright shade of red.

I haven't used a pencil in years: not since college.

In all those cases, an em dash would also work pretty well.

I've never been sure how to use whom—that pesky word.

My dad is a postal worker—so was his dad.

The robin's breast is red—a bright shade of red.

I haven't used a pencil in years—not since college.

For more on em dashes, see Chapter 19.

Not only are colons like greetings, but they're used in greetings: especially formal greetings. If you're writing a business letter, a letter of application, or anything formal, a colon should follow the greeting.

Dear sir:
To whom it may concern:
Dear Mr. Jenkins:
Dear Dr. Thompson:

Colons are also used in writing times.

I always take a nap at 3:30 in the afternoon.

My son was born at 1:43 A.M.

Football games usually start at 1:00.
Be home by 5:30! That's when Mom's making supper.

You may have seen the colon used in math class, since they are used in writing ratios. If there are twice as many peaches as apples, there's a 2:1 (2 to 1) ratio of peaches to apples.

In Congress, there's a 3:1 ratio of men to women.
The proportion of dogs to cats in my house is 4:1.
The ratio of water to other substances in your body is approximately 9:1.
I bet on the Bulls to win the NBA title and got 5:1 odds.

Colons are also used in many book titles, to separate the title and the subtitle.

Eleven Rings: The Soul of Success by Phil Jackson
Give and Take: A Revolutionary Approach to Success by Adam M. Grant
The Paleo Solution: The Original Human Diet by Robb Wolf and Loren Cordain
Running for Beginners: The Easiest Way to Start Running by Simon Adams

That's the colon: a useful, versatile form of punctuation.

Chapter Review Practice

A period is by far the most common way to end a sentence. Question marks end sentences that ask something; exclamation marks end sentences with a loud or emphatic point. Semicolons separate independent clauses or items in a list that contain commas. They only perform these two jobs. Colons introduce material, such as an independent clause, a phrase, or the body of a letter. Colons also appear in times (6:30), ratios (5:1), and many book and article titles.

Now let's practice what you learned in this chapter:

1. Supply the correct closing punctuation for these sentences.
    A. Hey
    B. Do you know what happened on this date
    C. I have a serious case of writer's block
    D. Your dog is a real happy boy

2. Which of the following is a proper use of a semicolon?
    A. I love pork chops; which are delicious.
    B. It's a beautiful; crisp fall day.
    C. This bubble tea tastes weird; it's like little balls of medicine.
    D. My favorite parts of writing are; revising, editing, and proofreading.
3. Which of the following is correct?
    A. Dear sir;
    B. Dear sir–
    C. Dear sir:
    D. Dear sir.
4. Which of the following is not an acceptable way to end a sentence?
    A. !
    B. ?
    C. .
    D. ;
5. Which of the following is the proper use of a colon:
    A. Dear sir:
    B. I don't know how to say this: we shouldn't see each other anymore.
    C. I hate three things: anxiety, depression, and spiders
    D. All of these

Answers

1. A. !
    B. ?
    C. .
    D. .
2. C
3. C
4. D
5. D

Quotation Marks and Apostrophes

Most punctuation is located or begins near the bottom of letters, like periods and commas. Quotation marks and apostrophes, on the other hand, appear near the tops of letters. These punctuation marks aren't as versatile as the comma, but they have a few specific jobs you'll need to learn and understand.

The most important thing about quotation marks is that they allow you to use the words of other people while giving full credit. If you use quotation marks correctly, you'll never have to worry about accidentally plagiarizing.

The most important thing about apostrophes might be that they drive people crazy when improperly used. There are many webpages devoted to misused apostrophes, with pictures of mistakes from signs and other sources. If you don't want to be similarly embarrassed, you'll have to get a handle on the apostrophe and its uses, most of which have to do with possession.

Enclosing Text in Quotation Marks

Quotation marks are important because they allow you to report exactly what someone else said or wrote. Newspapers, novels, and academic papers are full of quotation marks because those genres frequently report what others said. Quotation marks are the tools that allow you to quote people accurately.

Quoting a Person's Exact Words

As my grandmother used to say, "You have to use quotation marks when reporting what someone said or wrote." The preceding sentence is an example of how to use quotation marks. Here are some more:

> When I received the bad news, I said, "What? That can't be!"
>
> Shakespeare was the first writer to use the phrase "Something is rotten in the state of Denmark."
>
> On *Arrested Development*, Gob Bluth often says "I've made a huge mistake."
>
> Never say "I love you" just to be polite.

Quotation marks are used to document something that was said or written. Also—as in that last example about politeness—they can contain an example of something that might be said. Use quotation marks when the exact wording is important. Often, it's not. For example, sometimes you can be more general:

> My dad told me to always be respectful.

That sentence would be just fine in some situations. However, sometimes you might need to get more specific, like this:

> My dad told me, "Always respect your elders."

Punctuating Around Quotation Marks

There are a couple ways of punctuating around quotation marks: the logical way and the American way. In America, punctuation goes inside the quotation marks, as in the following examples:

> I hate when people use the expression "much to my chagrin."
>
> My brother said I was a "dork."
>
> He said I should grab the "thingamajig," which I couldn't find anywhere.

In British English, punctuation goes outside the quotation marks, like so:

> I hate when people use the expression "much to my chagrin".
>
> My brother said I was a "dork".
>
> He said I should grab the "thingamajig", which I couldn't find anywhere.

The British way is more logical because it excludes punctuation from the quotation marks if that punctuation is not part of the quotation. This makes more sense than the American way, but if you're writing for an American audience, put your punctuation before the quotation mark. The exception is when a quotation is part of a question:

Why do you like the phrase "stuck in your craw"?

Which president said the word "misunderestimate"?

Which superhero has the catchphrase "It's clobberin' time!"?

However, if the question mark is part of the quotation rather than part of the sentence, the question mark goes inside the final quotation mark:

Joe asked, "How did I get here?"

I was confused and said, "Mom?" to my Aunt Nancy.

"What is love?" asked the poet.

Dealing with Long Quotations: Block Quotes

Sometimes you'll need to use a long quotation. If a quotation goes on for many sentences, it would look kind of ugly, and it could create confusion. The solution to this problem is the block quote.

The exact format for block quotes varies in different style manuals, but the general idea stays the same: you put the quotation in a big block of text and indent it a few times. The following is a quotation from earlier in this chapter:

> Quotation marks are important because they allow you to report exactly what someone else said or wrote. Newspapers, novels, and academic papers are full of quotation marks because those genres frequently report what others said. Quotation marks are the tools that allow you to quote people accurately.

In Modern Language Association (MLA) style, you should use a block if the quotation takes up more than four lines. In American Psychological Association (APA) style, you use a block quote if the quotation is at least 40 words. *The Chicago Manual of Style* (CMS) guidelines are looser, suggesting a block quote for quotations 4 or 5 lines long but demanding it for quotations 10 lines long. Formats change with new editions, so always check the latest edition of the guide you're using.

In all formats, you don't need quotation marks for a block quote. The fact that the text is formatted as a block quote is enough to let readers know it's a quotation.

Dealing with Quotations Inside Quotations

What if you're quoting someone who is also quoting someone? How do you handle a quote within a quote? First, here's how not to handle it:

> The president said, "I met a woman today who said, "I hate taxes.""

Doesn't that look weird? Fortunately, there's a workaround. For quotes within quotes, switch to single quotes:

> The president said, "I met a woman today who said, 'I hate taxes.'"

This is the only use for single quotes, so remember to use them for this reason alone.

Enclosing Titles in Quotes

Titles of artworks often go in quotation marks, especially when you're talking about a part of a longer work. For example:

> "Teenage Riot" is the best song from the album *Daydream Nation*.
> My favorite *Seinfeld* episode is "The Yada Yada."
> The short story "Cousins from Hell" is part of the longer collection *Terrifying Families*.

As you can see from those examples, you should put longer or complete works—such as albums, TV shows, movies, and books—in italics.

Flagging Slang and Technical Terms

Sometimes quotation marks are used to highlight a term that is unusual for some reason. This could be a technical term, a slang term, or any word or phrase that is new or unusual.

> The businessman kept speaking about "synergistic paradigms."
> The senior citizens did not know what the teenager meant by "crunk."
> I can't stand the word "staycation."

When a word is discussed as a word, it can also be put in italics, which is the style used in this book. Follow the rules required by your format, teacher, or editor, but if you have a choice, italics look cleaner and less obtrusive:

> The businessman kept speaking about *synergistic paradigms*.
> The senior citizens did not know what the teenager meant by *crunk*.
> I can't stand the word *staycation*.

Quoting Someone Else

Inexperienced writers often forget quotation marks when attributing something to another speaker. For example, let's say a student wrote the following:

> According to Miller, high school football should be outlawed.

That's fine if this is a paraphrase of Miller, meaning the student put Miller's ideas into new words. However, if Miller wrote the exact words "High school football should be outlawed," then those words need quotation marks around them. By forgetting the quotation marks, the writer accidently plagiarized. Don't let this happen to you. Be very careful about using other people's words. Stealing words and ideas is as unethical as stealing physical property.

Practice

1. What is a long quote with its own format called?
   A. Questionable quote
   B. Special quote
   C. Conjugated quote
   D. Block quote
2. Which of the following is often followed by a comma?
   A. Nouns
   B. Verbs
   C. Introductory phrases
   D. Prepositions
3. What can proper use of quotation marks prevent?
   A. Forest fires
   B. Plagiarism
   C. Comma splices
   D. Run-on sentences

Answers

1. D
2. C
3. B

Using Apostrophes

The main job of the apostrophe is to create possessive words: words that establish that certain things, beings, or qualities belong to other things, beings, or qualities.

Forming Possessives

The following examples show nouns linked by apostrophes to create possessive words:

> The president's children were adorable.
> Have you seen my dog's toy?
> That coffee shop's mochas are delicious.
> My uncle's personality is depressing.
> France's best food is crêpes.

The apostrophe establishes the possessive relationship. These sentences could all be reworded in ways that read awkwardly but can help you remember the meaning.

> The children of the president were adorable.
> Have you seen the toy that belongs to my dog?
> The mochas made by that coffee shop are delicious.
> The personality of my uncle is depressing.
> The best food from France is crêpes.

Plural Nouns Ending in –s

A tricky case occurs when you have a noun that ends in –s. There are two ways to make that kind of word possessive, and you should check with the format or style guide you're using. The first way is simply to add an apostrophe.

> Jesus' apostles are mentioned in the Gospels.
> Where are my cats' toys?
> My parents' house is old.
> Is this Dennis' hat?
> That isn't my job. It's Congress' job.

Those words can also become possessive by adding *'s*.

> Jesus's apostles are mentioned in the Gospels.
> Where are my cats's toys?
> My parents's house is old.
> Is this Dennis's hat?
> That isn't my job. It's Congress's job.

If you have a choice, skip the extra *s*. Adding only an apostrophe looks a lot cleaner.

Adding apostrophes to plural words is a common mistake. The following examples are all mistakes because the apostrophes are not needed:

> The siblings' lost their cat.
> Most presidents' see their hair go gray while in office.
> Have you seen my guinea pigs'?

When using an apostrophe—or any punctuation mark—you should make sure you have a reason for using it. If you're not creating a possessive word or contraction, you likely don't need an apostrophe.

Indefinite Pronouns

Indefinite pronouns are pronouns that are general, not referring to a specific entity. You also need an apostrophe when making these words possessive.

> It's <u>anyone's</u> guess where my mom put it.
> <u>Someone's</u> coat is sitting on the chair.
> I respect <u>everyone's</u> human rights.

Dual Possession

In some sentences, you need to discuss two people or things that possess something. This can be punctuated two different ways, depending on the meaning of the sentences.

In some cases, the two entities equally possess something:

> Joe and Jenny's house is stylish.
> Gary and Stan's poker games are off the hook.
> I hate going to Jill and Joanne's knitting club.

Michael Jordan and Scottie Pippen's teams were impressive.
My mom and dad's car was broken down a lot.

In all these cases, the possession is truly a joint effort. For example, in the last sentence, the mom and dad equally owned the car. In the second-to-last example, Jordan and Pippen were part of the same teams, which won six championships. In cases like this, only the second item needs an apostrophe and *s*. Just as the two entities share whatever is in the rest of the sentence, they share the same punctuation.

On the other hand, sometimes you may need to write similar-looking sentences that have a different meaning because the two beings possess similar things that are not exactly the same. These examples need different punctuation:

Jordan's and Pippen's styles were different.
My mom's and dad's childhoods were difficult.
What's the difference between the quarterback's and linebacker's leadership roles?
How did the Bills' and Sabres' seasons go?

In these cases, the nouns each get their own *'s* because they possess distinctive, separate things. The Bills and Sabres may have both finished seasons, but they weren't the same season. Jordan and Pippen may have been on the same team, but their playing styles weren't identical. A mom and dad might have both had difficult childhoods, but they weren't the same difficult childhoods. They possess different things, so they get their own possessive punctuation.

Using apostrophes correctly allows readers to grasp your exact meaning so you can communicate effectively.

Practice

Punctuate the following sentences:

1. Have you seen my dog and sons toys?
2. Do your parents have a van?
3. How do the president and vice presidents roles differ?
4. Are Catholicism and Judaisms prayers similar?
5. Did Sally and Saras house—the one they grew up in—burn down?

Answers

1. Have you seen my dog's and son's toys? (Both get apostrophes, since they are probably not the same toys.)
2. Do your parents have a van? (No apostrophes, since *parents* is not possessive.)
3. How do the president's and vice-president's roles differ? (Both *president* and *vice-president* get their own apostrophe and *s*, since they have separate roles.)
4. Are Catholicism's and Judaism's prayers similar? (Both *Catholicism* and *Judaism* get their own apostrophe and *s*, since they are separate religions.)
5. Did Sally and Sara's house—the one they grew up in—burn down? (Only *Sara* gets an apostrophe and *s*, since Sally and Sara grew up in the same house, so they have joint possession.)

Time- and Money-Related Words

Sometimes you'll need to write about time or money in a way that requires an apostrophe, as in the following examples:

> I have two weeks' vacation coming to me.
> Can I buy one hundred dollars' worth of parakeets?
> In a month's time, you can get a lot of work done.

Converting Some Singulars into Plurals

Occasionally, you might see an apostrophe used to make a plural, like if you were talking about the 1700's or the 1960's. Resist this usage. You never need to use an apostrophe to make a plural word. Writing *1700s* and *1960s* is correct.

One of the most common mistakes in English is mixing up *its* and *it's*. That little apostrophe confuses many writers, partly due to an inconsistency in English. Here's the inconsistency: remember when we said apostrophes are for possessive words? Surprise! The exact opposite is true for *its* and *it's*. All the following sentences include possessive *its*—with no apostrophe—and they're all possessive.

> The building lost its awning in the storm.
> Freedom is its own reward.
> Your baby dropped its rattle.

The following sentences—all correct—have it's with an apostrophe, and they're not possessive.

> It's raining today.
> This color is bright. It's my sister's favorite.
> Getting older: it's not easy.

This can be confusing because *it's* does not use an apostrophe to make a possessive word; it uses an apostrophe to make a contraction. To find out which form is correct, see how the sentences sound with *it is*. The following examples sound pretty odd:

> The building lost it is awning in the storm.
> Freedom is it is own reward.
> Your baby dropped it is rattle.

Since that doesn't work, they were all correct with its. Now let's double-check the second batch.

> It is raining today.
> This color is bright. It is my sister's favorite.
> Getting older: it is not easy.

Those all make sense, so *it's* is correct.

Forming Contractions

Some words can be combined into one word with the help of an apostrophe, and these are called contractions. The following sentences all include a contraction:

> Don't touch that!
> I can't lift 500 pounds.
> My father didn't take me to the circus.
> My dog won't fetch my slippers.
> There isn't anything wrong with wearing a hat.
> Wouldn't you like some cake?
> I hadn't planned to go to the party.
> I shouldn't steal paper clips from work.
> There wasn't anything I could say to make my mother happy.
> Let's get some coffee.

Here's a look at those sentences with the contractions removed and the missing words spelled out.

<u>Do not</u> touch that!
I <u>cannot</u> lift 500 pounds.
My father <u>did not</u> take me to the circus.
My dog <u>will not</u> fetch my slippers.
There <u>is not</u> anything wrong with wearing a hat.
<u>Would not</u> you like some cake?
I <u>had not</u> planned to go to the party.
I <u>should not</u> steal paper clips from work.
There <u>was not</u> anything I could say to make my mother happy.
<u>Let us</u> get some coffee.

Some contractions are easier to remember than others. *Shouldn't* is close to *should not* and therefore easy to figure out. You'll have to memorize others. For example, *won't* is a contraction of *will not*.

Contractions are very common in speech and writing. However, in very formal types of writing, you should avoid contractions, which are considered too colloquial. When in doubt, ask the teacher or editor for their preference. As with most aspects of writing, there are different views on contractions, depending on your audience and purpose.

Chapter Review Practice

Quotation marks are used to distinguish someone else's exact words from your own. Apostrophes are used mainly for making words possessive, like if you were talking about a dog's dish: the dish that belongs to the dog. Apostrophes are also used to make contractions, as in changing *do not* to *don't*. *Its* is possessive, and *it's* is a contraction. This is a distinction you'll have to memorize. Contractions aren't welcome in very formal writing—fortunately, this book isn't that formal.

Now let's practice what you learned in this chapter:

1. Add quotation marks as needed to the following:
    A. My dad said, I have a headache.
    B. According to my friend Ben, robots will kill us all.
    C. I remember when a teacher said, Shakespeare said, The world must be peopled.
    D. I always misremember quotations.
    E. Crocodiles are like dinosaurs, said the intern.

2. What do apostrophes usually indicate?
    A. Plural
    B. Conjunction
    C. Possession
    D. Action
3. Which of the following words is not possessive?
    A. His
    B. Her
    C. Their
    D. It's

Answers

1. A. My dad said, "I have a headache."
   B. According to my friend Ben, "robots will kill us all."
   C. I remember when a teacher said, "Shakespeare said, 'The world must be peopled.'"
   D. I always misremember quotations.
   E. "Crocodiles are like dinosaurs," said the intern.
2. C
3. D

19

Hyphens, Dashes, Parentheses, and Brackets

This chapter deals with punctuation marks that cleave, which is an interesting word: it is its own antonym (opposite). To cleave is to bring together, and to cleave is also to separate.

The punctuation marks in this chapter cleave in both senses: hyphens, dashes, parentheses, and brackets bring together some elements of words or sentences while separating others. They are very useful in writing clear, flowing prose.

These marks are especially helpful in bringing some of the qualities of speech to writing. When you talk, it's easy to raise your voice, whisper, or dramatically pause to make a point. In writing, these punctuation marks can help readers hear your writing the way you want them to hear it: the way you hear it in your head.

This chapter is very important to style, since every writer has his or her own preferences when it comes to dashes, parentheses, and so on.

Putting Hyphens to Good Use

Hyphens are punctuation marks that connect words or parts of words. They are shorter than dashes, and they have totally different jobs. Don't confuse a hyphen (-) with a dash (—).

Breaking a Word at the End of a Line

Back in the days of typewriters, hyphens were used to break works at the end of lines, like so:

> I've had enough. When will you ever stop com-
> plaining about the weather?

Now that word processing programs wrap around text, this use of hyphens is very rare. You're only likely to see it in something quite old.

Hyphenating Compound Numbers

When spelling out numbers, hyphens help readers remember that the number is a single entity. The following is clear:

> I have eighty-one Batman action figures.

If you forget the hyphen, it's a little less clear:

> I have eighty one Batman action figures.

For just a second, the reader will think the number you're talking about is eighty, not eighty-one. Help your readers by remembering the hyphens in numbers.

You only need to hyphenate numbers from twenty-one to ninety-nine. If you're writing out a longer number, you should still hyphenate the part that includes a number from twenty-one to ninety-nine, as in the following examples:

> four hundred ninety-six
> one thousand twenty-nine
> one million, eighty thousand, forty-three

Practice

Write out the following numbers, hyphenating where necessary:

1. 306 _____
2. 87 _____
3. 102 _____
4. 9,000 _____
5. 37 _____

Answers

1. three hundred six
2. eighty-seven
3. one hundred two
4. nine thousand
5. thirty-seven

Setting Off a Prefix ... or Not

Prefixes are those little word parts that go on the front of words: like *pre–*, *mega–*, and *hyper–*. Do prefixed words need hyphens? Sometimes.

Language changes over time, and one of the most consistent changes is the disappearance of hyphens. For example, consider the word *email*. When electronic mail was new, it was consistently abbreviated as e-mail—the *e–* prefix standing for *electronic*. As time passed—and electronic mail became a commonplace, normal part of life—more and more people dropped the hyphen and spelled it *email*. Eventually, *email* became the norm.

Check *Merriam-Webster* if you're unsure whether or not a word should be hyphenated. It can also help to google both versions of a word to see which version is most popular. As mentioned elsewhere, if the masses make a change in English, the change will eventually stick.

See Chapter 20 for more on prefixes, suffixes, and infixes.

Hyphenating Compound Adjectives

One of the most helpful uses of hyphens is to link compound adjectives. All of the following examples hyphenate adjectives for the sake of clarity.

> I am a public-relations intern.
> My uncle is a free-wheeling traveler.
> Be careful of that spring-loaded bear trap.
> This voice-activated computer is nifty.
> That battery-operated light is cheap.

All these examples use hyphens to make the sentences read more smoothly and clearly. Here's the alternative without hyphens:

> I am a public relations intern.
> My uncle is a free wheeling traveler.
> Be careful of that spring loaded bear trap.
> This voice activated computer is nifty.
> That battery operated light is cheap.

Though these sentences look about the same, they're not as clear as the hyphenated batch. For example, take a closer look at this sentence:

> Be careful of that spring loaded bear trap.

As you start reading it, it seems as though the sentence is about some kind of spring: "Be careful of that spring …" Since *spring* and *loaded* are unattached, a reader can get tripped up. That hyphen lets readers know that *spring-loaded* is a single lexical item. Similar problems occur without the hyphen here:

> My uncle is a free wheeling traveler.

If you read this quickly, you might think *free* and *wheeling* have totally separate meanings in the sentence. You might wonder exactly how this uncle is free, and in what way he might be wheeling. You don't want to cause confusion in your readers, not even for a second. By hyphenating *free-wheeling*, you've made your meaning crystal clear.

The exception to this rule happens in the case of compound adjectives that are very established as words. For example, you can mention a *major league player* rather than a *major-league player*, since *major league* is so commonly used. When to use or omit a hyphen in a compound adjective is definitely a judgment call. Just make it an informed judgment.

Practice

1. Which of the following often need to be hyphenated?
    A. Numbers
    B. Countries
    C. Genders
    D. Restaurants
2. What does hyphenating compound adjectives prevent?
    A. Clarity
    B. Confusion
    C. Plagiarism
    D. Comma splices
3. Which of the following is often followed by a hyphen?
    A. Suffixes
    B. Prefixes
    C. Adverbs
    D. Articles

Answers

1. A
2. B
3. B

Making Good Use of the Dash

The hyphen's longer friend is the dash. There are two kinds of dashes, em dashes (—) and en dashes (–), and both are important to know. The dashes are (or once were, in typesetting days) about the width of the letters for which they are named, M and N. Read on to learn their uses.

Indicating a Range of Numbers

Although the en dash looks similar to and is occasionally used like a hyphen in making compound words, its main use involves writing a range of numbers:

> The students' ages range from 18–55.
> I have somewhere between 3–5 close friends.
> Someday I think I'd like 2–3 children.
> That family is so rich I think they own 2–3 mansions.
> This toy is designed for ages 5–8.

You also need to use an en dash when writing a range of years:

> The original *Star Wars* movies came out from 1972–1983.
> My uncle lived from 1934–1989.
> The best years of my life were from about 1990–1994.
> I wonder what TV will be like in the years 2050–2100.
> Picasso's blue period lasted from 1900–1904.

En dashes are also used to create a certain type of compound adjective—in cases where one word element consists of more than one word. For example:

> Rushdie is a Pulitzer Prize–winning author.
> I love reading about pre–World War II history.
> Buckner is still known for his World Series–losing play.

The em dash is more commonly used, so when I mention a dash from this point on, assume it's an em dash.

Introducing a Clarifying Statement

Em dashes are used introducing an idea that's meant to clarify, as in the following:

> I like action movies—especially superhero movies.
> Fall is the best season—the weather is just perfect.
> Spider-Man is the best superhero—he's heroic and relatable.
> I need coffee in the morning—it gets me going.
> I feel cranky—everything is getting on my nerves.

Enclosing Incidental (Nonessential) Text

The main job of parentheses is to set off nonessential text from the rest of the sentence. Parentheses aren't the only punctuation mark to do this job, so we need to talk again about dashes and commas.

Commas, Dashes, or Parentheses?

Here's one of the biggest judgment calls in writing: Should you set off a phrase with commas, dashes, or parentheses? In some cases, this is pretty clear. When the phrase is nonessential, as mentioned in the comma chapter, use commas:

> My uncle, the highest-ranked unicyclist in North Dakota, is coming for dinner.

Then again, using dashes in that sentence wouldn't exactly be wrong:

> My uncle—the highest-ranked unicyclist in North Dakota—is coming for dinner.

In that case, I would lean toward commas, since the information feels particularly trivial. Dashes create more emphasis than commas: they make the information stand out. Dashes are the best choice when you have information you'd like to highlight:

> The novelist—who has won the Pulitzer Prize—will be speaking at the university.
> Small dogs—no matter how well behaved at home—may run into trouble with big dogs at the park.
> The scandal—which involved drugs and prostitution—brought the administration to its knees.

Other times, parentheses would be a better choice:

> I like big dogs (mastiffs, Great Danes, etc.) more than little dogs.
> My great-aunt (my mom's aunt) is a designer of dresses.
> I love painting (usually with watercolors) on the weekends.

Think of what's in parentheses as almost a whispered aside. The material in parentheses adds a tiny bit of color or information to the sentence. These details help flesh out a thought, often by giving examples.

Ultimately, the choice between commas, dashes, or parentheses is a matter of taste. For example, some writers love dashes, while others hardly ever use them. As you read and write more, your style will emerge. Look at how other writers compose their sentences and you'll see ways you can improve your own prose.

When deciding if commas, dashes, or parentheses would work best, see which most enhance the meaning of your sentence. After that, consider variety. If a page of your writing has a half-dozen sentences with dashes, it might be time to start mixing it up with commas and parentheses.

Periods: In or Out?

One question that confuses even experienced writers is whether or not a period should go inside or outside the parentheses if the parentheses come at the end of the sentence. For some reason, this is a hard one to remember.

Here's the rule of thumb: If the material inside the parentheses is an independent clause, put the period inside the closing parenthesis, as in the following examples:

> I hate math. (It's the worst subject.)
> My uncle is a creep. (He's currently in jail.)
> Summer is the best. (I love swimming and boating.)
> My dog is fast. (He's won many races.)
> I feel sick. (My nose is running.)

If the material in parentheses is not an independent clause, put the period after the closing parenthesis, as in these examples:

> I love science fiction (especially Isaac Asimov).
> I have some strange symptoms (dizziness, odd pains).
> My doctor is handsome (and tall).

I like to swim in the lake (and ocean, when possible).

Bikers never seem to pay attention to traffic rules (especially stop signs).

Practice

In the following sentences, add the appropriate punctuation and capitalization if necessary:

1. I like tennis (it's so much fun to play)
2. My foot feels weird (and itchy)
3. My cat won't let me sleep (she always meows in the middle of the night)
4. Batman has awesome gadgets (like his batarangs)
5. Spring is coming soon (hopefully)

Answers

1. I like tennis. (It's so much fun to play.) (The period goes inside the closing parenthesis because "it's so much fun to play" is an independent clause.)
2. My foot feels weird (and itchy). (The period goes outside the closing parenthesis because "and itchy" is not an independent clause.)
3. My cat won't let me sleep. (She always meows in the middle of the night.) (The period goes inside the parenthesis because "she always meows in the middle of the night" is an independent clause.)
4. Batman has awesome gadgets (like his batarangs). (The period goes outside the parenthesis because "like his batarangs" is not an independent clause.)
5. Spring is coming soon (hopefully). (The period goes outside the parenthesis because *hopefully* is not an independent clause.)

Making Sure the Text Is Incidental

Now you know how to deal with incidental material, but how do you know if it really is incidental (in other words, nonessential)? There's an easy way to tell: pull it out of the sentence and see if you still have a complete thought:

My laptop—which is two years old—is getting slow.

My son (who is 10) has developed an annoying habit of whistling constantly.

If I had more money—much more money—I'd take a trip to Vegas.

Now let's take the material out:

> My laptop is getting slow.
> My son has developed an annoying habit of whistling constantly.
> If I had more money, I'd take a trip to Vegas.

In those cases, you're fine. The incidental material proved to be nonessential because its removal didn't result in an incomplete thought.

Using Brackets [Rarely, If Ever]

These aren't the kind of brackets that are so popular in March during the NCAA men's basketball tournament. Rather, brackets are a square friend of parentheses that are not used nearly as often.

One use of brackets is when you quote someone but need to add words for clarity. In the following examples, the material in brackets was not part of the original quotation:

> Jones wrote, "I hate it [basketball] so much. It's the worst sport."
> As the president said to the American people, "We're doomed. They [killer robots from the future] are on their way, and they're angry."
> His note said, "It [starting a Ponzi scheme] was the beginning of my downfall."

The brackets are a clear signal to readers that you're clarifying what's in the quotation but not changing the quotation.

Brackets help you find a middle way between two rules of thumb: you should always quote accurately, and you should always be clear. When an exact quotation is unclear, you're in a pickle. Using brackets to add clarifying material allows you to quote accurately while helping the reader understand what the author meant.

When it comes to quotations, using brackets is the opposite of using an ellipsis. Brackets are used to add information, like this:

> Frank said, "That so-and-so [Dave] is an evil, diabolical, demented, twisted maniac!"
> An ellipsis subtracts material from a quotation:
> Frank said, "That so-and-so is an evil … maniac!"
> Use both of these methods of quoting sparingly, since it's better to quote exactly what was said.

A word of caution: make sure the clarifying material you add is true to the source. It's dishonest to add material that changes or distorts the meaning. Only add bracketed material that will help readers understand what the writer intended.

Chapter Review Practice

Hyphens are used to make compound words such as *pre-board* and *battery-operated*. En dashes are used to indicate a range of numbers (like 2001–2005) and sometimes make compound words, like hyphens. Dashes are longer than hyphens and separate elements of a sentence—like this. Parentheses separate nonessential information from the rest of the sentence. Brackets are rarely used, but they help add information to a quotation that can make the meaning clearer.

Now let's practice what you learned in this chapter:

1. Write out the following numbers, hyphenating where necessary:
   A. 64 _____
   B. 872 _____
   C. 12 _____
   D. 3,980 _____
2. Add the appropriate punctuation to the following examples:
   A. I love sitting outside (only in the spring and summer)
   B. My dad loved the Red Sox (thank God they finally won the World Series a few times)
   C. Jamie liked to wear tall boots (especially in fall)
   D. I'm eating too many hamburgers (red meat isn't healthy)
   E. This would be a good day to go to the beach (my dog would love it)
3. Which of the following means about the same as *incidental*?
   A. Ameliorative
   B. Adjectival
   C. Nonessential
   D. Essential
4. What do brackets do to a quotation?
   A. Add information
   B. Omit information
   C. Modify information
   D. Invent information

5. Which of the following has the opposite job as brackets?
    A. Parentheses
    B. Em dashes
    C. En dashes
    D. An ellipsis

Answers

1. A. sixty-four
   B. eight hundred seventy-two
   C. twelve
   D. three thousand, nine hundred eighty
2. A. I love sitting outside (only in the spring and summer).
   B. My dad loved the Red Sox. (Thank God they finally won the World Series a few times.)
   C. Jamie liked to wear tall boots (especially in fall).
   D. I'm eating too many hamburgers. (Red meat isn't healthy.)
   E. This would be a good day to go to the beach. (My dog would love it.)
3. C
4. A
5. D

20

Spelling Rules, Tips, and Tricks

We can all sympathize with the terror of being in a spelling bee. "Spell that!" can feel like an impossible task, especially in a language with as many influences and ancestors as English.

Spelling is one of many areas where other people will judge you for mistakes. If you send an email application for a job and don't catch the spelling errors, you're not likely to get the job. Even in situations like dating, many people want nothing to do with someone who can't bother to spell words correctly. Spelling is a huge part of creating a positive impression in readers. Good spelling shows you're detail-oriented, careful, and respectful of your audience.

While spellcheckers solve a lot of spelling problems, you need a basic knowledge of the spelling rules and patterns in English. No one is a perfect speller, but with a little work and practice, you'll find spelling isn't as daunting as it seems.

Spelling Phonetically: A Challenge in English

Some languages—such as Spanish—have very consistent rules for spelling in which you can see a new word and immediately have a pretty good idea of how to pronounce it. In those languages, you can also hear a new word and have a pretty good idea how to spell it.

English isn't like that. Phonetic spelling will take you only so far: in other words, not far at all. Because English has a tangled history, involving borrowings from many languages—and more sounds than letters in the alphabet—English spelling is challenging, even to native speakers.

Buckle your seatbelts. It's time to take a closer look at English spelling.

Brushing Up on Spelling Rules

English is a tricky language to spell because for every rule, there's an exception—and usually more than one exception. However, there are some general rules you should know.

Vowel Sounds

There are two types of vowel sounds in English: long and short. The short sounds can be heard in *bat*, *bet*, *bit*, *bought*, and *but*. The long sounds can be heard in *bait*, *beet*, *bite*, *boat*, and *beaut*. Often, a short vowel sound becomes long with the addition of a final *e*, as shown in the following table.

Short Vowel	Long Vowel
bit	bite
cut	cute
din	dine
fad	fade
kit	kite
mat	mate
mop	mope
sat	sate
ton	tone
trip	tripe

Another way to spot long vowel sounds is to look out for double vowels. Double vowels are almost always long:

beep	feed	vacuum
creep	flee	

Of course, there are always exceptions. For example, the rare *aa* in *aardvark* is short, not long.

Doubling a Consonant

There's a special spelling rule for one-syllable words that end in a consonant: the final consonant gets doubled when adding a suffix:

I stop.	He's stopping.
He's fat.	I'm fatter.
She's hip.	He's hipper.

This rule does not apply to one-syllable words that end in a consonant blend:

He blends.	I blended.
You're fast.	I'm faster.
I grasp.	He grasped.

Practice

Write the present participle form of the following verbs by adding *–ing* and adjusting the spelling as needed:

1. clasp _____
2. coast _____
3. flip _____
4. stall _____
5. wade _____

Answers

1. clasping
2. coasting
3. flipping
4. stalling (Do not double the final consonant if it is doubled.)
5. wading (If the final consonant is followed by *e*, drop the *e*.)

Hard and Soft Consonants

Just as vowels can be short or long, many consonants can be soft or hard. While *b*, *m*, and others always sound the same, some consonants have two different sounds. For example, these are examples of a soft *c* sound, which sounds like an *s*:

cent	cinch	since
certain	sentence	

The following words feature the hard *c* sound, which is the same sound as a hard *k*:

apricot	caterpillar	corn
attic	cork	

G is another letter with a soft and hard sound. These words feature the soft sound:

genealogy	giant	gypsum
general	gym	

These words include the hard *g* sound:

again	goodness	great
aghast	gothic	

The *N* Sound

The letter *n* has only one sound, but that sound can be made by a few other sound blends. The following words all start with the same sound that begins *nun*, *nope*, *ninja*, and *noon*:

gnat	knife	know
gnostic	knight	pneumonia

In fact, *night* and *knight* are pronounced exactly the same way, though their meanings are pretty different. The opposite of day (*night*) is pretty different from a medieval warrior (*knight*).

Making Plurals

When making a word plural—like *words*, the plural of *word*—simply add an *s*. This is how you make the vast majority of words plural, as shown in the following table.

Singular	Plural
airplane	airplanes
basket	baskets
cat	cats
coffee	coffees
computer	computers
fire	fires
muffin	muffins
pumpkin	pumpkins

Singular	Plural
senator	senators
tangerine	tangerines

For words ending with the letters *–ch*, *–sh*, or *–s*, you need *–es* to make a plural word.

Singular	Plural
ax	axes
bass	basses
brush	brushes
crash	crashes
fax	faxes
glass	glasses
hatch	hatches
hex	hexes
latch	latches
stash	stashes

Words Ending in –Y

When you make a word ending in *–y* plural, you have to change the spelling to *–ie* in some cases.

Singular	Plural
dinghy	dinghies
puppy	puppies
symphony	symphonies
tragedy	tragedies
trophy	trophies

This rule does not apply to words that have a vowel before the final *y*. For example, the plural of *holiday* is *holidays*.

Practice

Make the following words plural:

1. bass _____
2. comedy _____
3. hitch _____
4. kitty _____
5. tax _____

Answers

1. basses
2. comedies
3. hitches
4. kitties
5. taxes

Irregular Plural Words

Many English words have an irregular plural form, which you'll have to memorize. The following table shows some of the most common irregular plural words.

Singular	Plural
child	children
foot	feet
goose	geese
man	men
matrix	matrices
mouse	mice
person	people
stratum	strata
tooth	teeth
woman	women

When Plural and Singular Are the Same

For some English words, the singular form doubles as the plural form. For example, while you could say the pond is full of fishes, you could also say the pond is full of fish. The following words have the same singular and plural forms:

aircraft	pants	species
barracks	salmon	swine
deep	scissors	
moose	sheep	

When *F* Becomes *V*

In the case of nouns that end with an *f* sound, turn the *f* into a *v* to make the plural:

Singular	Plural
elf	elves
knife	knives
life	lives
shelf	shelves
wife	wives

Exceptions to the Rules

There's no exception to the rule that there are always exceptions to the rules of English spelling. This creates challenges for anyone writing in English. You can learn every rule in the book, but there will always be words that don't fit the rules. These have to be memorized. For example, take the consonant blend *tw*. It's not that common in English, but it's used in *twaddle*, *tweet*, *twerp*, *twine*, *twist*, and *twitter*.

So what about the word *two*? The spelling of the number 2 looks like it should be pronounced with the *tw* sound, but it's not: *Two* sounds exactly like *too* and *to*. You just have to learn and memorize these exceptions. As you read, write, hear, and speak more English, it will get easier—even if it never makes total sense.

Attaching Prefixes and Suffixes

Affixes are lexical items that are attached to roots. They change the meaning of the word in some way. For example, if you add *–s* to *book*, you have *books*: more than one book.

Prefixes

Prefixes are attached to the beginning of a word. For example, the words *kilometer* and *nanometer* have the prefixes *kilo–* and *nano–*. There are many prefixes in English. For example:

> I'm super-excited for this movie.
> I prefer low-fat yogurt.
> Don't forget to pre-heat the oven.
> Stay tuned for the post-game show.
> Joe Biden was the vice president of the United States.
> My ex-husband is a jerk.
> Did you send an inter-office memo?
> I can't draw a semi-circle.
> Make sure to de-ice the car.
> In the movie, the hero fought the robo-monster.

As you can see, many prefixes are attached with a hyphen. (Look at Chapter 19 for more on hyphens.) However, this isn't always the case. Sometimes a word becomes so commonly accepted that the hyphen is no longer necessary. The prefixes in the following words all do their job without the help of a hyphen.

> The Peace Corps helps many underdeveloped countries.
> Have you heard this band? They're insane!
> I am an atheist.
> I'm sick. I need antibiotics.
> Coat hangers often become entangled.
> The United States is in the Western Hemisphere.
> Have you seen my overcoat?
> That singer is bewitching.
> I'm often unsure what to do.
> I enjoy many extracurricular activities.

Suffixes

Suffixes go on the end of words. As with prefixes, they often are attached to a word with the help of a hyphen.

>Many people are eating only gluten-free food.
>I believe all teaching should be student-centric.
>The toy is battery-operated.
>Make sure the whole house is child-proof.
>Is this restaurant family-friendly?

Even more than prefixes, it's very common for suffixes to not use a hyphen. Many of these are adjectives:

>I feel a little fluish.
>The couch is large and cumbersome.
>Hang the picture of lengthwise.
>Puppies are usually excitable.
>My sister has a theatrical background.

Others are nouns:

>My Uncle Jimmy is an alcoholic.
>Freedom is important to me.
>America is a democracy.
>In college, I studied biology.
>Do you believe in communism?

Suffixes are also attached to the back of verbs:

>I started Spanish classes today.
>Listen to the birds singing.
>Basketball players are good at running and jumping.
>My dog chased the squirrel into the tree.
>I learned to juggle in France.

Infixes

There's a far less common cousin of the prefix and suffix: the infix. While prefixes go on the front of the word, and suffixes go on the end, infixes are sandwiched in the middle. Infixes nearly always intensify the meaning of a word without adding additional meaning. Nothing intensifies like an obscenity, and many infixes are obscene, but there are a few examples we can list here.

>That movie was un-freaking-believable.
>My shirt is brand-spanking-new.
>I can't do that. It's im-bloody-possible!

How can you improve your spelling? Read, read, read. The best way to become a better speller is by becoming a better reader. The more you read, the more familiar you'll get with English spelling and quirky words. David Crystal's *Spell It Out: The Singular Story of English Spelling* is a remarkable look at the history of English spelling. Crystal puts the tangled history of spelling in context and shows the logic behind spelling that seems arbitrary. This book will help you become a better speller and more informed person about English in general.

Chapter Review Practice

Phonetic spelling will only take you so far in English, due to the many languages that have influenced English spelling. Get to know patterns in English, such as doubling the final consonant after a one syllable word that attaches a suffix (stopping, getting). Take some time to study irregular forms of words, such as *people*, a plural form of *person*. Prefixes are word parts that go on the front of the word, and suffixes go on the end. Suffixes and prefixes often, but not always, are linked to a word with hyphens.

Now let's practice what you learned in this chapter:

1. Add *–ing* to the following words:
   A. traipse _____
   B. move _____
   C. stop _____
   D. eat _____
2. Make the following words plural:
   A. matchstick _____
   B. cheese _____
   C. church _____
   D. knife _____

3. Why is English spelling so challenging?
   A. Teachers are evil.
   B. English kings are quirky.
   C. English borrows from many languages.
   D. To discourage students.
4. Why is the word *aardvark* unusual?
   A. Aardvarks are weird animals.
   B. Few words begin with *A*.
   C. Double vowels are usually a long sound.
   D. The *–vark* part is meaningless.
5. Over time, prefixes and suffixes tend to lose what?
   A. Their meaning
   B. Their pronunciation
   C. Their hyphens
   D. Their spelling
6. The infix is highly associated with what?
   A. Confusion
   B. Clarity
   C. Obscenity
   D. Plagiarism

Answers

1. A. traipsing
   B. moving
   C. stopping
   D. eating
2. A. matchsticks
   B. cheeses
   C. churches
   D. knives
3. C
4. C
5. C
6. C

21

Capitalization, Abbreviations, and Numbers

There are many choices available to writers in terms of sentence style, grammar, word choice, and punctuation. There is one final choice too: how to write a letter.

Understanding Capitalization

There are two ways to write letters in English: uppercase (ABC) and lowercase (abc). Uppercase letters are also called capital letters, and when you start a word with a capital letter, you're capitalizing it. Many situations in English demand capitalization, such as the beginning of a sentence or a proper noun, like *English*. There are also many ways to improperly capitalize.

FOR EXAMPLE, DOES THIS LOOK WEIRD?

how about this?

NoTice anyTHing oUt of wHacK heRe?

Using too many or not enough capital letters can cause confusion or annoyance in readers. Therefore, it's important to get a handle on the rules of capitalization, which are one of the most consistent areas of English. Once you get to know when and why to capitalize, you'll be prepared for most writing situations.

Capitalizing the First Word of Sentences and Quotations

One of the primary uses of capital letters is for the beginning of sentences. As you'll notice when looking at sentences—including this sentence—the first letter of the first word is capitalized. This is a signal to readers that a new sentence (and new thought) is beginning.

Also, the first word of a quotation is capitalized if the original was capitalized.

> Shakespeare wrote, "Something is rotten in the state of Denmark."

An Independent Clause Following a Colon

An independent clause that follows a colon is often capitalized:

> I followed my dreams: Fortunately, my dreams led to great things.

This is a judgment call, and you could punctuate the same sentence without capitalizing after the colon. The same judgement call applies to questions after a colon. You can either capitalize or not. Both of the following are okay:

> I have one question for you: Where did you get that jacket?
> I have one question for you: where did you get that jacket?

Capitalizing Proper Nouns and Adjectives

Another of the main uses of capital letters is for proper names. Capitalization distinguishes a proper noun (like *Joe*) from other nouns that are more general (like *guy*). Proper nouns can be people, places, or things.

> My brother's name is Albert.
> Susan and Jen went to dinner.
> I am from Buffalo, New York.
> Man, I would love to visit Australia.
> My computer is an Apple.

This includes the names of businesses and organizations:

> I work for Pepsi.
> Mark Zuckerberg founded Facebook.
> I am an ambassador to the United Nations.
> The legislative body of the United States is Congress.
> I'm a member of the Lakeview Book Club.

Even if the company or group uses all lowercase letters in their official name or logo, you should capitalize their name when you write it.

Nationalities, Races, and Religions

There are many kinds of proper nouns besides people and places. Religion and nationality give us many words that must be capitalized, such as *Canada*, *Muslim*, and *New Zealand*. Always capitalize the names of religions, races, and nationalities.

> My teacher was Jewish.
> The Pope is the leader of the Catholic Church.
> I think Mexican food is delicious.
> My teacher is African American.

Specific Places, Things, or Events

Some events are so historically important that they are capitalized:

> There are several museums dedicated to the Holocaust.
> The French Revolution changed world history.
> Brewing went underground in the United States during Prohibition.

Practice

1. Which of the following things is capitalized?
   A. People
   B. Places
   C. Nationalities
   D. Major historical events
2. Nouns that are always capitalized are called:
   A. Capital nouns
   B. Special nouns
   C. Proper nouns
   D. Significant nouns

Answers

1. All of these
2. C

Capitalizing *I*

One of the conventions of English spelling is that *I* is capitalized when it's used as a first-person pronoun:

> I hate when you show up late!
> Did you remember what I told you?
> I fell off the porch and broke my collarbone.
> What do I look like?
> I'm going to get you!

Sometimes when writing emails, texts, or tweets, people don't capitalize *I* and write like this:

> i like you!
> where should i go?
> i'm sleepy.

This may be acceptable in extremely informal messages to friends—and sometimes in poetry—but you should never forget to capitalize *I* in any writing that is public or written for anyone you might to impress. Using lowercase *i* is the writing equivalent of coming to a business meeting wearing ripped jeans and a shirt with mustard stains on it. It sends the wrong message and will make people think you're sloppy, ignorant, or just not smart.

Other First-Person Pronouns Are Not Capitalized

Though *me* and *myself* mean the same thing as *I*, they should not be capitalized:

> Don't you recognize me?
> Do I have to do everything myself?
> Kids today are always thinking, "me me me …."
> Sometimes I hate myself.
> You make me proud.

Also, note that the opposite of *I*—the word *you*—is not capitalized.

Capitalizing Titles

Titles are capitalized, too. This includes the titles of movies, TV shows, books, record albums, and other creations:

I loved *Iron Man 3* and *Star Trek: Into Darkness*.
Have you read *To Kill a Mockingbird*?
The best Sonic Youth album is *Daydream Nation*.
I once saw Kenneth Branagh play the lead in *Hamlet* in London.
The Book of Mormon is a musical by the creators of *South Park*.

Also, headlines and titles of articles are capitalized, though there are several ways to do it. The format varies, as you'll see in different magazines, journals, newspapers, and internet publications.

In some formats, only the very first word of the title is capitalized:

The mayor is caught embezzling
Study shows coffee cures the common cold
Dog rescues his owner

Other formats capitalize every single word:

The Mayor Is Caught Embezzling
Study Shows Coffee Cures The Common Cold
Dog Rescues His Owner

Many formats capitalize every important word, neglecting only the shortest and least significant words:

The Mayor is Caught Embezzling
Study Shows Coffee Cures the Common Cold
Dog Rescues his Owner

One of the trickiest elements of capitalizing is when different rules seem to contradict each other. You can resolve possible conflicts by following the rule that's most powerful, either overall or in that situation.

For example, names are always capitalized. So even if you're following a format where only the first word of a headline is capitalized, you still need to capitalize a name:

President meets Madonna
Fans mob Tim Duncan
Who really wrote Shakespeare's plays?
Was Emily Dickinson a vampire?

The personal pronoun *I* is always capitalized, but *myself* is not capitalized. However, *myself* would be capitalized in the title of a book, for example.

> *I Did It Myself: A Selfish Story*
> *From Myself to Yourself: Making a Connection*
> *Drinking Myself to Death: A Drunkard's Tale*
> *Myself, Me, and I: Pronouns of the Self*

In writing, there are very few rules that are followed 100 percent of the time. You have to examine the situation, think about your audience and purpose, and decide what makes sense. The more you read and write, the better your judgment will be.

Personal Titles Are Sometimes Capitalized

A person's title is capitalized if it's part of their name, as in these examples:

> I'd love to meet President Barack Obama.
> Where is Congressman Wilson?
> Is Mayor Bloomberg vegan?
> Editor-in-Chief Jameson is strict.

In those cases, the titles are part of the person's name. Since names are always capitalized, you should capitalize the titles, too. You don't need to capitalize a title that comes after the name:

> Jameson, the editor-in-chief, is strict.
> Bloomberg, the mayor, is in the gazebo.
> Wilson, a congressman, has no morals.
> Barack Obama was elected president in 2008.

You can capitalize some familial words if they're being used as proper nouns. The following are correct:

> Hey Dad, what are you doing?
> I need to get off the phone, Mom.
> Where's Uncle Fred?

These are also correct:

> My mom likes to leave voicemails.
> I wish my dad had more money.
> Is my aunt around?

This is the rule: if you refer to your mom or dad as a mom or dad (almost like you'd refer to a banker, quarterback, or editor) then you don't capitalize them. If you refer to them directly—using *Mom* or *Dad* as a name—then you should capitalize them.

Words Referring to God

Names that refer to God or any other deity are capitalized, too:

> I've been praying to God for a new car.
> Please help me, Jesus.
> The Scandinavian people used to worship Odin.
> By the beard of Zeus, my head hurts!

You don't capitalize *god* if you're simply referring to a god or gods, as in the following examples:

> The ancient Greeks worshipped many gods, such as Apollo.
> Thor is the only god who became a major superhero.
> Christians consider Jesus half-human, half-god.
> Athena was a goddess.

Practice

1. Whose names are always capitalized?
   A. People
   B. Pets
   C. Gods
   D. All of these
2. In which of the following does capitalization vary from publication to publication?
   A. Headlines
   B. Introductions
   C. Classified ads
   D. Photo descriptions

Answers

1. D
2. A

Working with Abbreviations

An abbreviation is a shortening of a word or group of words, either by removing letters or using only the first initials of all or some of the words. Abbreviations are used when it would look or sound clumsy to write something long over and over.

Many types of abbreviations are not capitalized. For example, if you wrote *dept.* to abbreviate *department*, you don't need to capitalize it. (Unless it's part of a proper name, like the Arts Dept.)

The following table shows a few common abbreviations.

Abbreviation	Term
Ave.	avenue
Dr.	doctor
E.	east
fridge	refrigerator
plane	airplane
pres.	president
prof	professor
sec	second
US	United States
W.	west

An acronym is a type of abbreviation that is capitalized; in fact, acronyms use all capital letters. Acronyms are also pronounced like a regular word. The following table shows some common acronyms.

Acronym	Term
AIDS	acquired immune deficiency syndrome
FEMA	Federal Emergency Management Agency
NASA	National Aeronautics and Space Administration
POTUS	President of the United States
SIDS	sudden infant death syndrome

Other acronyms abbreviate phrases.

Acronym	Phrase
ASAP	as soon as possible
FAQ	frequently asked questions
FOMO	fear of missing out
NIMBY	not in my backyard
YOLO	you only live once

Acronyms have a close relation: the initialism. Initialisms also use all capital letters, but they have one difference: initialisms are not pronounced like a regular word. You have to spell initialisms out when you say them. You have to say every initial.

Initialism	Term
CEO	chief executive officer
CIA	Central Intelligence Agency
IED	improvised explosive device
MRI	magnetic resonance imaging
NFL	National Football League

Like acronyms, some initialisms abbreviate phrases.

Initialism	Phrase
BYOB	bring your own booze
MIA	missing in action
OMG	oh my God
PDA	public display of affection
RIP	rest in peace

Practice

Identify which of the following are acronyms, initialisms, or just plain abbreviations?

1. I enjoy TV, movies, etc.
2. Are you a fan of the NHL?
3. Want to go scuba diving?
4. I was born Jan. 11, 1981.
5. Could you send me that file as a gif?

Answers

1. Abbreviation: *Etc.* is a shortening of *etcetera*, and TV is a shortening of *television*.
2. Initialism: NHL stands for National Hockey League and is pronounced one letter at a time.
3. Acronym: Scuba stands for self-contained underwater breathing apparatus and is pronounced as a regular word.
4. Abbreviation: *Jan.* is a shortening of *January*.
5. Acronym: gif stands for graphics interchange format and is pronounced as a regular word.

Working with Numbers, Dates, and Times

Even if you prefer English class to math class, you're still going to have to deal with numbers. Fortunately, there are only a few ways of writing numbers. For the first nine numbers and zero, write them out as a word: zero, one, two, three, etc. For larger numbers, use the numerals: 10, 15, 67, 114, etc. When writing numbers that are four digits or more, add a comma every three digits starting from the right-hand side: 1,000, 400,000,000, 481,878,231,000,000, etc.

There will often be exceptions to these rules, depending on the style guide you're using. You might sometimes have to write ten thousand instead of 10,000. As always, follow the appropriate rules for your writing situation.

When writing a date, you need to use commas on both sides of the year:

> On January 14, 1987, I was married.
> Is August 5, 1971, your birthday?
> December 18, 1999, was the worst day of my life.

Times are written with a colon, and often followed by *A.M.* or *P.M.*:

> Where were you at 3:00 P.M.?
> I keep waking up at 2:30 in the morning.
> 9 A.M. is the starting time for my job.

Watch for redundancy when speaking or writing times. You should say "10 A.M." or "10 in the morning," not "10 A.M. in the morning."

Chapter Review Practice

Capitalize proper names: the names of specific people, places, religions, and works of art. Abbreviations are a type of shorthand, like writing Dr. Miller instead of Doctor Miller. Acronyms like POTUS are pronounced as a word; initialisms like CIA are pronounced by spelling letter by letter. In general, write out single-digit numbers such as nine and use numerals for numbers of two or more digits such as 17 and 861.

Now let's practice what you learned in this chapter:

1. Which is not true about acronyms?
   A. They're abbreviations.
   B. They're all capital letters.
   C. They're pronounced like a word.
   D. They're passive voice.
2. Which of the following is correct?
   A. My Mom loves to leave voicemail messages.
   B. Where's your Dad?
   C. Hi, mom!
   D. Can we change the channel, Dad?

3. Identify the following as acronyms, initialisms, or abbreviations:
   A. Capt. _____
   B. ASAP _____
   C. NASA _____
   D. MVP _____

Answers

1. D
2. D
3. A. Abbreviation
   B. Acronym
   C. Acronym
   D. Initialism

A

Glossary

adjective   A word that modifies nouns.

adverb   A word that modifies verbs, adjectives, and other adverbs.

affix   An element attached to the beginning, middle, or end of a root or word that modifies its meaning. Affixes include prefixes, infixes, and suffixes.

agreement   The condition when parts of a sentence have the same case, gender, number, or person.

analogy   A comparison between two different entities or processes, usually based on a similarity between the two.

antecedent   The referent of a pronoun—the noun to which it refers.

appositive   A grammatical construction that puts a subject or object in different words. Appositives rename.

auxiliary verb   These include forms of *be*, *do*, and *has*. Auxiliary verbs add meaning to other verbs in some forms, such as "I had been studying." In that sentence, *had* and *been* are auxiliary verbs.

bias-free language   Language that is offensive or insensitive to any gender, race, religion, or sexuality.

case   How a noun or pronoun functions in a sentence. The case is different if a noun or pronoun is used as subject, object, or appositive.

clause   A group of words with a subject and a predicate.

cliché   A worn-out, overused word or expression that has become almost meaningless.

collective noun   A singular noun that also functions as a plural, such as *people*.

comparative   A word such as *better*, *bigger*, *faster*, or *taller*.

complete sentence   A group of words that has a subject and predicate and expresses a complete thought.

complex sentence A sentence with an independent clause and a dependent clause.

compound sentence A sentence with two independent clauses.

compound-complex sentence A sentence with two independent clauses and at least one dependent clause.

conjugate To show or produce the different forms of a verb.

conjunction A word used to connect other clauses, phrases, or words—two common conjunctions are *and* and *but*.

connotation The flavor or undertones of a word—the associations of a word. Connotation isn't the explicit meaning, which is denotation.

contraction A shortened version of a word or words, like *don't* (do not) and *can't* (cannot).

dangling modifier A word or phrase that modifies an entity other than the subject of the sentence. This error causes confusion.

demonstrative A word that points to or stands for another. In English, the demonstratives are *this*, *that*, *these*, and *those*. Demonstratives can act as either adjectives or pronouns.

denotation The literal meaning of a word, as opposed to the connotation, which consists of the associations of a word.

dependent clause A group of words that has a subject and predicate but cannot stand on its own as a sentence.

diction Word choice. This is why a word book is called a dictionary.

direct object The entity acted upon by the subject of a sentence.

elliptical clause A clause with some words eliminated for the sake of the sentence's sound. An elliptical clause is acceptable if it makes sense to readers.

euphemism A softer, vaguer word for something, like saying employees were downsized instead of fired.

exclamation A word or sentence with great emphasis, usually punctuated with an exclamation mark, such as "Hey!" or "My foot hurts!"

gerund The *–ing* form of a verb used as a noun, as in "Swimming is fun."

grammar The total structure of a language, including syntax and morphology.

imperative A command, such as "Give me that!" or "Help me move this couch." The implied subject of an imperative is *you*.

imperfect The verb form for an action that's still happening but isn't finished.

indefinite pronoun   A pronoun without a specific antecedent, such as *who*, *whom*, and *that*.

independent clause   A group of words with a subject and predicate that can stand on their own as a sentence. An independent clause is a complete thought.

indicative   A verb mood that states or declares something. "I am hungry" and "Squirrels are gross" are in the indicative mood.

indirect object   An entity affected by the action of the sentence. The indirect object is *Jim* in this sentence: "I threw the ball to Jim."

infinitive   The form of a verb that includes *to*, such as *to eat* and *to defend*.

infix   An affix that is inserted into the middle of a word.

interjection   A word, usually short, that expresses an emotion. Interjections are often used as sentences in themselves. They include *mmm*, *ow*, *hey*, *uh*, and *yep*.

interrogative   A question or any form of a word related to questions.

interrogative pronoun   A pronoun such as *how*, *what*, *when*, *where*, *who*, and *why*. These pronouns are often used in questions.

intransitive verb   An intransitive verb can be used alone, with no object or complement, unlike a transitive verb, which must be done to someone or something. In "I stood," *stood* is an intransitive verb.

irony   A literary device that involves saying the opposite of what you mean, often for the sake of humor.

jargon   The language of a profession. This word can also refer to empty, pretentious language.

linking verb   A verb used to convey a state of being—the most common linking verb is *be*.

mechanics   The nuts and bolts of language, especially areas such as formatting and punctuation.

metaphor   A comparison that does not involve *like* or *as*, such as calling a crowd a swarm of people.

misplaced modifier   When a modifier is placed too far away from the word it should be modifying, creating confusion.

mixed metaphor   A metaphor that is inconsistent, like if you were comparing love to an ocean, and then suddenly the comparison shifted to a sandwich.

modifier   A word, phrase, or clause that changes the meaning of other words, often by describing them. Grammatically, modifiers are optional.

mood   A feature of verbs that signals the speaker's point of view or attitude. In English, the moods are indicative, imperative, and subjunctive.

noun   Not just persons, places, and things, nouns are also states of being and conditions. Nouns serve as subjects, objects, and direct objects in sentences.

object   The entity acted upon by the subject of the sentence.

parallel structure   When parts of a sentence have the same form, especially in a series.

participle   A verb used as an adjective, as in *screaming maniac* and *stalled car*.

phrase   A group of words with a specific function but lacking a subject and predicate.

possessive   The form of a word that indicates it belongs to another word. Many possessive words are created with the apostrophe and *s*.

possessive adjective   Adjectives such as *his*, *her*, *my*, *your*, *our*, *their*, and *its*. These convey a relationship of ownership or belonging.

possessive pronoun   A pronoun that indicates what belongs to someone, such as *his*, *her*, or *their*.

predicate   The second half—and second essential part—of a sentence. (The first is the subject.) The predicate, which starts with a verb and sometimes only consists of a verb, tells what the subject does or is.

prefix   An affix that is attached to the beginning of a root.

preposition   A word signifying a relationship between other words, such as *between*, *of*, *on*, and *for*.

pronoun   A word used in place of another noun, such as referring to a man as *he* or a group of people as *them*.

punctuation   Marks such as commas, periods, and quotation marks that help convey meaning in writing.

redundancy   A repetitive quality in writing when the same information appears more than once while adding no additional meaning.

reflexive pronoun   A pronoun used when the subject performs an action on the subject—these include *myself*, *yourself*, *himself*, *herself*, *ourselves*, and *themselves*. For example, "I hurt myself."

relative clause   A dependent clause that modifies another element in a sentence. Also called an adjective clause.

relative pronoun   A pronoun such as *that*, *who*, *what*, *whatever*, *whom*, or *whomever*. Relative pronouns introduce relative clauses.

root   The smallest form of a word with meaning; *small* and *mean* are roots.

run-on sentence   An ungrammatical sentence in which two or more independent clauses are put together incorrectly.

sentence   A group of words that express a complete thought, usually consisting of a subject and predicate. A sentence can be a statement, question, or command (imperative).

sentence fragment   A group of words that does not comprise a complete thought. A sentence fragment is usually considered an error.

sexist language   Use of language that is insulting or unfair in some way toward women.

simile   A comparison using the words *like* or *as*.

simple sentence   A sentence consisting of one independent clause.

slang   Informal, humorous language that binds a social group.

split infinitive   When a word comes between the two parts of an infinitive, as in the famous example of *Star Trek*'s "To boldly go …"

style   A distinctive way of using language, such as the style of a magazine or an individual writer.

subject   The main actor of a sentence. The subject performs the action of a sentence.

subjunctive   A verb mood that expresses wishes and possibilities, such as "If I were you, I'd be careful," and "You should be home by 8:00."

subordinate clause   A clause that adds meaning to an independent clause but cannot stand on its own as a grammatical sentence. Also called a *dependent clause*.

suffix   An affix that is attached to the end of a word.

superlative   A word such as *fastest* or *greatest* that compares more than two things.

syntax   The way words, phases, and clauses are arranged in a language.

tense   The forms of a verb that indicate when an action occurs, such as past, present, or future. There are also several more complex tenses under the umbrellas of perfect and progressive.

tone   The level of emotion or formality in a piece of writing. Love letters have a romantic tone, while letters of application have a formal tone.

transitive verb   A verb that must have an object or complement to be used correctly. For example, you can't just schedule—you have to schedule a meeting.

usage   How a word is actually used in a language. This also refers to usage levels, which have different levels of formality.

verb   A word that conveys action or a state or being. Verbs make subjects active.

verbal A word derived from a verb but used as another part of speech.

voice Whether a sentence is active or passive. In active voice, the subject performs the action, and in passive voice, the subject is hidden or absent.

Resources

Books

Aarts, Bas. *Oxford Modern English Grammar*. New York: Oxford University Press, 2011.

Adams, Michael. *Slang: The People's Poetry*. New York: Oxford University Press, 2009.

Birchard, Bill. *Writing for Impact: 8 Secrets from Science That Will Fire Up Your Readers' Brains*. New York: HarperCollins, 2023.

Casagrande, June. *Grammar Snobs Are Great Big Meanies: A Guide to Language for Fun and Spite*. New York: Penguin, 2006.

———. *It Was the Best of Sentences, It Was the Worst of Sentences: A Writer's Guide to Crafting Killer Sentences*. New York: Ten Speed Press, 2010.

The Chicago Manual of Style, 18th Edition. Chicago: University of Chicago Press, 2024.

Clark, Roy Peter. *Writing Tools: 50 Essential Strategies for Every Writer*. New York: Little, Brown & Co., 2008.

Crystal, David. *Spell It Out: The Story of English Spelling*. London: Profile Books, 2013.

———. *The Story of English in 100 Words*. New York: Picador, 2013.

Dryer, Benjamin. *Dreyer's English: An Utterly Correct Guide to Clarity and Style*. New York: Random House, 2020.

Fogarty, Mignon. *Grammar Girl's 101 Misused Words You'll Never Confuse Again*. New York: St. Martin's Griffin, 2011.

———. *Grammar Girl's Quick and Dirty Tips for Better Writing (Quick & Dirty Tips)*. New York: Holt Paperbacks, 2008.

Goldberg, Natalie. *Writing Down the Bones: Freeing the Writer Within*. Boston: Shambhala, 2005.

Gordon, Karen Elizabeth. *The Deluxe Transitive Vampire: The Ultimate Handbook of Grammar for the Innocent, the Eager, and the Doomed*. New York: Pantheon, 1993.

Greene, Robert Lane. *You Are What You Speak: Grammar Grouches, Language Laws, and the Politics of Identity*. New York: Delacorte Press, 2011.

Hacker, Diana, and Nancy Sommers. *A Writer's Reference with Writing in the Disciplines*. New York: Bedford/St. Martin's, 2011.

Hale, Constance. *Sin and Syntax: How to Craft Wickedly Effective Prose*. New York: Broadway Books, 2001.

King, Stephen. *On Writing: 10th Anniversary Edition: A Memoir of the Craft*. New York: Scribner, 2010.

Klinkenborg, Verlyn. *Several Short Sentences About Writing*. New York: Vintage, 2013.

Lammot, Anne. *Bird by Bird: Some Instructions on Writing and Life*. New York: Anchor, 1995.

Lanham, Richard A. *Revising Prose, Fifth Edition*. New York: Longman, 2006.

Liberman, Mark, and Geoffrey K. Pullum. *Far From the Madding Gerund and Other Dispatches from Language Log*. New York: William, James & Company, 2006.

McCann, Colum. *Letters to a Young Writer: Some Practical and Philosophical Advice*. New York: Random House, 2017.

Miller, Brenda. *Tell It Slant, Second Edition*. New York: McGraw-Hill, 2012.

MLA Handbook for Writers of Research Papers, Seventh Edition. New York: Modern Language Association, 2009.

O'Conner, Patricia T. *Woe Is I: The Grammarphobe's Guide to Better English in Plain English*. New York: Riverhead Books, 2019.

Pinker, Stephen. *The Sense of Style: The Thinking Person's Guide to Writing in the 21st Century*. New York: Penguin Books, 2015.

Publication Manual of the American Psychological Association, Seventh Edition. Washington, DC: American Psychological Association, 2019.

Pullum, Geoffrey. *The Great Eskimo Vocabulary Hoax*. Chicago: University Of Chicago Press, 1991.

Stamper, Kory. *Word by Word: The Secret Life of Dictionaries*. New York: Vintage, 2018.

Strunk Jr., William, with E. B. White and Roger Angell. *The Elements of Style, Fourth Edition*. New York: Longman, 1999.

Thurman, Susan, and Larry Shea. *The Only Grammar Book You'll Ever Need: A One-Stop Source for Every Writing Assignment*. Avon, MA: Adams Media, 2003.

Trimble, John R. *Writing with Style: Conversations on the Art of Writing, 3rd Edition*. New York: Longman, 2010.

Walsh, Bill. *The Elephants of Style: A Trunkload of Tips on the Big Issues and Gray Areas of Contemporary American English*. New York: McGraw-Hill, 2004.

———. *Yes, I Could Care Less: How to Be a Language Snob Without Being a Jerk*. New York: St. Martin's Griffin, 2013.

Williams, Joseph M., and Gregory G. Colomb. *Style: Lessons in Clarity and Grace, 10th Edition*. New York: Longman, 2010.

Yagoda, Ben. *How to Not Write Bad: The Most Common Writing Problems and the Best Ways to Avoid Them*. New York: Riverhead Trade, 2013.

Zinsser, William. *On Writing Well, 30th Anniversary Edition: The Classic Guide to Writing Nonfiction*. New York: HarperPerennial, 2006.

Websites

Dictionary of American Regional English
dare.wisc.edu
This website contains samples from and news on DARE, which collects Americanisms that are not used across the entire country.

Grammar Girl
quickanddirtytips.com/grammar-girl
This website contains helpful advice on grammar written in an accessible, enjoyable style.

Green's Dictionary of Slang
greensdictofslang.com
The largest slang dictionary in the world.

Language Log
languagelog.ldc.upenn.edu/nll
Professional linguists discuss a variety of language-related topics.

Merriam-Webster
merriam-webster.com
The most trusted and authoritative general-use dictionary.

OWL (Online Writing Lab)
owl.english.purdue.edu/owl
Though aimed at undergraduate students, there's help available for anyone on grammar, style, and citation formats.

Oxford English Dictionary
oed.com
The largest dictionary in the world, this is the ultimate authority on the history of the English language.

Index

A

abbreviations, 15, 322–323
absolutes, 257–258
acronyms, 322–323
action verbs, 45–46
actions, adverbs and, 141
active voice, 30, 123
addresses, commas, 270
adjective clauses, 77, 173–174
adjective phrases, complements, 148
adjectives, 50, 129–130. *See also* articles
   adverbs, transforming, 141
   capitalization, 316
   commas, 267
   common, 131
   comparisons and, 137
   complements, 149
   compound, 131–132, 293–294
   described by adverbs, 142
   indefinite, 133
   predicate adjectives, 51
   prepositional phrases as, 158
   proper, 131
   selecting, 135–136
   syntax and, 13
   to be and, 135
   when not to use, 138
adverb clauses, 77, 175

adverbs, 52
   actions and, 141
   adjectives, transforming from, 141
   as conjunctions, 143
   conjunctive adverbs, 80
   describing adjectives, 142
   describing adverbs, 142
   prepositional phrases as, 158
advertising copy writing, 27
ageism in language, 254
alliteration, 32
allusion, 32
American Psychological Association (APA), 187
antecedents, 242
   pronouns, 41, 90
      agreement, 91
apostrophes
   contractions, 288–289
   indefinite pronouns, 285
   money-related words, 287
   plural nouns ending in –s, 284
   plurals, converting to, 287–288
   possessives, 284
      dual possession, 285
appositives, 73, 162–163
argument, 188
articles, 51
   definite, 51, 139
   indefinite, 51, 139

article writing
- magazine articles, 27
- news articles, 26
- scholarly journals, 27

assonance, 32

A Writer's Reference (Hacker), 187

B

biases in language
- ageism, 254
- disabilities, 255
- ethnic, 253–254
- gender, 247–251
- gender identity, 254–255
- generalizations, 252–253
- medical conditions, 255
- politically correct (PC), 253
- racial bias, 253–254
- sexual orientation, 254–255

blog posts, 28

brackets, 299–300

business writing, 26

C

capitalization, 15
- adjectives, 316
- deities, 321
- first word, 315
- independent clause following colon, 316
- pronouns, first person, 318
- proper nouns, 39, 316
  - events, 317–318
  - nationalities, 317
  - places, 317
  - races, 317
  - religions, 317
- titles, 318–320
  - personal titles, 320

case
- objective, 44
- possessive, 44
- subjective, 44

Chicago Manual of Style, The (CMS), 187

citing sources, 196

clarifying statements, dashes, 296

clarity
- clauses, 176
- in writing, 183–184
- phrases, 164

clauses, 54
- adjective, 173–174
- adverb, 175
- arranging/rearranging, 176
- comma splices, 239–240
- dependent (subordinate), 76, 156, 170–171
  - adjective, 77
  - adverb, 77
  - elliptical, 78
  - infinitive, 78
  - nonrestrictive, 77
  - noun, 77
  - restrictive, 77
- independent, 76, 156, 169
  - capitalization, 316
  - colons, 274
  - commas, 267–268
  - coordination, 241
  - semicolons, 271–272
  - subordination, 241
- nonessential, commas, 268
- noun, 172–173
- placement, 17–18
- subordinate, 173, 241
- versus phrases, 156–157

clear writing, 183–184

clichés, 206–208

Index 339

collective nouns, 40
   subject-verb agreement, 120
colons, 275–276
   formal statement, 274
   independent clauses, 274
   lists, 274
   long quotations, 274
comedy writing, 28
commands, subject omission, 89
comma splices, 239–240
commas
   addresses, 270
   adjectives, 267
   compound sentences, 80
   dates, 270
   direct quotations, 270
   independent clauses, 267–268
   introductory elements, 268–269
   items in a series, 266
   misplaced, 20
   nonessential clauses, 268
   numbers, 270
   omitted, 20
   serial commas, 20
common adjectives, 131
common nouns, 39
communication, conventions and, 16, 22
comparisons
   adjectives and, 137
   parallelism in, 222
compelling writing, 185
complements, 69
   adjective phrases, 148
   direct objects, 69
   indirect objects, 69
   noun phrases, 148
   object complements, 70, 148–149
   subject complements, 147–148
      predicate adjective, 70
      predicate nominative, 70
   verb complements
      gerunds, 150
      infinitives, 150
      noun phrases, 151
completeness in writing, 191
complete predicate, 66
complex sentences, 80
compound adjectives, 131–132, 293–294
compound nouns, 40
compound numbers, 292
compound sentences, 80
   commas, 80
   conjunctions, 80
   conjunctive adverbs, 80
   semicolons, 80
compound subjects, subject-verb agreement, 119
compound/complex sentences, 81
conciseness in writing, 189
conjunctions
   adverbs as, 143
   combining short sentences, 226
   compound sentences, 80
   coordinating, 54–55
      parallelism, 221
   correlative, 56
      parallelism, 222–223
conjunctive adverbs, 80
connotation, 204
consistency in writing, 186–188
consonance, 32
consonants
   double, 304
   hard/soft, 305
contractions, 288–289

conventions
   abbreviations, 15
   capitalization, 15
   clause placement, 17–18
   comma usage, 20
   communication and, 16, 22
   dangling modifiers, 19
   numbers, 15
   parallel construction, 21
   phrase placement, 17–18
   punctuation, 15
   spelling, 15
   syntax, 16
   verb tense, 18–19
convincing writing, 189
coordinate clauses, 54
coordinating conjunctions, 54–55
   parallelism, 221
coordination, 241
correctness in writing, 191–192
correlative conjunctions, 56
   parallelism, 222–223
creative writing, 27

D

dangling modifiers, 19, 243
dashes
   clarifying statements, 296
   incidental (nonessential) text, 296–297
   numbers, 295–296
dates
   commas, 270
   writing, 324
definite articles, 51, 139
deities, capitalization, 321
demonstrative pronouns, 42
denotation, 204

dependent (subordinate) clauses, 76, 156, 170–171
   adjective, 77
   adverb, 77
   elliptical, 78
   infinitive, 78
   nonrestrictive, 77
   noun, 77
   restrictive, 77
descriptive nature of grammar, 12
diction
   clichés, 206–208
   connotation, 204
   denotation, 204
   dictionaries, 201
   double negatives, 205
   eggcorns, 211
   euphemisms, 208
   jargon, 210
   reading with dictionaries, 203
   slang, 209–210
   thesauruses, 202
   word choice, 203
diction consistency, 187
dictionaries, 201
   reading with, 203
direct objects, 69
double consonants, 304
double negatives, 205

E

editorial writing, 26
eggcorns, 211
elliptical clauses, 78
emphasis
   clauses, 176
   phrases, 164
error-free writing, 190

essay writing, 27
ethnic biases in language, 253–254
euphemisms, 208
events, capitalization, 317
evidence of claims, 258
exaggeration in writing, 190
exclamation points, 265
expletive expressions, 94–95

F

facts in writing, 190
figurative language, 32
first-person pronouns, capitalization, 318
flow of writing, 29
formal statements, 274
format consistency, 187
fragmented sentences, 237–238
    positive aspects, 238
future perfect progressive tense, 116
future perfect tense, 113
future progressive tense verbs, 107

G

gender
    nongendered nouns, 248–249
    pronouns and, 93
gender equality in language, 247–248
gender identity, 254–255
gender neutrality in language, 248–249
    pronouns, 249–251
general-use dictionaries, 202
generalizations, 190, 257–258
gerunds, 21, 40, 73–74, 160
    as subject, 160–161
    verb complements, 150
grammar, 11
    consistency, 186
    descriptive, 12
    prescriptive, 12

grammatical correctness, 191
grant writing, 28

H

helping verbs, 45, 48
historical dictionaries, 201
humor in writing, 185
hyperbole, 32
hyphens
    compound adjectives, 293–294
    compound numbers, 292
    end-of-line, 291
    prefixes, 293

I

I, capitalization, 318
idioms, 32
imperative mood, 122
incidental material, 298
incidental (nonessential) text, dashes, 296–297
indefinite adjectives, 133
indefinite articles, 51, 139
indefinite pronouns, 42, 120
    apostrophes, 285
    subject-verb agreement, 120
independent clauses, 76, 156, 169
    colons, 274
    capitalization, 316
    comma splices, 239–240
    commas, 267–268
    coordination, 241
    semicolons, 271–272
    subordination, 241
indicative mood, 122
indirect objects, 69
infinitives, 161
    bare, 74
    clauses, 78

verb complements, 150
verbs, 49, 102
inflection, verbs, 45
initialisms, 323
intensive pronouns, 42
interjections, 60–61
interrogative pronouns, 42, 88
intransitive verbs, 48
introductory elements, commas, 268–269
irregular verbs, 103–106
items in a series, semicolons, 273

J–K

jargon, 210
journalism, column writing, 26

L

lie vs. *lay*, 117
linking verbs, 45–47
lists, colons, 274
literary devices, 31–33

M

magazine articles, 27
mechanics, 11
    abbreviations, 15
    capitalization, 15
    numbers, 15
    punctuation, 15
    spelling, 15
metaphors, 32
misplaced modifiers, 243
Modern Language Association (MLA), 187
modifiers
    dangling, 19
    misplaced, 243
mood, 122
morphology, 12
    morphemes, 12

N

n sound, 306
nationalities, 317
news articles, 26
nonessential clauses, commas, 268
nonessential material, 298
nonrestrictive clauses, 77
noun clauses, 77, 172–173
noun phrases
    complements, 148
    verb complements, 151
noun-verb agreement, 118
    collective nouns, 120
    compound subjects, 119
    indefinite pronouns, singular, 120
    singular and plural forms, 121
nouns
    appositives and, 162–163
    case, 44–45
    collective, 40, 120
    common, 39
    compound, 40
    form changes, 43
    gerunds and, 40, 160
    nongendered, 248–249
    object complements, 149
    plurals, 284, 309
    prepositions and, 58–59
    proper, 39
        capitalization, 316–318
    starting sentences, 87–90
        plural subject, 88
numbers, 15
    commas, 270
    compound, 292

dashes, 295–296
writing, 324

O

object complements, 70, 148–149
object questions, 88
objective case, 44
objective personal pronouns, 41–42
onomatopoeia, 32
outlines, 184
Oxford comma, 266

P

paradox, 32
parallelism, 21–22
   comparing items, 222
   coordinating conjunctions, 221
   correlative conjunctions, 222–223
   prepositional phrases, 219
   résumés, 220–221
   series, 217–218
paraphrasing, 194–195
parentheses
   periods, 297–298
participles, 74, 160
   past, 74
   present, 74
parts of speech. *See also specific parts of speech*
   adjectives, 50
   adverbs, 52
   articles, 51
   conjunctions
      coordinating, 54–55
      correlative, 56
   interjections, 60–61
   nouns
      collective, 40
      common, 39
      compound, 40
      gerunds and, 40
      proper, 39
   prepositions, 58–59
   pronouns
      antecedent, 41
      demonstrative, 42
      indefinite, 42
      intensive, 42
      interrogative, 42
      personal, 41
      possessive, 41
      reciprocal, 43
      reflexive, 42
      relative, 42
   sentences, 65
      clauses, 76–78
      complements, 69–71
      compound, 80
      compound subjects, 67
      phrases, 71–76
      predicate, 66
      simple, 79
      subject, 66
      subject identification, 67, 69
   verbs, 45
      action, 46
      helping, 48
      infinitives, 49
      intransitive, 48
      linking, 46
      transitive, 48
passive voice, 30, 123
past participles, 74
past perfect progressive tense, 115
past perfect tense, 113
past progressive tense, 114
pauses in sentences, commas, 270

perfect tenses
  future perfect, 113
  past perfect, 113
  present perfect, 112
periods, 263–264
  parentheses, 297–298
personal pronouns, 41
personal titles, capitalizing, 320
person-centric language, 94
personification, 32
phonetic spelling, 303
phrases, 54, 155
  abbreviations, 323
  appositives, 162–163
  arranging/rearranging, 164
  infinitives, 161
  nonessential, commas, 268
  placement, 17–18
  prepositional, 58, 72, 157–159
    as adjectives, 158
    as adverbs, 158
  verb phrases, 71
    gerunds, 160
    participles, 160
  versus clauses, 156–157
places, capitalization, 317
plagiarism
  checkers, 197
  quotes, 193–194
plural nouns
  ending in –s, 284
  subject-verb agreement, 121
plural subject starting sentence, 88
plurals
  collective nouns, 40
  converting from singular, 287–288
  spelling rules, 306–307
    irregular, 308
    same as singular, 309

politically correct (PC) language, 253
possessive case, 44
possessives
  apostrophes, 284
    dual possession, 285
  pronouns, 41
predicate, 66
predicate adjective subject complements, 70
predicate adjectives, 51
predicate nominative subject complements, 70
prefixes, 293
  spelling rules, 310
prepositional phrases, 58, 72, 157–159
  arranging/rearranging, 164
  as adjectives, 158
  as adverbs, 158
  complements, 149
  parallelism, 219
prepositions, 58–59
  object, 58
prescriptive nature of grammar, 12
present participles, 74
present perfect progressive tense, 115
present perfect tense, 112
present progressive tense, 114
progressive tenses
  future perfect progressive, 116
  future progressive, 114
  past perfect progressive, 115
  past progressive, 114
  present perfect progressive, 115
  present progressive, 114
pronouns
  antecedents, 41, 90–91, 242
  case, 44–45
  combining short sentences, 227–228
  consistency, 187
  demonstrative, 42
  first-person, capitalization, 318

form changes, 43
gender and, 93
gender neutrality, 249–251
indefinite, 42
    apostrophes, 285
    subject-verb agreement, 120
intensive, 42
interrogative, 42, 88
personal, 41
possessive, 41
prepositions and, 58–59
reciprocal, 43
reflexive, 42, 92
relative, 42
starting sentences, 90–93
subjective, 90
third-person, 90
proper adjectives, 131
proper nouns, 39
    capitalization, 316
        events, 317
        nationalities, 317
        places, 317
        races, 317
        religions, 317
        things, 317
punctuation, 15
    apostrophes
        contractions, 288–289
        indefinite pronouns, 285
        plural nouns ending in –s, 284
        plurals, converting to, 287–288
        possessives, 284–285
        time-related words, 287
    brackets, 299–300
    colons, 275–276
        formal statements, 274
        independent clauses, 274
        lists, 274
        long quotations, 274
    commas
        addresses, 270
        adjectives, 267
        dates, 270
        direct quotations, 270
        independent clauses, 267–268
        introductory elements, 268–269
        items in a series, 266
        nonessential clauses, 268
        numbers, 270
        pauses in sentences, 270
    dashes
        clarifying statements, 296
        incidental (nonessential) text, 296–297
        numbers, 295–296
    exclamation points, 265
    hyphens
        compound adjectives, 293–294
        compound numbers, 292
        end-of-line, 291
        prefixes, 293
    parentheses, 297–298
    periods, 263–264
    quotation marks, 264
        block quotes, 281
        exact words, 279
        punctuation around, 280–281
        quotations within quotations, 281
        quoting others, 283
        technical terms, 282
        titles, 282
    semicolons, 271
        independent clauses, 271–272
        items in a series, 273
purpose in writing, 192

Q

question marks, 264
questions
    interrogative pronouns, 88
    object questions, 88
    subjects, 88
    subject questions, 88
quotation marks
    block quotes, 281
    exact words, 279
    punctuation around, 280–281
    quotations within quotations, 281
    quoting others, 283
    technical terms, 282
    titles, 282
quotes
    blending in, 194
    block quotes, 281
    capitalization, 315
    citing sources, 196
    colons, 274
    commas, 270
    paraphrasing, 194–195
    quotations within quotations, 281
    sources, 193
    summarizing, 196
quoting others, 283
quoting sources, 194

R

races, 317
racial biases in language, 253–254
reading, dictionaries and, 203
reciprocal pronouns, 43
reflexive pronouns, 42, 92
regular verbs, 102
relative pronouns, 42
religions, 317
    deities, capitalizing, 321

repetition, style and, 29
research paper writing, 27
restrictive clauses, 77
résumés, parallelism, 220–221
rhythm, 32
run-on sentences, 239

S

scholarly journal articles, 27
semicolons, 271
    combining short sentences, 227
    compound sentences, 80
    independent clauses, 271–272
    items in a series, 273
sentence fragments, 237–238
    positive aspects, 238
sentence structure
    long sentences, breaking up, 229–230
    short sentences, 226
        combining with colon, 227
        combining with conjunction, 226
        combining with pronoun, 227–228
        combining with semicolon, 227
    syntax, 225–226
    varying, 30
        sentence beginnings, 232
        sentence type, 231
sentences, 65
    appositives, 73
    capitalization, 315
        independent clause following colon, 316
    clauses
        dependent (subordinate), 76–79
        independent, 76
    complements, 69
        direct objects, 69
        indirect objects, 69
        object complements, 70
        subject complements, 70

complex, 80
compound, 80
   commas, 80
   conjunctions, 80
   conjunctive adverbs, 80
   semicolons, 80
compound-complex, 81
nouns starting, 87–90
   plural subject, 88
pauses, commas, 270
phrases
   prepositional, 72
   verb, 71
predicate, 66
pronouns starting, 90–93
run-on, 239
simple, 79
subject, 66
   compound subjects, 67
   identifying, 67–69
   gerunds, 160–161
verbals, 73
   bare infinitives, 74
   gerunds, 73
   infinitives, 74
   participles, 74
serial comma, 20, 266
series, parallelism, 217–218
sex equality in language, 247–248
sex neutrality in language, 248–249
sexist language, 249–251
sexual orientation, 254–255
similes, 32
simple predicates, 66
simple tenses, 110–112
singular subject starting sentence, 87
singular words, spelling same as plural, 309
slang, 209–210
slang dictionaries, 201

source citations, 196
spaces after period, 264
specific language, 184
spelling, 15
   capitalization
     adjectives, 316
     first word, 315
     I, 318
     independent clauses, 316
     proper nouns, 316–317
   consonants
     double, 304
     hard/soft, 305
   exceptions, 309
   n sound, 306
   phonetically, 303
   plurals, 306–307
     irregular, 308
     same as singular, 309
   prefixes, 310
   suffixes, 311
   vowel sounds, 304
style, 25
   active/passive voice, 30
   advertising copy, 27
   blog posts, 28
   business writing, 26
   comedy writing, 28
   creative writing, 27
   developing, 26
   editorials, 26
   essay writing, 27
   flow, 29
   grant writing, 28
   guidelines, 29–30
   humor in, 185
   improving, 30–31
   journalism columns, 26
   language use, 185

literary devices, 31–33
magazine articles, 27
news articles, 26
precision with words, 30
repetition use, 29
research papers for school, 27
scholarly journal articles, 27
structure variances, 30
text messages, 28
theatrical writing, 27
tweets, 28
vague language, 184
variety and, 233–234
word meanings, 30
style guides, 187–192
subject complements, 147–148
    linking verbs and, 46
    predicate adjectives, 70
    predicate nominatives, 70
subject questions, 88
subject-verb agreement, 88, 118
    collective nouns, 120
    compound subjects, 119
    indefinite pronouns, singular, 120
    singular and plural forms, 121
subject-verb combinations, 30
subjective case, 44
subjective personal pronouns, 41
subjective pronouns, 90
subjects, 66
    compound subjects, 67
    fragmented sentences, 237–238
    gerunds, 160–161
    identifying, 67–69
    in commands, 89
    placement, 16
    plural, starting sentence, 88
    questions, 88
    singular, starting sentence, 87

    verbals as, 89
    verbs and, 45
subjunctive mood, 122
subordinate clauses, 54, 173
subordination, 241
suffixes, spelling rules, 311
summarizing, 196
supporting evidence, 258
synonyms, 202
syntax, 12–14, 16, 225–226
    adjectives and, 13
    poetry, 16

T

technical terms, 282
tenses, 18–19
    forming, 108
    perfect
        future, 113
        past, 113
        present, 112
    perfect progressive
        future, 116
        past, 115
        present, 115
    progressive
        future, 114
        past, 114
        present, 114
    shifting, 243
    simple, 110–112
tense shifts, 116
terminology consistency, 187
text messages, 28
that, when to use, 96
theatrical writing, 27
thesauruses, 202
    careful use, 204

thesis statements, 188
things, capitalization, 317
third-person pronouns, 90
time, writing, 324
titles, 282
   capitalization, 318–320
   personal, 320
to be, adjectives and, 135
transitive verbs, 48
tweets, 28

U

usage, 11
usage levels, 14–15

V

vague language, 184
value judgments, 258
verb complements
   gerunds, 150
   infinitives, 150
   noun phrases, 151
verb phrases, 71
   gerunds, 160
   participles, 160
verb tenses, 18–19
   forming, 108
   past, 101
   past participle, 101
   perfect
     future, 113
     past, 113
     present, 112
   perfect progressive
     future, 116
     past, 115
     present, 115
   present, 101
   present participle, 101
   progressive
     future, 114
     past, 114
     present, 114
   shifts, 116
   simple, 110–112
verb-noun agreement, 118
   collective nouns, 120
   compound subjects, 119
   indefinite pronouns, singular, 120
   singular and plural forms, 121
verbals, 73
   as subject, 89
   bare infinitives, 74
   gerunds, 73
   infinitives, 74
   participles, 74
     past participles, 74
     present participles, 74
verbs
   action, 45–46
   fragmented sentences, 237–238
   helping, 45–48
   infinitive, 49, 102
   inflection, 45
   intransitive, 48
   irregular, 103–106
   linking, 45–47
   mood, 122
   regular, 102
   shifting tense, 243
   subject and, 45
   subject-verb agreement, 88
   subject-verb combination, style, 30
   to be, 109–110
   transitive, 48

voice
   active, 30, 123
   passive, 30, 123
vowel sounds, spelling, 304

W–Z

word choice, 203
   double negatives, 205
word meanings, style and, 30
word usage
   lie vs. *lay*, 117
   that, 96
   which, 96
   who, 96-97
   whom, 97
   whomever, 97
word use
   clichés, 206–208
   connotation, 204
   denotation, 204
   dictionaries, 201
   double negatives, 205
   eggcorns, 211
   euphemisms, 208
   jargon, 210
   reading with dictionaries, 203
   slang, 209–210
   thesauruses, 202
   word choice, 203
writing style
   active/passive voice, 30
   advertising copy, 27
   blog posts, 28
   business writing, 26
   comedy writing, 28
   creative writing, 27
   developing, 26
   editorials, 26
   essay writing, 27
   flow, 29
   grant writing, 28
   guidelines, 29–30
   humor in, 185
   improving, 30–31
   journalism columns, 26
   language use, 185
   literary devices, 31–33
   magazine articles, 27
   news articles, 26
   precision with words, 30
   repetition use, 29
   research papers for school, 27
   scholarly journal articles, 27
   structure variances, 30
   text messages, 28
   theatrical writing, 27
   tweets, 28
   vague language, 184
   variety and, 233–234
   word meanings, 30
writing well
   absolutes, 257–258
   ageism, 254
   clarity, 183–184
   comma splices, 239–240
   compelling writing, 185
   completeness, 191
   conciseness, 189
   consistency, 186–188
   convincing writing, 189
   coordination, 241
   correctness, 191–192
   diction, 202–204, 207–208, 212
      clichés, 206–208
      connotation, 204
      denotation, 204
      dictionaries, 201–202
      double negatives, 205

eggcorns, 211
  euphemisms, 208
  jargon, 210
  slang, 209–210
  thesauruses, 202, 204
  word choice, 203
  word meanings, 203
directions and guidelines, 188
disabilities, 255
ethnic bias, 253–254
fragmented sentences, 237–238
gender references, 247–251, 254–256
generalization avoidance, 252–253
medical conditions, 255
modifiers, 243
parallelism, 217–218, 222
  comparing and contrasting, 222
  coordinating conjunctions, 221
  correlative conjunctions, 222–223
  lists, 217
  prepositional phrases, 219
  series, 217
plagiarism
  avoidance, 193–195
  checkers, 197
pronoun references, 242
racial bias, 253–254
referring to people, 252–253
run-on sentences, 239
sentence structure
  breaking up, 230
  colons, 227
  conjunctions, 226
  long, 229
  pronouns, 227–228
  semicolons, 227
  sentence beginnings, 232
  syntax, 225

  variety in, 233–234
  varying types, 231
specific language, 184
style guides, 192
subordination, 241
summarizing, 196
supporting evidence, 258
tense shifts, 243
value judgments, 258